Self-Scoring Study Guide
and Student Activities Manual
to accompany

Psychology and the Challenges of Life: Adjustment and Growth

Eleventh Edition

by

Jefferey S. Nevid

and

Spencer A. Rathus

prepared by

Gary W. Piggrem
Devry University, Columbus, Ohio

John Wiley & Sons

.

ISBN-13 978-0-470-59231-1

Printed in the United States of America

10 9 8 7 6 5 4 3 2 1

Printed and bound by Malloy Incorporated

TO THE STUDENT
by Spencer A. Rathus and Gary W. Piggrem

This study guide is designed to accompany your *Adjustment and Growth: The Challenges of Life, Tenth Edition* textbook. It will help you study the text material, review this material systematically, and check how well you've covered the material. The study guide covers all the important points covered in the corresponding chapters of the text, but it is **NOT** a substitute for reading and studying the text and attending class. If you read the text conscientiously, attend class regularly, and use the study guide to strengthen your learning, you should do very well in the course.

This study guide also contains two sections that will be of broader interest to you. They are intended not only to help you do well in psychology but in your other courses as well. They are "**Some Study Tips**" and "**Test Anxiety**." Many students who are motivated to do well in their courses are concerned that because they never had to study seriously before they entered college, they have not acquired the study skills they need to do well in college. By following the suggestions in this section on study tips these students can acquire and strengthen their study skills. Other students are concerned because they study hard and learn the material well, but are prevented from adequately demonstrating the depth and extent of their knowledge on tests because of test anxiety. Test anxiety is a cruel handicap for students who work hard to learn the material. The section on test anxiety will help the test-anxious student develop ways of coping with test anxiety and achieving higher grades.

HOW TO USE THIS STUDY GUIDE

Each chapter in this study guide corresponds to a chapter in your text. There are eighteen chapters in the text and in the study guide. Each chapter in the study guide contains a number of features: a chapter outline, learning objectives, key terms, a key terms review, a chapter review, and a sample test.

The Chapter Outline: A Preview of the Chapter

The outline serves to give you a feel for the general thrust of each chapter by highlighting chapter subheadings and topic areas. It is a skeleton outline which can serve as an "advance organizer" for you as you study the chapter.

The Chapter Overview: Putting Some "Meat" on the Bones

The overview gives you a brief description of each of the key topics and subheadings covered in the chapter. It is **not** a substitute for reading the chapter, but it provides you with a more detailed description of the various topics in the chapter than does the chapter outline.

Learning Objectives: What You Should Learn from the Chapter

This section will give you an idea of what you should know when you have finished your study of the chapter. You should read these objectives carefully **BEFORE** you read the chapter in your text, since they will help make you "ready" for the material by allowing you to recognize the main points. Once you have read the chapter in the text, it will be useful to reread the learning objectives in the study guide and ask yourself whether you have met them. If you have not, you may wish to return to the chapter and seek out the missing information before you proceed any further in your studying.

The learning objectives are varied, but tend to fall into a number of categories. Some ask you to define or compare and contrast important terms. Some ask you to describe or explain an experimental procedure or to summarize the results of a number of experiments. Others ask you to identify a number of items that may require memorization.

As you read these objectives, it will be helpful for you to write out your answers and to say them aloud. Try to be precise. This will be especially helpful if your instructor uses essay questions on the tests. Essay questions commonly involve comparing and contrasting important terms and describing research that may be used to support or contradict particular points of view. The learning objectives are easily converted into essay questions and many of your instructor's essay questions are likely to be similar, if not identical, to the learning objectives presented in this study guide.

Key Terms: Important Words and Phrases

Each chapter has a list of important or "key" terms. Many of these terms are found in the running glossary (the words and terms defined in the margins) of your text. All are found in the reading matter of the chapter. Some are repeated in a number of chapters. This indicates that these terms, such as psychoanalysis, social-cognitive theory, or self-actualization, have applications in a variety of areas studied by psychologists.

Ideally, you should be able to define each key term precisely and, often, provide an example of its use. The example may indicate how the term fits into psychological theory or how it relates to psychological research that has been conducted. Your definitions need not be in the exact words used in the text. However, the words must be similar enough in meaning so that it is clear that you have not confused the term with another term.

The Key Terms Review: Defining Your Terms

This section tests your knowledge of many of the key terms presented in the chapter. Since so much of your ability to do well in a course such as this depends on your mastery of the vocabulary, it is important that you be able to define accurately key concepts and ideas presented in the textbook material. In this section, key terms and phrases are presented from the original "Key Terms" section following the chapter outline. There are usually 20 key terms in a "Key Terms Review" exercise. You must write a definition for each of the terms listed in this section. ***Note:*** *Some chapters contain so many terms that more than one "Key Terms Review" is provided for those chapters. Chapter 2 contains three such exercises.*

The Chapter Review: A Step-by-Step Approach

This section summarizes the chapter in a fill-in-the-blank and matching question format. This permits you to test your knowledge of the chapter in a systematic way. The material is presented in the same sequence as it normally appears in the text. We suggest you try filling in the blank and matching questions after you first read the chapter and then reread any parts of the chapter which presented you with difficulties. Several challenging formats are presented in either "fill-in-the-blank" or "matching" questions.

The Practice Test: Taking a Stab at It

In each chapter, there is a sample test with twenty multiple-choice questions, five true-false questions, and an essay question. This test is designed to test your abilities to recognize accurately major principles as well as more detailed information from the chapter, such as names, statistics, etc. Your performance on these practice tests should be a relatively accurate predictor of how well you will perform on your instructor's tests, especially if she or he uses mostly multiple-choice items.

In grading your practice test, you should formulate a letter grade only for the 25 objective questions. You should compare the essay question with the answer outlined in the answer key (at the back of the study guide) and see if any required information was lacking, but grading these can be tricky and it will be easier to grade yourself just on the objective questions in the sample test. For the objective portion of the test, you will need to get the following number of items correct to achieve the letter grade indicated:

$$
\begin{array}{lll}
A & = & 23, 24, \text{ or } 25 \quad (90–100\%) \\
B & = & 20, 21, \text{ or } 22 \quad (80–89\%) \\
C & = & 18 \text{ or } 19 \qquad\;\; (70–79\%) \\
D & = & 15, 16, \text{ or } 17 \quad (60–69\%) \\
F & = & 14 \text{ or below} \;\;\;\; (\;0–59\%)
\end{array}
$$

In answering multiple-choice items there are a few factors you might keep in mind in order to do as well as you are able. First, carefully read the entire question, including **ALL** of the possible choices. Do **NOT** just focus on a single key word or term and jump to conclusions about what is being asked. Second, keep in mind that you must select the answer that **BEST** answers a question or completes a sentence. Try to select a full, satisfying answer, not an inexact answer. If you have time, you may find it helpful to find a reason for eliminating each of the incorrect choices. If you cannot find a reason for eliminating a choice, it may be the correct answer.

Today, most professors prefer multiple-choice questions. However, some use a variety of types of questions and some others prefer fill-in-the-blank, matching, true-false, or essay questions. If your professor prefers the fill-in-the-blank or matching formats, you should probably spend more time on the chapter review section. If your professor prefers essay questions, pay attention to the essay question in your sample test and spend more time reviewing the learning objectives (converting them into essays and trying to answer them).

Student Activities: Critically Thinking About the Material

These activities are designed to help you apply the knowledge you have gained from the chapter and to help you further explore key issues raised in the chapter. They are often thought provoking, and in many cases, there is no single correct answer to the questions they pose. Many of the exercises are designed to help you explore your own feelings and experiences related to important issues raised by the text. Hopefully they will help you in your personal adjustment and growth process.

SOME STUDY TIPS

Imagine participating in a one-person experiment in which you first put some water in a bathtub and then sit in the tub. You wait a few moments and then look around. You notice that the water is still there, although you may have displaced a bit.

You may have been dry when you sat in the tub, but you are a person and not a sponge. You will not simply soak up the water. You would have to take rather active measures to get it inside you—perhaps a straw, patience, and a great deal of single-mindedness would help. It is also a task that must be accomplished gradually.

The problem of "soaking up" knowledge in psychology and in your other courses is not entirely dissimilar. You will not accomplish a great deal by sitting on your textbook, except perhaps looking an inch or so taller. It will not even help to flip through your textbook a dozen times unless you are doing some active searching for answers to questions.

Some tips on studying effectiveness follow. They involve taking an active approach to studying and using the SQ3R method.

An Active Approach to Studying

Begin your active approach to studying by assessing the amount of material you must master during the academic term and then measure the rate at which you plan to learn. How long does it take for you to read a chapter or a book in each of your courses? How much time must you spend studying each day? Does it add up correctly? Will you make it?

Once you have determined how much study time you will need for each of your courses for the academic term, try to space your study periods evenly. For most of us, spaced or distributed learning is more efficient than cramming or massed studying. Psychologists do not yet know exactly why, but it takes some time for learning to be "consolidated." Continuing to study when prior learning has not yet been consolidated may be less efficient than distributing, or breaking up, your study times. So try to outline a study schedule that will provide an approximately equal amount of study time each weekday. Leave weekends relatively free. Weekends will provide you with extra hours for reviewing notes and working on assignments that may be causing more difficulty than had been anticipated. If you have kept to your study schedule, you have probably earned some "reward" time for yourself and your friends.

Try to avoid studying psychology all day Monday, composition all day Tuesday, chemistry all day Wednesday, and so on. Psychology is so fascinating that you may have difficulty ripping yourself away from the text, but it may be more efficient to spend some time studying several subjects each day for at least two reasons. First, switching to a new subject may allow time for what you have learned in the previous subject to consolidate, so you will remember more of it later. Second, research indicates that old learning can interfere with new learning and new learning can interfere with old learning, particularly if it is all similar material. Switching subjects should reduce the amount of "interference" between old and new learning.

If you have difficulty pushing yourself to study for the required amount of time each day, begin with a more comfortable amount of time and build your study time gradually. Find a place to study that is relatively quiet, comfortable, and free from distractions. Try to do nothing but study in this place (that is, do not munch on chips, talk, listen to music, and fantasize about the weekend here), and try to remain in this place for the required amount of time. Then this place will come to mean studying to you.

Set specific goals for what you want to accomplish during your time in this study place and push yourself to achieve those goals. Your goals should focus on topics *learned*, not just topics *covered.* After you have accomplished an immediate goal, such as studying and learning two topics, you may want to reward yourself with a break. In general, you should take a ten-minute break (not 15 or 20 minutes) each hour you study, just to get up, stretch your muscles, get a snack, or go to the bathroom, etc. This can relieve fatigue, help refresh you, and improve your concentration during the next hour. You should try to reward yourself somehow for meeting your daily study goals, even if only by putting off your dessert until after you have studied. Do not try to be a martyr and put off all pleasures until the end of the academic term. Some people are capable of doing this, but most of us are not, and if you have never spent much time in nonstop studying you may be demanding too much for yourself and setting yourself up for failure.

SQ3R: SURVEY, QUESTION, READ/WRITE, RECITE, REVIEW

Educational psychologist Francis Robinson (1970) of Ohio State University originated a method of studying called SQ3R—Survey, Question, Read/Write, Recite, Review—in which you are encouraged to become more active in soaking up academic material. Essentially, you phrase questions about the material as you first survey it. Then you answer these questions as you study. SQ3R has helped many college students study more effectively and raise their grades.

SURVEY: Some people short-circuit their pleasure in reading mystery novels by turning to the last pages of the novel to find out "whodunit" when their curiosity gets the best of them. While skipping through the pages of a novel may harm the dramatic impact by revealing information before the suspense has been adequately built, skipping through the pages can be an excellent prelude to learning textbook material. More and more textbooks are being written specifically to stimulate the student to survey the material before reading it.

Your adjustment and growth textbook and this study guide have chapter outlines at the beginning of each chapter. Your textbook also has "Truth or Fiction?" sections at the beginning of each chapter. These provide a preview of what is to come when you read the chapter. Familiarity with the outline of the chapter will provide you with a framework, or advance organizers, for learning the substance of the chapter as you later absorb it page by page.

QUESTION: Phrase questions for each of the major and minor headings in the chapter outline. If you were to do this for the headings in the beginning of Chapter 1, the beginning of a list of questions might look like this:

> What are psychology and adjustment and how are they related?
> > What is the difference between adjustment and personal growth?
> > How is nature different from nurture? Is biology/heredity destiny?
> > How is the clinical approach different from the healthy personality approach?
> Why is human diversity important to the study of adjustment?
> > Why is ethnic diversity important?
> > Why is gender important?
> > What other kinds of diversity are there?

You may have phrased the questions differently. Your method of phrasing may be more efficient for you. With some practice you will learn to form questions that work well for you.

Textbooks for your other courses may not begin with chapter outlines. Some may not have headings for clearly defined sections. If the book lacks headings, get into the material page by page and phrase relevant questions as you go along.

READ/WRITE

READ: Once you have phrased each question, read the relevant subject matter with the purpose of answering the question. This will help you attend to the central points of the section of the chapter. If the material is fine literature, such as a novel, you may wish to read it once to appreciate its poetic features fully. Then you may wish to skim it and phrase questions so that you may read it in order to answer those questions later on.

WRITE: As you read, write down your questions and write the answers to those questions. This helps you actively focus on important questions raised by the section or the chapter while at the same time providing you with a written record for later study.

A more formal way to do this is to wait until you have thoroughly read the chapter, then go back and take notes from it just as you would normally take notes in a classroom. It is better to take notes from a chapter after you have read it thoroughly because then you will know what is important and needs to be written down. If you take notes before you have thoroughly read the chapter, it is more difficult to know what is really important, and most students tend to write down too many irrelevant items, making it more difficult to study effectively later on.

If you prefer to highlight your text rather than to take notes from it, you should do it here, *after* having read the material thoroughly. Again, students who highlight their text as they read it for the first time tend to highlight too much, making it difficult to figure out what is really important when they are studying later on. In general, the rule of thumb is that you should highlight no more than 10 percent of the material in your text. Most study skills experts prefer that students take notes instead of highlighting because taking notes is more active and involves more concentration and focused thinking whereas highlighting can become mechanical, passive, and requires little focus or concentration. Taking notes may be more efficient than highlighting for gathering information from your text.

RECITE: Once you have read the appropriate section or chapter and highlighted it or taken notes from it, put it down and answer the question or questions you have phrased as clearly and briefly as possible. Jot down a few key words that will "telegraph" the answer to you when you review your notes. Recite your answer aloud if possible. Your willingness to recite aloud may depend on where you are, who is near you, and how you feel about the reaction you expect from those who are near you.

REVIEW: Review the material briefly at the conclusion of each study session, and then on a reasonable schedule—perhaps weekly—cover the key response words and read your questions like a quiz. Perhaps you can enlist friends to read them. Then recite the answers and check them for accuracy against the key response words. Reread the relevant subject matter if the key response words are not sufficiently meaningful to you. Forgetting the answers to too many questions may mean a number of things: that you are not phrasing your questions in an appropriate way, that you did not read the textbook material carefully, that you did not fully understand the textbook material, that you chose your key response words carelessly, or that you did not recite the material on a schedule that is efficient for you.

Once you have actively studied your material, you may feel less anxious about the prospect of taking quizzes and examinations. But if you suffer from test anxiety, you will find the following section useful.

TEST ANXIETY

There are few experiences more frustrating than test anxiety. When a student works diligently to prepare for a test, it can seem particularly unfair that concern about taking the test can be linked to poor performance. This section presents a lengthy treatment of methods that may be used to cope with test anxiety for students who have this problem.

Tests are practically inescapable. From achievement and intelligence tests in the elementary schools to SATs, GREs, and civil service examinations, tests seem built into every corner of our society. It is not entirely unusual for graduate students to boast about their test scores or even to introduce themselves by their test scores. We know of a statistics professor who said that one of the first pieces of information she and her future husband shared when they met were their scores on the Miller Analogies Test, a test often used for entry into graduate schools. Students who have done poorly on the SATs and GREs have often told us that they wonder whether they "have what it takes" for college work. They take their test scores very seriously. Unfortunately, their concern about the importance of tests often becomes part of the problem.

Is It All in Your Mind?

Why do some people become so upset about tests? Can it be explained through principles of classical conditioning (which you will learn about in Chapter 2)? That is, do a few bad experiences with tests lead a person to automatically experience a fear response at the thought of taking another test? Experiments in test anxiety suggest that what people tell themselves while they are taking tests may be a more important factor.

Psychologist Kenneth Holroyd of Ohio University and his colleagues (1978) recruited seventy-two women taking introductory psychology for an experiment in test anxiety. Thirty-six of the women showed high test anxiety as measured by Irwin Sarason's (1972) Test Anxiety Scale, and thirty-six showed low test anxiety. All the women were then given anagrams (jumbled words) to solve as quickly as they could. ATSR, for example, is an anagram for STAR, ARTS, or RATS. It had been shown earlier that high test anxiety interferes with the ability to solve anagrams, but how it did so was not entirely clear (Sarason, 1973).

In the Holroyd study, the high-test-anxious women were down on themselves regardless of how well they actually did. High-test-anxious women and low-test-anxious women showed similarity in bodily signs of anxiety as a result of the stress of the test-taking situation, as measured by heart rate and by sweat in the palms of their hands. This study and others (Bandura, 1977; Sarason, 1978) suggest that highly critical self-evaluation during the test situation may impede test performance.

It appears reasonable to conclude that persons who report themselves to be highly test anxious are more critical of themselves during tests and allow themselves to be somewhat distracted from their tasks by self-criticism and worry. It makes sense that there could be an interaction between self-criticism and high bodily arousal such that these two variables may cause each other to increase, perhaps in a vicious cycle. A standard method for coping with test anxiety focuses on changing highly critical self-evaluations and other troublesome thoughts.

Rational Restructuring of Test Taking

Psychologist Marvin Goldfried of the State University of New York at Stony Brook and his colleagues (1978) reported a technique that was successful in reducing test anxiety among college women and men attending either Stony Brook or Catholic University: rational restructuring. Essentially, these students were taught to restructure or reshape their thoughts while taking tests.

Participants in the study first selected fifteen anxiety-evoking situations taken from the Suinn Test Anxiety Behavior Scale (Suinn, 1971). Items from the Suinn scale (which is presented in Chapter 11 of the text) include the following:

> waiting for the test to be handed out
> studying for a quiz
> hearing the announcement of the coming test
> reading the first item on a final examination
> discussing the approaching test with friends a few weeks before the test is due

Students then listed items in a hierarchy from least anxiety-inducing to most anxiety-inducing. Then, during each of the five clinical treatment sessions, three of the items were presented for four one-minute trials. During each trial, students did the following: they noted their self-defeating, anxiety-producing thoughts as they imagined themselves in the situation, and they attempted to replace each self-defeating thought with a rational alternative. For instance, one self-defeating thought was, "I'm going to fail this test, and everyone's going to think I'm stupid!" An example of rational restructuring of this thought is, "Chances are I probably won't fail. And even if I do, people probably won't think I'm stupid." Students noted their levels of anxiety before and after rational restructuring and discussed their problems and progress with other students.

You can rationally restructure test-taking situations with the following steps:
1. pinpoint your self-defeating thoughts
2. construct rational alternative thoughts
3. practice the rational alternatives *before* you take the test as well as during the test
4. reward yourself for your efforts

Pinpointing Self-Defeating Thoughts: Imagine yourself in a variety of test-taking situations. Sit back, relax, and fill in the details of the situation as vividly as possible. Search for any thoughts that cause you concern. Write down these thoughts after a minute or so. Perhaps some of the items on the Suinn scale cause you concern. Imagine yourself in these situations. Here are other situations that may cause you concern:

the proctor writing down the time left on the blackboard
students discussing their answers after class
not being able to think of the answer to an easy question immediately
a student who has completed the test leaving the room
not being able to answer the first question of a test

Constructing Rational Alternatives: Carefully examine each of your anxiety-producing thoughts. Note how they may distract you from focusing on the test items themselves. Construct rational alternatives for these thoughts, as in the following examples:

Self-Defeating Thoughts	**Rational Alternatives**
"I'm the only one who's going to go bananas over this thing!"	"Nonsense! Lots of people have test anxiety. Just don't let it distract you from the test itself!"
I'm running out of time!"	"Time is passing, but take it item by item and answer what I can. Panicking won't help."
"This is impossible! Are all the items going to be like this?"	"Just take it item by item. They're all different. There's no reason to assume the worst."
"I just can't remember a thing!"	"Just slow down and think about it for a moment. It may come back. If not, go on to the next item. Getting upset won't help.
"Everyone is smarter than I am!"	"That's an exaggeration, but they may not be distracting themselves from taking the test by worrying. Just do the best I can, item by item."
"I've got to get out of here. I can't take it any longer!"	"Even if I feel that way now and then, I don't have to act on it. Just focus on the items, one by one."

"I just can't do well on tests!"	"That's only true if I believe it's true! Now get back to the items. One at a time."
"There are a million items left!	"Quite a few, but not a million! Worrying about how many items are left just leaves me with less time to complete them. Now get back to the items and answer as many as I can, one by one."
"Everyone else is leaving. They're all finished before I am."	"Fast work does not guarantee correct work. The first people done do not usually get the best grades. I must work at my own pace taking each item one at a time, finishing what I can."
"If I flunk, everything is ruined!"	"I won't be happy if I fail but it's not the end of my life either. Distracting myself by worrying about failure just increase my chances of failure. My best chance to pass is to answer each item as best I can, one at a time!"

Practicing Rational Alternatives: Arrange practice tests in your courses that are as close to actual testing conditions as possible. Time yourself. If the tests are Graduate Record Exams, or civil service type exams, obtain practice tests and make the testing conditions as realistic as you can.

You may wish to use one of the practice tests in each chapter of this study guide to practice rational alternatives for the tests in your psychology course. If so, allow yourself as much time as your professor would permit you and try to take the test in the actual room (or a room similar to) where you take your psychology tests.

Pay close attention to the thoughts you experience as you take the practice test. For each self-defeating thought, think firmly of a rational alternative. Repeat the rational alternative aloud, firmly, and then return to working on the test items, item by item. If you feel anxious, you need not allow your anxiety to distract you from working on the test items.

When you have finished the first ten or fifteen items, you may wish to run through the list of self-defeating thoughts you had identified to see if you left any out. If so, you may think through them purposefully, then follow them with rational alternatives. Then return to the test and continue, item by item, as before.

Self-Reward: When you have firmly thought a rational alternative to a self-defeating thought, say to yourself, "That's better! Now I can return to the test," or "I don't have to allow anxiety to distract me after all." When you have completed the test, think something like, "Well, I did it! Regardless of the grade I get, I certainly got through that test feeling much better than I usually do. And I may have done better than usual as well! Now there's no reason why I can't do even better on my future tests!"

Now it's up to you. Psychology is the most exciting part of our lives, and we sincerely hope that you find it stimulating and rewarding. If you work your way through the sections of each chapter of the study guide, one at a time, you should thoroughly master the material for the course. Your performance on the practice test at the end of each chapter should serve as a relatively accurate predictor of how you will do in the actual tests in your course.

References

Bandura, A. *Social Learning Theory*. Englewood Cliffs, NJ. Prentice-Hall, 1977.

Doerr, H.O. and Hokanson, J.E. "A relation between heart rate and performance in children." *Journal of Personality and Social Psychology*, 1965, *2*, pp. 70-76.

Goldfried, M.R., Linchan, M.M., and Smith, J.L. "Reduction of test anxiety through cognitive
restructuring." *Journal of Counseling and Clinical Psychology*, 1978, *46*, pp. 32-39.

Holroyd, K.A., Westbrook, T., Wolf, M., and Badhorn, E. "Performance, cognition, and physiological responding to test anxiety." *Journal of Abnormal Psychology*, 1978, *87*, pp. 442-451

Robinson, F.P. *Effective Study*, 4th ed. New York: Harper & Row, 1970.

Sarason, I.G. "Experimental approaches to test anxiety: Attention and uses of information." In C.D. Spielberger (ed.), *Anxiety and Behavior* (vol. 2). New York: Academic Press, 1972.

Sarason, I.G. "Test anxiety and cognitive modeling." *Journal of Personality and Social Psychology*, 1973, *28*, pp. 58-61.

Sarason, I.G. "The test anxiety scale: Concept and research." In C.D. Spielberger and I.G. Sarason (eds.), *Stress and Anxiety* (vol. 5). New York: Halstead-Wiley, 1978.

Suinn, R.M. *The Suinn Test Anxiety Behavior Scale*. Fort Collins, CO: Rocky Mountain Behavioral Science Institute, 1971.

Contents

1

Psychology and the Challenges of Life

Chapter Outline

Module 1.1: Psychology and Adjustment

Module 1.2: Human Diversity and Adjustment

Module 1.3: Critical Thinking and Adjustment

Module 1.4: How Psychologists Study Adjustment

Module 1.5: Psychology in Daily Life: Becoming a Successful Student

Chapter Overview

Psychology, Adjustment, and Personal Growth. Psychology is the science of behavior and mental processes. Adjustment is behavior that permits us to meet the challenges of life. Adjustment is also referred to as coping or coping behavior. Adjustment is reactive—coping with the challenges of life. Personal growth is proactive. It involves conscious, active self-development.

The Role of Biology. Biology is not destiny. Genes may determine the ranges for the expression of traits, but environmental conditions and our chosen behavior patterns minimize the influence of genetic risk factors, and maximize our genetic potential.

The Clinical and Healthy Personality Approach. The clinical approach focuses on ways in which problems can be corrected, whereas the healthy-personality approach focuses on optimizing our development along personal, social, physical, and vocational lines.

Studying Human Diversity. Human diversity refers to many sources of differences among people, including ethnic or racial differences, gender differences, and differences in disability status and sexual orientation. Awareness of the richness of human diversity enhances our understanding of the individual and enables students to appreciate the cultural heritages and historical problems of various ethnic groups. Knowledge of diversity helps psychologists understand the aspirations and problems of individuals from various groups so they can successfully intervene to help group members.

The Ethnic Group. An ethnic group comprises people who share factors such as cultural heritage, history, race, and language in common. Minority ethnic groups have frequently experienced prejudice and discrimination by members of one dominant culture.

Prejudice Against Women. There have been historic prejudices against women. The careers of women have been traditionally channeled into domestic chores, regardless of women's wishes as individuals. Much of the scientific research into gender roles and gender differences assumes that male behavior represents the norm.

Critical Thinking. Critical thinking is the adoption of a skeptical questioning attitude and evaluation of arguments of claims in the light of evidence. Critical thinking is the hallmark feature of psychology and other sciences. Critical thinking involves examining definitions of terms, examining the premises or assumptions behind arguments, and scrutinizing the logic with which arguments are developed. Critical thinkers are cautious in drawing conclusions from evidence. They do not oversimplify or overgeneralize. Critical thinking guides us to examine evidence for and against astrology and other pseudosciences.

The Scientific Method. The scientific method is an organized way of expanding and refining knowledge. Psychologists reach conclusions about their research questions or the accuracy of their hypotheses on the basis of their research observations or findings.

The Case Study Method. The case study method involves the crafting of carefully constructed portraits of individuals to help shed light on their behavior.

The Survey Method. The survey method involves the administration of questionnaires or interviews to large numbers of individuals to learn more about their attitudes and behavior patterns.

Using Samples to Represent Populations. The subjects who are studied are referred to as a sample. A sample is a segment of a population. Women's groups and health professionals argue that there is a historic bias in favor of conducting research with men. Research samples have also tended to underrepresent minority ethnic groups in the population. Researchers use random and stratified samples to represent populations. In a random sample, each member of a population has an equal chance of being selected to participate. In a stratified sample, identified subgroups in the population are represented proportionately.

The Naturalistic Observation Method. The naturalistic-observation method involves careful and unobtrusive observation of behavior where it happens—in the "field."

The Correlational Method. The correlational method reveals relationships between variables, but does not determine cause and effect. In a positive correlation, two variables increase together; in a negative correlation, one variable increases while the other decreases.

The Experimental Method. Experiments are used to discover cause and effect—that is, the effects of independent variables on dependent variables. Experimental groups receive a specific treatment, whereas control groups do not. Blinds and double blinds may be used to control for the effects of the expectations of the subjects and the researchers. Results can be generalized only to populations that have been adequately represented in the research samples.

Becoming a Successful Student. Succeeding in meeting the academic challenges of college requires taking an active approach to learning, as well as skill in managing time and studying effectively. This involves planning ahead, studying different subjects each day, becoming an active note taker, expanding your attention span, eliminating distractions, practicing self-reward, and sticking with it.

SQ3R. The SQ3R study method is a widely used study technique designed to help students develop more effective study habits. The steps in this method are: survey, question, read, recite, and review.

Coping with Test Anxiety. Test anxiety can make it difficult for us to perform to the best of our ability. Learning to manage irrational, catastrophic thoughts and practicing relaxations techniques can be helpful in coping with test anxiety.

Learning Objectives

After studying this chapter your students should be able to:

1. Explain what psychology is, what psychologists do and how psychology can be helpful in exploring adjustment and growth issues.

2. Define multitasking. Identify and describe the various positive and negative effects of multitasking. Are we better at multitasking some activities than others? Why or why not?

3. Compare and contrast adjustment and personal growth.

4. Explain what genes and chromosomes are and what they do. Also discuss why biology is not necessarily destiny.

5. Compare and contrast the differences between the clinical and healthy-personality approaches to adjustment.

6 Discuss the focus and goals of positive psychology. Briefly explain the three the three fundamental challenges in boosting happiness, and describe at last three techniques for boosting happiness.

7. Summarize research findings on what does, or does not, make people happy

8. Define "ethnic group" and discuss why it is important to study human diversity.

9. Define "gender" and discuss the various prejudices experienced by women historically and in scientific research.

10. Explain what critical thinking is and why it is essential to your adjustment.

11. Identify and briefly explain the eight principles of critical thinking.

12. Show how critical thinking can be used to examine the claims made by supporters of astrology and other pseudosciences.

13. Explain at least five ways that critical thinking can be used to protect yourself from the false claims made in many self-help books.

14. Analyze how critical thinking can help protect people while surfing online.

15. Explain what the scientific method is and describe the various steps involved in it.

16. Explain and provide some examples of the various sampling bias problems present in scientific research in regard to women.

17. Identify and briefly explain the various methods of observation used by psychologists.

18. Explain the case study method of research in terms of its purposes and its limitations.

19. Describe the survey method of research in terms of its purposes and its limitations.

20. Describe the relationship between samples and populations and explain how researchers ensure that their samples represent target populations.

21. Describe the naturalistic-observation method of research in terms of its purposes and its limitations.

22. Describe the correlational method of research in terms of its purposes and limitations, and explain what a positive correlation, a negative correlation, and a correlation coefficient are.

23. Describe the experimental method of research in terms of its purposes and limitations, and explain what control subjects, experimental subjects, and placebo treatments are.

24. Identify and briefly describe 7 things you can do to become a successful student.

25. Describe the purpose of the SQ3R method and briefly describe each of its steps.

Key Terms

bulimia nervosa	correlation	correlation coefficient
psychology	selection factor	positive correlation
multitasking	replicate	negative correlation
adjustment	case study method	experimental method
gene	social desirability bias	independent variable
chromosome	surveys	dependent variable
predisposition	generalize	treatment
positive psychology	sample	random assignment
ethnic groups	population	experimental group
gender	stratify	control group
critical thinking	random sample	placebo
pseudoscience	volunteer bias	sugar pill
Barnum effect	naturalistic observation	blind
scientific method	unobtrusive measures	double blind
hypothesis	correlational method	SQ3R

Key Terms Review

Define each of the following terms:

1. Bulimia Nervosa: _____

    _____

2. Psychology: _____

    _____

3. Adjustment: _____

    _____

4. Gene: _____

    _____

5. Chromosome: _____

    _____

6. Ethnic Groups: _____

    _____

7. Gender: _____

    _____

8. Hypothesis: _____

    _____

9. Critical Thinking: _____

    _____

10. Pseudoscience: _____

    _____

11. Scientific Method: _____

_____

12. Stratify: _____

_____

13. Population: _____

_____

14. Correlation: _____

_____

15. Sample: _____

_____

16. Independent Variable: _____

_____

17. Dependent Variable: _____

_____

18. Treatment: _____

_____

19. Control Group: _____

_____

20. Placebo: _____

_____

Chapter Review

1. Psychology is the science that studies _____ and _____ processes.

2. _____ involves trying to do two or more things at once.

3. _____ is coping behavior that permits us to meet the demands we face in the environment.

4. The problem of overloading our mental resources is especially keen when it comes to tasks that engage _____ parts of the brain.

5. _____ is essentially reactive, whereas _____ is proactive.

6. When psychologists refer to the nature versus nurture controversy, nature reflects _____ influences, and nurture reflects _____ influences.

7. _____ are segments of DNA which represent the basic units of heredity, and the stuff of which our _____ are composed.

8. Genetic factors interact with _____ influences and personal _____ to affect behavior.

9. Genes create a _____ that certain traits, abilities, or psychological disorders will develop.

10. The _____ approach to psychology primarily focuses on ways in which psychology can help people correct personal problems and cope with stress.

11. The _____-_____ approach to psychology primarily focuses on healthful patterns of personal growth and development.

12. _____ psychology focuses on the study of love, optimism, hope, helping behavior, and human happiness.

13. _____ _____ are subgroups within the population that have a common cultural heritage.

14. Four reasons for studying ethnic diversity are:

   a. _____

   b. _____

c. _____

d. _____

15. The two fastest growing ethnic groups right now in the United States consist of

_____ Americans and _____ Americans.

16. _____ is the state of being male or female.

17. One of the hallmarks to a scientific approach to life is _____ thinking.

18. The eight principles of critical thinking are:

a. _____

b. _____

c. _____

d. _____

e. _____

f. _____

g. _____

h. _____

19. Astrology is an example of a _____.

20. The tendency to believe a generalized but phony personality report is called the

_____ effect.

21. Psychology is a _____.

22. Science demands that beliefs about behavior be supported by _____.

23. Five ways to separate what is meaningful from what is not in self-help books are:

a. _____

b. _____

c. _____

d. _____

e. _____

24. Critical thinkers don't suspend their _____ attitude when they go online.

25. The _____ _____ is a method for obtaining scientific evidence in which a hypothesis is formed and tested.

26. The four basic steps of the scientific method are:

   a. _____

   b. _____

   c. _____

   d. _____

27. _____ is a statistical association or relationship between variables.

28. A source of bias that may occur in research findings when subjects are allowed to determine for themselves whether or not they will receive a treatment condition is a _____ _____.

29. Researchers are obligated to provide enough details of their work that others will be able to _____ it.

30. Most of the large sample research on the relationships between lifestyle and health has been conducted with _____.

31. Sigmund Freud developed his theory of personality largely on the basis of _____ _____.

32. In surveys, naturalistic observation, and other research methods, the actual participants in a study are called the _____, and they represent a larger group of people called the _____.

33. Samples in which each member of a target population has an equal chance of being chosen to participate in an experiment are called _____ samples.

34. A source of bias or error in research that reflects the prospect that people who offer to participate in research studies differ systematically from people who do not is

known as _____ bias.

35. The naturalistic observation method provides _____ information, but it is not

the best method for determining a behavior's underlying _____.

36. A correlation coefficient is a number that varies between _____.

37. Researchers have found that as a person's height increases, so does his or her

weight. This is an example of a _____ correlation.

38. Researchers have found that as stress levels increase, immune system functioning

decreases. This is an example of a _____ correlation.

39. Most scientists agree that the preferred method for determining cause and effect

relationships it the _____ method.

40. **Matching:** Match the name of the psychological research method with its corresponding definition:

   a. _____.   A method in which organisms are   1.   the case study method
                     observed in their natural environments

   b. _____.   A biography compiled from interviews,   2.   the survey method
                     questionnaires, and psychological tests

   c. _____.   A method that studies the relationships 3.   the correlational method
                     between variables

   d. _____.   A method in which large numbers of people 4. naturalistic observation
                     are questioned with verbal or written
                     questionnaires   5.   the experimental method

   e. _____.   A method that seeks to discover
                     cause and effect relationships

41. A condition in a scientific study that is manipulated so that effects may be observed is

a(n) _____ variable.

42. Ideal experiments use _____ groups and _____ groups.

43. In many experiments, some subjects are given a "sugar pill," or _____ treatment, to control for the effects of their expectations.

44. Studies in which neither the subjects nor the experimenters know who has obtained the treatment are called _____-_____ studies.

45. Seven steps in taking an active approach to learning are:

    a. _____

    b. _____

    c. _____

    d. _____

    e. _____

    f. _____

    g. _____

46. The five steps of the SQ3R method are:

    a. _____

    b. _____

    c. _____

    d. _____

    e. _____

47. Four steps in coping with test anxiety are:

    a. _____

    b. _____

    c. _____

    d. _____

Sample Test

Multiple-Choice Questions

1. An eating disorder characterized by cycles of binge eating and a dramatic method for purging, such as vomiting, is _____.
   a. anorexia nervosa
   b. hypoglycemia
   c. Korsakoff's syndrome
   d. bulimia nervosa

2. Psychology is the study of _____.
   a. the subjective activities of the mind
   b. observable behavior, but not mental processes
   c. mental processes, but not observable behavior
   d. mental processes and observable behavior

3. The strongest and most effective forms of adjustment involve _____.
   a. seeing pressures and problems for what they are
   b. avoiding problems for as long as possible
   c. using psychological defense mechanisms
   d. confronting problems without relying on others for help

4. Physical traits such as height, race, and eye color are genetically transmitted from generation to generation by _____.
   a. endorphins
   b. antigens
   c. genes
   d. leukocytes

5. A psychologist focuses mainly on ways in which psychology can help people correct personal problems and cope with stress. This psychologist is using the _____.
   a. primary process
   b. healthy-personality approach
   c. organic approach
   d. clinical approach

6. Gender is _____.
   a. neither a psychosocial nor a biological concept
   b. biological concept, not a psychosocial concept
   c. psychosocial concept, not a biological concept
   d. both a psychosocial and a biological concept

7. Each of the following is true of critical thinking EXCEPT _____.
   a. it means taking nothing for granted
   b. it means expressing all your feelings
   c. it refers to thoughtfully analyzing the statements and terms of other people
   d. it is essential to your adjustment

8. A specific prediction about behavior or mental processes that is tested through research is called _____.
   a. an opinion
   b. a paradigm
   c. a theory
   d. a hypothesis

9. A researcher finds that more aggressive children tend to watch more violent television. While she is tempted to conclude that violent television causes aggressive behavior in children, she realizes that it might be that children who choose to watch violent television may be more aggressive to begin with. If this is true, it is a classic example of a _____.
   a. selection factor
   b. latency effect
   c. cue-controlled stimulus
   d. volunteer bias

10. A psychologist studies one, or a handful of people, in great depth, seeking factors that contribute to notable or rare behavior patterns, putting together a carefully drawn biography or compilation of the person or persons being studied. The psychologist is using the _____ method.
   a. naturalistic observation
   b. case study
   c. correlational
   d. experimental

11. The research method used by psychologists that involves the use of questionnaires, interviews, or public records to examine people's behaviors, attitudes, opinions, or feelings is the _____ method.
   a. case study
   b. correlational study
   c. survey
   d. experiment

12. To apply observations based on a small research sample to a much larger population is to _____ the research observations.
   a. stratify
   b. verify
   c. generalize
   d. validate

13. The research method that focuses on using **unobtrusive** measures in observing subjects' behaviors is the _____ method.
   a. naturalistic observation
   b. laboratory observation
   c. experimental
   d. survey

14. A correlation coefficient measures _____ of the relationship between two variables.
   a. neither the strength nor direction
   b. the strength, but not the direction
   c. the direction, but not the strength
   d. both the strength and direction

15. A weakness of correlational studies is that _____.
   a. they are expensive to set up and time consuming to run
   b. they are subject to high levels of bias and distortion
   c. they often require the use of deception, raising several ethical issues
   d. they cannot be used to prove cause and effect

16. If a researcher could ethically conduct research to find out what **CAUSES** the relationship between lung cancer and cigarette smoking, what method of research would be most effective for doing this?
   a. an experimental study
   b. a case study
   c. a correlational study
   d. a laboratory observation study

17. In an experiment, if there are two groups being studied and one group is given alcohol to measure its effects while the other group is not given alcohol, the people receiving the alcohol would be considered the _____ group.
   a. dependent
   b. experimental
   c. independent
   d. control

18. Which of the following is **NOT** used to help control for subjects' behavior and expectations in an experimental study?
   a. placebo
   b. blind
   c. random assignment
   d. a selection factor

19. In experiments, some subjects are kept unaware of whether or not they have received an experimental treatment. This is known as keeping the subjects _____.
   a. confused
   b. generalized
   c. blind
   d. generalized

20. In a study to measure the effects of a new drug to treat anxiety, some subjects are given the real drug while others are given sugar pills. In this situation, the sugar pills are being used as _____.
   a. a placebo
   b. a selection factor
   c. a blind
   d. a pablum

True-False Questions

21. Biology is destiny. _____

22. Fewer than half of today's post-secondary students are women. _____

23. Research findings with men can usually be generalized to women. _____

24. You use the naturalistic observation method every day of your life. _____

25. Numerous studies report positive correlations between stress and health. _____

Essay Question

26. Identify the differences between the clinical and healthy-personality approaches to adjustment.

Student Activities

Name _____ **Date** _____

1.1 What Is Challenging?

Nevid and Rathus begin their first chapter with several examples of individuals facing challenges. They illustrate the nature of challenge for Beth, John, Maria, Lisa, and David, and they also review a litany of problems and opportunities that could serve as a checklist. Have you considered which ones apply to you? Some can be regarded as concerns, some as hassles, some as crises, and some as openings for growth. Try this: skip any issues that do not concern you, but count the number of issues in the list below that are (1) issues you have had to adjust to and are examples of your growth, and (2) issues that remain a challenge.

Interpersonal relations	Test taking
Family	Premarital living arrangements
Health	Career goals
Economics	Child care
Career	Life goals conflicts
Self-worth	Grades
School	Moral decisions
Environmental pollution	Food and eating
Sex	Insomnia
Politics	Motivation
Ethics	Depression
Emotions	Suicide
Concern for others	Role conflicts
Constraints of time	Self-esteem
Sexual orientation	Changing technology
AIDS and/or safe-sex practices	Religion
Alcohol	Personal budget
Divorce	Aging
Exercise	Drug abuse
Heart disease	Marriage
Cigarette smoking	Values
Job interviews	Studying
Tranquilizer use	Family planning
Social approval	Mental health
Gender issues in the workplace	Cultural diversity

How many issues fit category (1)?_____ How many issues fit category (2)?_____

Pat yourself on the back for each issue you have faced and managed. For those issues you still must face, consider the following possibility. Look in the index of the text and see if this text promises to discuss issues relevant to you. You may wish to look ahead, or even to visit the library or bookstore for references to supplement your reading.

It might be valuable to ask your classmates how many issues they recorded in each case. Everyone could submit their results anonymously, so it could be made apparent that everyone has some challenge to face. That might help your instructor to recognize which directions to take a class.

Activity continued on the back

Follow-Up Questions:

1. Which of the above issues were **not** faced by your parents?

2. Which of the above issues were **not** faced by people 150 years ago?

3. How are these issues more (or less) difficult than those faced by your parents or by people 150 years ago?

4. In what way were some of the issues faced by your parents or by people 150 years ago more difficult than those you face today?

5. What classes on your campus address any of these challenges?

1.2 A Learning Theory Assessment of Your Studying

Learning theorists encourage us to analyze how reinforcers and punishments affect our behavior, and Chapter 1 recommends we use self-rewards for encouraging studying. It might be useful to attempt a "behavioral assessment" of studying behavior by asking ourselves these questions and recording our answers:

1. What are my rewards for studying and how powerful are they?

2. How soon after studying do I receive these rewards?

3. What behaviors do I do instead of studying (to avoid it)?

4. What are my rewards for these incompatible behaviors, and how soon do they get rewarded?

5. Which comes first, studying or other behaviors? Why?

Activity continued on the back

Now consider these general principles from learning theories:

1. Rewards are more effective when they are immediate.

2. Bigger rewards are more effective and weak rewards are less effective.

3. If we engage in less rewarding behavior before a more rewarding behavior, we may grow to like the less rewarding behavior and do it more and more.

In other words, if our main rewards for studying are grades, graduation, and maybe the approval of others, all of which are delayed, we can choose to follow studying with entertainment or socializing which are immediate and attractive rewards. Now if you will create a simple plan for organizing activities that can serve as immediate rewards for studying, you will have taken your first step as a behavioral technician. Write your plan here:

Name _____ **Date** _____

1.3 Research: A Way of Knowing

Chapter 1 explains the value of the scientific approach, and especially the role of research. Being able to read, understand, and conduct research can put you on the leading edge of knowledge, which is valuable in our "information age," whether your career takes you into business, human services, science, or industry.

To explore research as a tool for knowledge, follow the outline for research in Chapter 1, and pick one of the issues mentioned in the chapter.

1. First, what is the nature of the problem?

2. Formulate a research question.

3. Form a hypothesis.

4. Design an experiment to test your hypothesis. Present your experimental design here:

Activity continued on the back

5. Imagine the hypothesis is supported, what can you conclude?

6. How can you be sure that the results are due to the factors you are studying, instead of outside variables that you could not control for in your experiment?

1.4 Gender Issues in Challenges to Adjustment

Fifty years ago, the expectations for what men and women should become in our society were very clear cut, and often very different from each other. Today, many of those expectations have changed, while some have remained remarkably similar.

1. Identify three major expectations for men that you believe have substantially changed since the 1950s and briefly explain what impact you believe that has had on males growing up in our society today.

    a.

    b.

    c.

2. Identify three major expectations for women that you believe have substantially changed since the 1950s and briefly explain what impact you believe that has had on females growing up in our society today.

    a.

    b.

    c.

Activity continued on the back

3. Identify two major expectations for men that you believe have remained similar to those of the 1950s and briefly explain what impact you believe they have on males growing up in our society today.

    a.

    b.

4. Identify two major expectations for women that you believe have remained similar to those of the 1950s and briefly explain what impact you believe they have on females growing up in our society today.

    a.

    b.

5. Many people in our culture still have somewhat different expectations for males and females and how they should fulfill social roles. Given this, who do you think has the more difficult task in adjusting in our society today, males or females? Why?

Name _____ **Date** _____

1.5 Planning Your Study Time

Taking an active rather than passive approach to studying can begin with the mastery of the material in this text. To organize your study plans, use a chart such as the one below to fill in the planned amount of study time and the planned number of pages to read at the beginning of the week. Fill in the **actual** amount of study time and the **actual** number of pages read each day. At the end of the week, compare the totals from the "planned" columns and the "actual" columns.

Adjust next week's plans according to how much leftover and new material remain to be studied. Each day that your "actual" total is equal to or greater than your "planned" column, you have met your study goals for that day and are entitled to reward yourself.

	Planned Amount of Study Time	Planned Number of Pages Read	Actual Study Time	Actual Number of Pages Read	Reward?
Monday					
Tuesday					
Wednesday					
Thursday					
Friday					
Saturday					
Sunday					

2

Theories of Personality

Chapter Outline

Module 2.1: Psychodynamic Theories

Module 2.2: Learning Theories

Module 2.3: Humanistic Theory

Module 2.4: Trait Theories

Module 2.5: The Sociocultural Perspective

Module 2.6: Assessing Personality

Module 2.7: Psychology in Daily Life: Understanding Yourself

Chapter Overview

The Psychodynamic Model. Freud's theory is termed psychodynamic because it assumes that we are driven largely by unconscious motives and forces within our personalities. People experience conflict as basic instincts of hunger, sex, and aggression come up against social pressures to follow rules and moral codes. At first this conflict is external, but as we develop it is internalized.

Freud's Structure of Personality. The personality consists of three mental states: the id, the ego, and the superego. The unconscious id represents psychological drives and seeks instant gratification. The ego, or the sense of self or "I," develops through experience and takes into account what is practical and possible in gratifying the impulses of the id. Defense mechanisms such as repression protect the ego from anxiety by repressing unacceptable ideas and distorting reality. The superego is the moral conscience and develops largely through the Oedipus complex and identification with other important figures in one's life.

Freud's Theory of Psychosexual Development. People undergo psychosexual development as psychosexual energy, or libido, is transferred from one erogenous zone to another during childhood. There are five stages of development: oral, anal, phallic, latency, and genital. Fixation in a stage leads to development of traits associated with the stage.

Other Psychodynamic Theorists. Carl Jung's theory, analytical psychology, focuses on a collective unconscious and archetypes, both of which reflect the history of our species. Alfred Adler's theory, individual psychology, focuses on the inferiority complex and the compensating drive for superiority. Karen Horney's theory focuses on parent-child relationships and the possible development of feelings of anxiety and hostility. Erik Erikson's theory of psychosocial development highlights the importance of early social relationships rather than the gratification of childhood sexual impulses. Erikson extended Freud's five developmental stages to eight, including stages that occur in adulthood.

The Psychodynamic View of Healthy Personality. Psychodynamic theorists equate healthy personality with the abilities to love and work, ego strength, a creative Self (Jung and Adler), compensation for feelings of inferiority (Adler), and positive outcomes to various psychosocial challenges (Horney and Erikson).

Traits. Traits are elements of personality that are inferred from behavior and account for consistency in behavior. Heredity is believed to play a large role in the development of traits.

The Trait Theory View of Personality. Hans Eysenck described personality in terms of two broad personality dimensions: introversion–extraversion and emotional stability–instability (neuroticism). The major contemporary model, the five-factor model, posits five key factors of personality: extraversion, agreeableness, conscientiousness, emotional stability, and openness to experience.

The Trait Theory View of Healthy Personality. Trait theorists to some degree equate the healthy personality with having the fortune of inheriting traits that promote adjustment. The focus of trait theory is description of traits people possess, not the origins or modification of traits.

The Behaviorist View of Personality. To behaviorists, personality is the sum total of an individual's response repertoire, which is developed on the basis of experience. Behaviorists believe we should focus on observable behavior rather than hypothesized unconscious forces, and that we should emphasize the situational determinants of behavior. They also consider the sense of personal freedom or ability to exercise free will to be an illusion.

Classical Conditioning. Classical conditioning is a simple form of associative learning in which a previously neutral stimulus (the conditioned stimulus, or CS) comes to elicit the response evoked by a second stimulus (the unconditioned stimulus, or US) as a result of repeatedly being paired with the second stimulus.

Operant Conditioning. Operant conditioning is a form of learning in which organisms learn to engage in behavior that is reinforced. Reinforced responses occur with greater frequency.

Types of Reinforcers. These include positive, negative, primary, and secondary reinforcers. Positive reinforcers increase the probability that operant responses will occur when they are applied. Negative reinforcers increase the probability that operant responses will occur when they are removed. Primary reinforcers have their value because of the organism's biological makeup. Secondary reinforcers such as money and approval acquire their value through association with established reinforcers.

Punishment Versus Negative Reinforcement. Punishment and negative reinforcement are not the same thing. Punishments are defined as aversive events that suppress behavior; punishments decrease the probability that the targeted behavior will occur. Negative reinforcers increase the probability that the targeted behavior will occur—when they, the negative reinforcers, are removed.

The Social-Cognitive View of Personality. Social-cognitive theory focuses on cognitive and social influences on behavior, such as expectancies and learning by observing others in social environments. To predict behavior, social-cognitive theorists believe we need to consider both situational variables (rewards and punishments) and person variables, such as competencies, expectancies, and self-regulatory processes.

The Learning Theorist View of Healthy Personality. Learning theorists prefer to speak of adaptive behaviors rather than a healthy personality. Nevertheless, they would probably concur that the following will contribute to a "healthy personality": having opportunities for observational learning, acquiring competencies, encoding events accurately, having accurate expectations, having positive self-efficacy expectations, and regulating behavior productively to achieve goals.

The Humanistic View of Personality. Humanistic theorists argue that our personalities are shaped by what we make of our lives. To the humanists, we are all capable of free choice, self-fulfillment, and ethical behavior. Humanistic psychologists draw upon the philosophy of existentialism, the belief that humans are free to determine their lives and cannot escape responsibility for the choices and the meaning or lack of meaning with which they imbue their lives. Both psychodynamic and behavior theorists believe that our behavior is determined, either by internal forces within the personality, as Freud believed, or by external forces in the environment as the behaviorists maintained. But humanistic psychologists believe that people can exercise personal choice and strive for self-actualization.

Self Theory. According to Rogers, the self is an organized and consistent way in which a person perceives his or her "I" in relation to others. Self theory begins by assuming the existence of the self and each person's unique frame of reference. The self attempts to actualize (develop its unique potential) and best does so when the person receives unconditional positive regard. Conditions of worth may lead to a distorted self-concept, to disowning of parts of the self, and to anxiety.

The Humanistic View of Healthy Personality. Humanistic-existential theorists view the healthy personality as experiencing life here and now, being open to new experience, expressing one's genuine feelings and ideas, trusting one's feelings, engaging in meaningful activities, making adaptive changes, and being one's own person.

Sociocultural Theory. One cannot fully understand the personality of an individual without understanding the cultural beliefs and socioeconomic conditions that have affected the individual. Sociocultural theory encourages us to consider the roles of ethnicity, gender, culture, and socioeconomic status in the development of personality and behavior.

Individualism Versus Collectivism. Individualists define themselves in terms of their personal identities and give priority to their personal goals. Collectivists define themselves in terms of the groups to which they belong and give priority to the group's goals. Many Western societies are individualistic and foster individualism in personality. Many Eastern societies are collectivist and foster collectivism in personality.

Acculturation and the Adjustment of Immigrant Groups. Relationships are complex, with negative outcomes associated both with high and low levels of acculturation. Healthier adjustment may be related to maintaining ethnic identity while balancing the demands of living in the host country.

The Sociocultural View of Healthy Personality. Sociocultural theorists would view the healthy personality as functioning adaptively within one's cultural setting, balancing competing cultural demands, coping with discrimination, and becoming adequately acculturated in a new society while at the same time, retaining important traditional values and customs.

Personality Assessment. Various methods are used to assess personality, including observation and interviewing techniques, behavior rating scales, and objective and projective tests of personality. Objective tests, such as the MMPI, present sets of items or questions that allow for only a limited range of responses, so that they can be objectively scored. The examiner compares the individual's scores to relevant norms in order to determine how an individual places on particular psychological traits or to identify areas of concern. Projective tests, such as the Rorschach and the TAT, present ambiguous test materials that are answered in ways that may reveal underlying aspects of the individual's personality.

Learning Objectives

After studying this chapter, your students should be able to:

1.   Explain Freud's "iceberg" view of consciousness, identifying each level of consciousness and explaining its functions.

2.   Identify the three psychic structures in Freud's personality theory and how each structure functions.

3.   Identify and briefly explain, and give an example of, 5 of the defense mechanisms proposed by Sigmund Freud.

4.   Identify the stages of Freud's theory of psychosexual development and describe what happens at each stage.

5.   Briefly explain the views of the various neo-Freudians in terms of their major concepts and how they differed from Freud.

6.   Explain Erikson's view of development, identifying each of his stages of development and the life crisis characterizing that stage.

7.   Summarize the elements that psychodynamic theorists feel are essential for a person to have a healthy personality.

8.   Discuss the views of the behaviorists in terms of their focus and how they differ from the other personality perspectives.

9.   Explain how classical conditioning works. In your explanation, be sure to briefly discuss what extinction and spontaneous recovery are.

10.   Explain how operant conditioning works and discuss the differences among positive and negative reinforcers, primary and secondary reinforcers, and punishment.

11.   Describe the views of social-cognitive theorists in terms of their focus, concepts, and how they differ from the other personality perspectives.

12.   Summarize the elements that social-cognitive theorists believe are necessary for a person to have a healthy personality.

13.   Describe the views of humanistic theorists in terms of their focus and common features, and how they differ from the other personality theories.

14. Explain the major ideas of Abraham Maslow's theory of personality.

15. Explain the major ideas of Carl Rogers' self theory.

16. Summarize the elements that humanistic theorists believe are essential for a person to have a healthy personality.

17. Discuss the views of trait theorists in terms of their focus and how they differ from the other personality perspectives.

18. Explain what the "five-factor" model is, briefly describing each of the five factors in the model and discussing how the model is currently being used.

19. Summarize the elements that trait theorists feel are necessary for a person to have a healthy personality.

20. Describe the views of sociocultural theorists in terms of their focus and common features, and how they differ from the other personality theories.

21. Summarize the elements that sociocultural theorists believe are essential for a person to have a healthy personality.

22. Compare and contrast objective tests with projective tests.

Key Terms

personality	genital stage	person variables
psychodynamic theory	analytic psychology	situational variables
preconscious	collective unconscious	competencies
unconscious	archetypes	encode
repression	inferiority complex	expectancies
psychoanalysis	drive for superiority	self-efficacy expectations
resistance	creative self	outcome expectancies
psychic structures	individual psychology	humanism
id	psychosocial development	existentialism
pleasure principle	ego identity	self-actualization
ego	free association	hierarchy of needs
reality principle	behaviorism	self
defense mechanism	classical conditioning	frames of reference
superego	unconditioned stimulus	unconditional positive regard
identification	unconditioned response	conditional positive regard
eros	conditioned stimulus	conditions of worth
libido	conditioned response	client-centered therapy
erogenous zone	extinction	self-ideals
psychosexual development	spontaneous recovery	traits
oral stage	operant conditioning	neuroticism
fixation	reinforcement	introversion
anal stage	positive reinforcers	extraversion
anal retentive traits	negative reinforcers	conscientiousness
anal expulsive traits	primary reinforcers	neuroticism
phallic stage	secondary reinforcers	neurotransmitter
Oedipus complex	punishment	sociocultural theory
Electra complex	social cognitive theory	individualists
displaced	reciprocal determinism	collectivists
latency	observational learning model	acculturation

Key Persons

Sigmund Freud
Carl Jung
Alfred Adler
Karen Horney
Erik Erikson

John B. Watson
Ivan Pavlov
Little Albert
B.F. Skinner
Albert Bandura

Abraham Maslow
Carl Rogers
Hans Eysenck
Hermann Rorschach

Key Terms Reviews: Due to the complexity of this chapter, there are three different exercises in this section. The first exercise deals with terms related to psychodynamic and biological theories. The second exercise presents terms related to behavioral, social-cognitive, and phenomenological theories. The third exercise presents the people associated with the various theories discussed in this chapter.

Key Terms Review #1

Define each of the following terms:

1. Preconscious: _____

   _____

2. Unconscious: _____

   _____

3. Repression: _____

   _____

4. Resistance: _____

   _____

5. Psychic Structure: _____

   _____

6. Id: _____

   _____

7. Ego: _____

   _____

8. Superego: _____

_____

9. Libido: _____

_____

10. Psychosexual Development: _____

_____

11. Fixation: _____

_____

12. Oedipus complex: _____

_____

13. Collective unconscious: _____

_____

14. Archetypes: _____

_____

15. Inferiority Complex: _____

_____

16. Drive for Superiority: _____

_____

17. Psychosocial Development: _____

_____

18. Traits: _____

_____

19. Introversion: _____

_____

20. Neuroticism: _____

_____

Key Terms Review #2

Define each of the following terms:

1. Behaviorism: _____

_____

2. Classical Conditioning: _____

_____

3. Unconditioned Stimulus: _____

_____

4. Unconditioned Response: _____

_____

5. Conditioned Stimulus: _____

_____

6. Conditioned Response: _____

_____

7. Extinction: _____

_____

8. Spontaneous Recovery: _____

_____

9. Operant Conditioning: _____

_____

10. Reinforcement: _____

_____

11. Negative Reinforcers: _____

_____

12. Secondary Reinforcers: _____

_____

13. Person Variables: _____

_____

14. Reciprocal Determinism: _____

_____

15. Self-efficacy Expectations: _____

_____

16. Existentialism:_____

_____

17. Self-Actualization: _____

_____

18. Hierarchy of Needs: _____

_____

19. Frames of Reference: _____

_____

20. Unconditional Positive Regard: _____

_____

Key Persons Review

Identify the theory, technique, or ideas most closely associated with each of the following people:

Example: Sigmund Freud: Psychoanalysis, psychodynamic theory, and the influence of

unconscious urges and sexuality on personality.

1. Alfred Adler: _____

_____

2. Abraham Maslow: _____

_____

3. Erik Erikson: _____

_____

4. B. F. Skinner: _____

_____

5. Albert Bandura: _____

_____

6. Carl Jung: _____

_____

7. Carl Rogers: _____

_____

8. Ivan Pavlov: _____

_____

9. John B. Watson: _____

_____

10. Karen Horney: _____

_____

11. Hans Eysenck: _____

_____

12. Hermann Rorschach: _____

_____

13. Little Albert: _____

_____

Chapter Review

1. Each psychodynamic theory owes its origins to the thinking of _____.

2. Each psychodynamic theory teaches that personality is characterized by a dynamic _____ between different elements within the personality.

3. Freud was trained as a _____.

4. Freud pictured the human mind as similar to a(n) _____.

5. Freud divided the mind into three levels of awareness: the _____, the _____, and the _____.

6. Freud believed that most of the human mind lies in the _____.

7. Freud believed that people keep unacceptable urges or impulses from conscious awareness through the process of _____.

8. Freud's method of exploring human personality is known as _____.

9. Freud labeled the three psychic structures that control personality the _____, the _____, and the _____.

10. According to Freud, the _____ is the only psychic structure present at birth and it operates under the _____ principle.

11. According to Freud, the ego is guided by the _____ principle.

12. According to Freud, an unconscious function of the ego that protects it from anxiety-evoking material by preventing accurate recognition of this material is a _____ _____.

13. According to Freud, the _____ develops during early childhood by incorporating the moral standards of the parents through the process of _____.

14. **Matching:** Match each defense mechanism with its proper definition.

_____ a.	Repression	1.	The use of self-deceiving justifications for unacceptable behavior
_____ b.	Regression	2.	The channeling of primitive impulses into positive, constructive efforts
_____ c.	Rationalization		
_____ d.	Displacement	3.	Thrusting one's own unacceptable impulses onto others
_____ e.	Projection	4.	The ejection of anxiety-evoking ideas from awareness
_____ f.	Reaction Formation	5.	Refusal to accept the true nature of a threat
_____ g.	Denial	6.	The return, under stress, to a form of behavior characteristic of an earlier stage of development
_____ h.	Sublimation	7.	Assumption of behavior that is opposite of one's genuine impulses
		8.	The transfer of ideas and impulses from threatening or unsuitable objects to less threatening objects

15. Freud believed that there is a major life instinct called _____, which contains a certain amount of energy called _____.

16. The five stages of psychosexual development postulated by Freud are the _____ stage (age 0-1), the _____ stage (1-2), the _____ stage (3-5), the _____ stage (6-11), and the _____ stage (12 and over).

17. Freud believed that inadequate or excessive gratification in any stage can lead to _____ in that stage.

18. According to Freud, issues of self-control and delaying gratification are paramount during the _____ stage.

19. Four psychodynamic theorists other than Freud are _____, _____,

    _____, and _____.

20. Carl Jung believed in a unifying force of personality called the _____.

21. Carl Jung believed in two levels of the unconscious mind: a _____ unconscious

    and a _____ unconscious.

22. Adler believed that children develop a drive for _____ to overcome an

    _____ _____.

23. Adler believed that self-_____ plays a major role in the formation of
    personality.

24. Karen Horney argued that it is not _____ envy that makes women feel inferior

    to men, but rather the envy of social _____ and _____ that men hold in society.

25. Karen Horney believed that _____ _____ were crucial to children's
    development.

26. Erik Erikson described eight stages of _____ development.

27. **Matching:** Match the conflict with the stage of development in which Erikson
    thought it would occur.

_____	a. Infancy	1.	Ego identity vs. role diffusion
_____	b. Early childhood	2.	Initiative vs. guilt
_____	c. Preschool years	3.	Integrity vs. despair
_____	d. Grammar school years	4.	Industry vs. inferiority
_____	e. Adolescence	5.	Generativity vs. stagnation
_____	f. Young adulthood	6.	Trust vs. mistrust
_____	g. Middle adulthood	7.	Intimacy vs. isolation
_____	h. Late adulthood	8.	Autonomy vs. shame and doubt

28. The five elements of a healthy personality according to the psychodynamic model are:

a. _____

b. _____

c. _____

d. _____

e. _____

29. John Watson was the founder of the _____ movement.

30. _____ conditioning was discovered by accident by Ivan Pavlov.

31. **Matching:** Match the term on the left with its appropriate descriptor on the right taken from Pavlov's research with dogs.

_____ a. Unconditioned stimulus   1. A bell

_____ b. Unconditioned response   2. A piece of meat

_____ c. Conditioned stimulus   3. Salivation to a bell

_____ d. Conditioned response   4. Salivation to a piece of meat

32. **Matching:** Match the term on the left with the appropriate definition on the right.

_____ a.	Extinction	1.	a stimulus that increases the frequency of a behavior when it is presented
_____ b.	Spontaneous recovery	2.	a pleasant stimulus that increases the frequency of a behavior
_____ c.	Classical Conditioning	3.	an unlearned reinforcer, such as food or water
_____ d.	Operant conditioning	4.	repeated presentation of a conditioned stimulus in the absence of the unconditioned stimulus, leading to suspension of the conditioned response
_____ e.	Reinforcement	5.	a technique for extinguishing fear in which a person is continuously exposed to fear-evoking, but harmless, stimulation
_____ f.	Primary reinforcer	6.	an unpleasant stimulus that suppresses behavior
_____ g.	Secondary reinforcer	7.	a simple form of learning in which the frequency of behavior is increased by means of rewards or reinforcement
_____ h.	Positive reinforcer	8.	a stimulus that gains a value as a reinforcer as a result of being associated with established reinforcers (i.e., money)
_____ i.	Negative reinforcer	9.	a form of conditioning in which previously desirable objects become repugnant as a result of being paired with unpleasant stimulation
_____ j.	Punishment	10.	the eliciting of an extinguished response by a conditioned stimulus after some time has elapsed
_____ k.	Reward	11.	a simple form of learning in which one stimulus brings about a response usually brought forth by a second stimulus as a result of being paired repeatedly with the second stimulus
		12.	a reinforcer that increases the frequency of a behavior when it is removed
		13.	a stimulus that increases the frequency of a behavior

33. Social-cognitive theory focuses on the importance of learning by _____.

34. Person variables include _____, _____ strategies, _____,

and self-_____ systems and plans.

35. Social-cognitive theorists see the following five elements as essential to a healthy personality:

a. _____

b. _____

c. _____

d. _____

e. _____

36. Humanistic psychologists focus our attention on _____

_____.

37. The view that people are capable of free choice, self-fulfillment, and ethical behavior

is known as _____.

38. Maslow's hierarchy of needs, from lowest to highest within the hierarchy, include

_____, _____, _____, _____, and _____-_____

needs.

39. Carl Rogers' views of personality are labeled _____ theory.

40. When parents show children _____ positive regard, they learn to disown the

thoughts and behaviors rejected by the parents and may develop _____

_____ _____, which make them feel as if they are acceptable **ONLY** if

they behave in certain ways. However, if parents show children _____ positive

regard, it can help them develop high _____-_____.

41. Getting in touch with our genuine feelings, accepting them, and acting on them to

achieve self-actualization is the goal of _____-_____ therapy.

42. Humanistic-existential theorists see the following six qualities as essential healthy
personalities:

a. _____

b. _____

c. _____

d. _____

e. _____

f. _____

43. A relatively stable element of personality that is inferred from behavior is a

    _____.

44. Hans Eysenck focused much of his research on the relationships between two
    personality traits: _____-_____, and _____.

45. Recent research on traits suggests that there are five basic personality factors:

    _____, _____, _____, _____, and _____

    to new experiences.

46. Critics contend that trait theory _____ behavior but does not _____ it.

47. The view that focuses on the roles of ethnicity, gender, culture, and socioeconomic

    status in personality, behavior, and adjustment is _____ theory.

48. Cross-cultural research indicates that people in the United States and many northern

    European countries tend to be _____, whereas people from Africa, Asia, and

    Central and South America tend to be _____.

49. Among immigrants, those who identify with the _____ pattern of acculturation
    have the highest self-esteem.

50. Sociocultural theorists view the healthy personality in terms of three issues:

    a. _____

    b. _____

    c. _____

51. _____ tests present respondents with a standard group of test items in the form of a
    questionnaire, with a limited range of answers for each question.

52. In _____ tests, people are asked to interpret ambiguous stimuli and there is no
    one correct response

53. The _____ and the _____ are two types of projective tests.

Sample Test

Multiple-Choice Questions

1. A psychologist believes that personality is the result of an active struggle between various conscious and unconscious forces moving through the mind. This psychologist believes in the _____ model of personality.
    a. psychodynamic
    b. social learning
    c. phenomenological
    d. biological

2. Freud's psychic structures of personality can _____.
    a. not be seen nor measured directly
    b. be seen, but not measured directly
    c. be measured, but not seen directly
    d. both be seen and measured directly

3. In psychodynamic theory, the unconscious assumption of another person's behavior, usually the behavior of the parent of the same gender, is _____.
    a. a reaction formation
    b. catharsis
    c. displacement
    d. identification

4. A man who is scolded by his boss and then yells at the employees who work for him, rather than the boss who upset him in the first place is using the defense mechanism of _____.
    a. projection
    b. a reaction formation
    c. sublimation
    d. displacement

5. For Freud, the term for the instinct to preserve and perpetuate life is _____.
    a. libido
    b. eros
    c. thanatos
    d. animus

6. Which of the following is the correct order of Freud's stages of development?
    a. anal, oral, phallic, genital, latency
    b. oral, anal, latency, genital, phallic
    c. anal. oral, latency, phallic, genital
    d. oral, anal, phallic, latency, genital

7. Irene is perfectionistic, overly self-controlled, as well as excessively neat and clean. She is _____, according to Freud.
    a. orally fixated
    b. an anal expulsive
    c. an anal retentive
    d. fixated in the phallic stage

8. Each of the following theorists was a follower of Sigmund Freud except _____.
    a. Carl Jung
    b. Karen Horney
    c. Fritz Perls
    d. Alfred Adler

9. Early psychodynamic theory taught that women who sought to compete with men in the workplace were suffering from _____.
    a. unconscious penis envy
    b. an inferiority complex
    c. excessive libido
    d. psychosocial retardation

10. Erikson labeled each of his developmental stages _____.
    a. according to the life crisis that must be resolved at that stage
    b. according to the moral dilemma that had to be resolved at each stage and how the person resolved it
    c. according to cognitive abilities possessed by a person at each stage
    d. according to the underlying psychosexual conflict that had to be resolved at each stage

11. The conflict that Erikson felt characterized young adulthood was _____.
    a. industry versus inferiority
    b. intimacy versus isolation
    c. integrity versus despair
    d. identity versus role diffusion

12. A scientist says that he can shape a child's personality into whatever he wants it to be through manipulation of the child's environment. The scientist also claims that psychology should focus on measurable, testable actions and reject "mentalistic" concepts that cannot be proven. This psychologist's views are most similar to those of a _____.
    a. behaviorist
    b. psychodynamic theorist
    c. humanist
    d. trait theorist

13. In Pavlov's research with dogs, salivation to the meat was _____.
    a. the unconditioned stimulus
    b. the unconditioned response
    c. the conditioned stimulus
    d. the conditioned response

14. In _____, an organism learns to engage in a certain behavior because of the effects of that behavior.
    a. classical conditioning
    b. flooding
    c. observational learning
    d. operant conditioning

15. Which of the following is **NOT** seen by learning theorists as a danger to the use of punishment in shaping behavior?
    a. punishment does not teach alternative, acceptable behaviors
    b. punishment may be imitated as a way of solving problems or coping with stress
    c. punishment only suppresses unwanted behavior under limited circumstances
    d. punishment does not rapidly suppress undesirable behavior

16. In social-cognitive theory, knowledge and skills that are needed to adjust in our social environment are known as _____.
    a. expectancies
    b. self-efficacy
    c. encoding strategies
    d. competencies

17. The old U.S. army recruiting ads that claimed in the army you can "be all that you can be" were utilizing Maslow's concept of _____ to try to get people to enlist.
    a. authentic living
    b. self-efficacy
    c. psychological congruence
    d. self-actualization

18. A parent wants to help her child develop self-esteem. If she follows Carl Rogers' guidelines, she will most likely provide the child with _____.
    a. unconditional positive regard
    b. conditional positive regard
    c. conditions of worth
    d. a peak experience

19. From the trait theory perspective, healthy personality is mainly the result of _____.
    a. a creative self
    b. good genetic inheritance
    c. ego strength
    d. self-actualization

20. Individualism is most likely to be fostered by growing up in a _____ society.
    a. communist
    b. socialist
    c. cloistered
    d. capitalist

True-False Questions

21. Freud believed that children encounter conflict during each stage of development. _____

22. The definition of reinforcement relies on "mentalistic" assumptions about what a person or lower organism finds pleasant or unpleasant. _____

23. Behaviorists typically speak in terms of a healthy personality. _____

24. The greatest value of the humanistic approach may also be its greatest weakness. _____

25. The Rorschach is the best known projective personality test. _____

Essay Question

26. Describe the views of humanistic-existential theorists in terms of their focus and common features, and how they differ from the other personality theories.

Student Activities

Name _____ **Date** _____

2.1 What Is Your Theory of Human Nature?

In the second chapter, Nevid and Rathus describe some of the most important theories of personality developed in this century by psychologists. We all have our own theories of human nature, whether they are explicit or implicit. Just as the people who construct such theories for a living, we tend to begin with observations and then hypotheses. What theories are we working with? Explore this by simply asking yourself if you think humans are more inclined to be kind and benevolent or more inclined to be egotistical, selfish, and only interested in "number one." To provoke some thinking here, decide which description of people you think is more accurate.

Sigmund Freud said:

". . . men are not gentle friendly creatures wishing for love, who simply defend themselves if they are attacked, but . . . a powerful measure of desire for aggressiveness has to be reckoned with as part of their instinctual endowment. The result is that their neighbor is to them not only a helper or sexual object, but also a temptation to them to gratify their aggressiveness . . . to seize his possessions, to humiliate him, to cause him pain, to torture and to kill him . . . Anyone who calls to mind the atrocities of the early migrations of the invasions of the Huns or by the so-called Mongols under Ghengis Khan and Tamurlane, of the sack of Jerusalem by the pious crusaders, and even the horrors of the last world war, will have to bow his head humbly before the truth of this view of man . . . We see man as a savage beast to whom the thought of sparing his own kind is alien" (*Civilization and Its Discontents,* 1930).

Carl Rogers wrote:

"I have little sympathy with the rather prevalent concept that man is basically irrational, and that his impulses, if not controlled, will lead to destruction of others and self. Man's behavior is exquisitely rational, moving with subtle and ordered complexity toward the goals his organism is endeavoring to achieve" (*Journal of Consulting Psychology,* 1957).

Questions:

1. Which position do you think is more accurate? Why?

Activity continued on the back

Questions (continued)

2. Since Freud cited historical cases to support his view, what examples could be used to refute him?

3. How could either of the arguments use case histories, correlated observations, or research findings to support the theories (provide some specific examples)?

4. Is there any way to resolve this debate? If so, how? If not, why not?

5. What would the consequences be should the followers of each theorist, Freud and Rogers, be placed in charge of education? What if each point of view were represented by presidential candidates? Where else in society might big differences be created by the applications of these different models?

2.2 Researching Human Nature

We have been much encouraged to think that research is an important and powerful tool for answering questions about ourselves and others. If we use case histories to support one side or the other, it seems it will become a draw. There are lots of nice people in the world and lots of dangerous people. A tougher test of theories is to create hypotheses and to test them.

What hypotheses could address such basic issues as those raised by Freud and Rogers? Consider the following possibility as we engage in each of the four basic steps to the scientific method:

1. **Formulate a research question.** When people are given a chance to be helpful, are they as ruthless as Freud says, or as benevolent as Rogers pictures? What do you think? Why?

2. **Developing a hypothesis.** When people find a wallet with identification and money in it, they are in a position to be helpful. What hypothesis would Freud and Rogers likely create to predict if we were purposely to drop wallets at various locations around campus? Also, what is your prediction? Express your predictions as percentages of wallets returned intact with money and identification inside. Explain why you feel the way you do?

3. **Testing a hypothesis.** Where will you place or drop the wallets? How much money would you place in each, or would you choose different amounts? How will finders be able to return wallets if they choose to do so, and can they be returned anonymously?

Activity continued on the back

4. **<u>Drawing conclusions about the hypothesis.</u>** Since this is speculation, unless you have vast resources upon which to draw, just imagine the outcomes fit your own predictions even better than Freud's and/or Rogers'. What could you conclude about the alternative theories? What other hypotheses and tests could you now create?

5. While your experiment has done a good job of explaining the "what" of your hypothesis (how many people picked up the wallet and returned it), has it been able to explain the "why"? One drawback of many psychological research studies is that they do little to reveal why people act as they do. Is there any way you could empirically discover the "why" in your study? If so how? If not, why not?

2.3 Creating Classical Conditioning

It is useful to start this exercise by reading about Pavlov's work on classical conditioning, described in Chapter 2. He used dogs in his research, but we can use roommates and friends to explore classical conditioning. Simply ask a friend to hold out his or her hands with the palms turned up. Tell your subject to resist the moderate pressure you exert downward on his or her hands with your own hands. Each time, before you push down, say the word "Now!" then immediately press down. Repeat this four times. On the fifth occasion, sharply say "Now!" without pressing down. Did the hands rise up to meet yours? (If not, pronounce your friend less than a dog, and try another.) Now tell your subject that you will continue to place your hands just above his or hers and sharply say "Now!" until he or she no longer responds by raising the hands upward. Note how many trials until you "extinguish" his or her hand response. Finally, ask your friend to explain what happened and to write down what he or she tells you.

Follow-Up Questions:

1. Using the above exercise and the textbook, identify the:

    a. Conditioned stimulus:　　　 _____

    b. Unconditioned stimulus:　　 _____

    c. Conditioned response:　　　 _____

    d. Unconditioned response:　　 _____

2. If the hand response extinguishes immediately after telling the subject not to respond to the stimulus "Now!", how would you explain the extinction? However, if it takes more than one trial to extinguish the response, what explanation would you use?

Activity continued on the back

3. What results did your classmates get?

4. How did your subject explain what happened? Is it a behavioral, social-cognitive, phenomenological, or psychodynamic explanation, or some combination of them?

5. What theory is best supported by your results? Why?

Name _____ **Date** _____

2.4 Nature versus Nurture?

Various psychological theories conceptualize people as being inherently "good" or "evil." They also have different views about how much of personality is learned (nurture) as opposed to being genetically inherited (nature). Given what is discussed in Chapter 2 of your text, state where you think each of the following theories falls on the issue of nature versus nurture and then briefly explain why you feel as you do:

a.   Freudian Psychodynamic Theory:

b.   Trait Theory:

c.   Phenomenological Theory:

d.   Social-Cognitive Theory:

e.   Behavioral Theory:

Activity continued on the back

f.   Sociocultural Theory:

Which of the above theories' views makes the most sense to you? Why?

2.5 Free Will or Not?

The various theories of personality have widely opposing views of whether or not people have free will. Freud's theory implies that we are basically prisoners of our unconscious instincts, drives, and impulses with little conscious control (or free will) over our actions. Learning theorists are nearly as pessimistic in that many of them see us as prisoners of the conditioning imposed on us by the environment, with little or no ability to rise above that conditioning. Phenomenological theorists and cognitive theorists are somewhat more optimistic, arguing that we do have the ability to rise above biological needs and social conditioning. How do you feel about this?

1. Do you believe that people have free will? Why or why not?

2. If people do have free will, what implications does this have for society in areas such as education, religion, politics, and the criminal justice system? Explain why you feel as you do.

3. If people do not have free will, what implications does this have for society in areas such as education, religion, politics, and the criminal justice system? Again, explain why you feel as you do.

3

Stress: What It Is and How to Manage It

Chapter Outline

Chapter Overview

Sources of Stress. These include daily hassles, life events, acculturative stress, pain, frustration, conflict, Type A behavior, natural and technological disasters, and environmental factors such as noise, extremes of temperature, pollution and overcrowding.

Life Changes and Daily Hassles. Too many positive life changes can affect one's health because life changes require adjustment, whether they are positive or negative. In contrast to daily hassles, life changes occur irregularly. Research shows that hassles and life changes are associated with health problems such as heart disease and cancer, although causal connections remain murky.

Acculturative Stress is associated with physical and psychological health problems among African Americans. Developing a strong ethnic identity can serve to buffer the effects of this stress.

Pain is a major adjustment problem for many people. Obtaining accurate information, using distraction and fantasy, using hypnosis, practicing relaxation training and biofeedback training, taking control of your thoughts, and closing the "gate" on pain, are all methods for dealing with persistent pain.

Frustration occurs when a person's attempts to achieve a goal are thwarted. Activities such as commuting, as well as psychological barriers such as fear and anxiety can be persistent sources of frustration. People who have learned to surmount barriers or find substitute goals are more tolerant of frustration.

Conflict is frustrating and stressful. It occurs when people are pulled in two or more directions by opposite motives. Psychologists have classified conflicts into four types: approach-approach, avoidance-avoidance, approach-avoidance, and multiple approach-avoidance.

Irrational Beliefs. Albert Ellis shows that negative activating events (A) can be made more aversive (C) when irrational beliefs (B) compound their effects. People often catastrophize negative events. Two common irrational beliefs are excessive needs for social approval and perfectionism. Both set the stage for disappointment and increased stress.

Type A people create stress for themselves, in part, because they hold the irrational belief that they must be perfectly competent and achieving in everything they do.

Disasters. There are natural and technical disasters. Not only do such disasters do physical and personal damage when they strike, they also damage our support systems and our sense of control over our situations and our lives. The effects of disasters may linger for years after the physical damage is done. Terrorism is a source of stress that can shake our sense of living securing in our homes and communities.

Environmental Factors. High noise levels are stressful and can impair learning and memory, as well as lead to health problems such as hearing loss, hypertension, and neurological and intestinal disorders. Loud noise also dampens helping behavior and heightens aggressiveness. Extremes of temperature tax the body, are a source of stress, and impair performance. High temperatures are also connected with aggression. The lead in auto fumes may impair learning and memory. Overcrowded living conditions are experienced as aversive and lead to feelings that one's personal space is intruded upon. Perhaps because of crowding, noise, and so on, city dwellers are less likely than people who live in small towns to interact with or help strangers. A sense of control or choice—as in choosing to attend a concert or athletic contest—helps us cope with the stress or high density.

Self-Efficacy Expectations. Self-efficacy expectations encourage us to persist in difficult tasks and to endure discomfort. Self-efficacy expectations are also connected with lower levels of adrenaline and noradrenaline, thus having a braking effect on bodily arousal. When we feel capable of accomplishing tasks and meeting challenges, we are more likely to persist in difficult tasks and endure discomfort.

Psychological Hardiness. Suzanne Kobasa found that psychological hardiness among business executives is characterized by commitment, challenge, and control.

Humor. Evidence is not conclusive about the potential health benefits of humor or laughter. However, humor does make people feel good, and there is something to be said for feeling good.

Predictability. Predictability allows us to brace ourselves for stress. Control permits us to plan and execute ways of coping with stress.

Optimism has been linked to higher resilience to stress. It is also associated with lower levels of emotional distress among cancer patients and fewer postoperative complications among coronary bypass surgery patients.

Social Support. Social support has been shown to help people resist infectious diseases such as colds. It also helps people cope with the stress of cancer and other health problems. Kinds of social support include expression of emotional concern, instrumental aid, information, appraisal, and simple socializing.

Stress management seeks to help people more effectively manage stress, not eliminate it. While defensive coping techniques reduce the immediate impact of a stressor, they do so at a cost, and can sometimes be harmful in the long run. These techniques include withdrawal, denial, substance use, and aggression. Active coping techniques tend to be more effective because they deal directly with stress and its sources. Active coping techniques include keeping stress at manageable levels, becoming more aware of your body's response to stress, developing a social support system, exercising regularly, developing rational alternatives to stress-causing thoughts, expressing your feelings, practicing meditation, and practicing deep breathing and progressive relaxation.

Learning Objectives

After studying this chapter your students should be able to:

1. Define stress and identify eight different sources of stress.

2. Compare and contrast daily hassles and life changes and explain how each of them affects us.

3. Explain what acculturative stress is, what its effects are, and what can be done to better cope with it.

4. Discuss what pain and discomfort are, how they are transmitted to the brain, and how they affect us.

5. Identify and briefly discuss physiological and psychological methods of pain management.

6. Compare and contrast frustration and conflict, identifying the four types of conflict discussed in the text.

7. Explain Ellis's A-B-C model and discuss how irrational beliefs affect one's stress levels and one's ability to deal with stress

8. Compare and contrast Type A and Type B behavior, and explain how Type A behavior affects us.

9. Identify and briefly discuss the various environmental stressors and how they affect us.

10. Discuss what self-efficacy expectations are and how they affect us.

11. Explain what psychological hardiness is and discuss how it helps us cope with stress.

12. Explain how control, predictability, humor, optimism, and social support can help people cope with stress.

13. Compare defensive coping with active coping in terms of their types, uses, and advantages and disadvantages

14. Explain what meditation is, how it works, and summarize research findings on its effectiveness.

Key Terms

stress
daily hassles
uplifts
life changes
acculturative stress
prostaglandins
analgesic
endorphins
hypnosis

biofeedback training (BFT)
gate theory of pain
acupuncture
frustration
tolerance for frustration
conflict
approach-approach conflict
approach-avoidance conflict
avoidance-avoidance conflict

multiple approach-avoidance conflict
type A behavior pattern
self-efficacy expectations
psychological hardiness
locus of control
defensive coping
active coping
meditation
progressive muscle relaxation

Key Terms Review

Define each of the following terms:

1. Stress: _____

    _____

2. Daily Hassles: _____

    _____

3. Uplifts: _____

    _____

4. Life Changes: _____

    _____

5. Acculturative Stress: _____

    _____

6. Prostaglandins: _____

    _____

7. Analgesic: _____

    _____

8. Endorphins:_____

_____

9. Hypnosis: _____

_____

10. Biofeedback Training (BFT):_____

_____

11. Acupuncture: _____

_____

12. Frustration: _____

_____

13. Conflict: _____

_____

14. Approach-Approach Conflict: _____

_____

15. Avoidance-Avoidance Conflict: _____

_____

16. Approach-Avoidance Conflict: _____

_____

17. Multiple Approach-Avoidance Conflict: _____

_____

18. Type A Behavior: _____

_____

19. Self-Efficacy Expectations: _____

_____

20. Psychological Hardiness: _____

Chapter Review

1. In physics, _____ is a pressure or force exerted on a body.

2. In psychology, stress is the demand made on an organism to _____,

   _____, or _____.

3. Seven sources of stress are:

   a. _____

   b. _____

   c. _____

   d. _____

   e. _____

   f. _____

   g. _____

4. _____ is the number-one reason that college students seek help at college counseling centers.

5. Eight types of daily hassles are:

   a. _____

   b. _____

   c. _____

   d. _____

   e. _____

   f. _____

g. _____

h. _____

6. Life changes differ from daily hassles in the following two ways:

   a. _____

   b. _____

7. Research shows that African Americans who have an African-American viewpoint but who can befriend European Americans experience the _____ acculturative stress.

8. People aged 18 to 34 are most likely to attribute pain to _____ or _____, whereas people over age 65 are most likely to attribute pain to getting _____.

9. _____ facilitate transmission of pain messages to the brain and heighten blood circulation to an injured area.

10. _____ drugs such as aspirin and ibuprofen work by inhibiting the production of _____ and thus decreasing fever, inflammation, and pain.

11. Neurotransmitters that are functionally similar to morphine are _____.

12. Traditionally, the primary treatment for coping with pain has been _____.

13. Seven methods for improving pain management are:

    a. _____

    b. _____

    c. _____

    d. _____

    e. _____

    f. _____

    g. _____

14. According to _____ theory, the nervous system can process only a limited amount of stimulation at a time.

15. The benefits of acupuncture can best be explained by a _____ effect.

16. The emotion produced by the thwarting of a motive is _____.

17. Anxiety and fear can serve as _____ barriers that prevent us from effectively meeting our goals.

18. Too many stressors at once _____ our tolerance for frustration.

19. _____ is the feeling of being pulled in two or more directions by opposing motives.

20. Four types of conflict which can contribute to stress are:

    a. the _____-_____ conflict (the least stressful)

    b. the _____-_____ conflict

    c. the _____-_____ conflict

    d. the _____ _____-_____ conflict (the most stressful)

21. All forms of conflict entail motives that aim in _____ directions.

22. Albert Ellis notes that our _____ about events can be stressors that challenge our ability to adjust.

23. In Ellis's "A-B-C" model, the "A" refers to an _____ event, the "B" refers to _____, and the "C" refers to _____.

24. Ellis argues that many of us carry _____ _____ that magnify our current problems, and can give rise to new ones.

25. Researchers have found connections between irrational beliefs and feelings of _____ and _____.

26. People with _____ behavior pattern are competitive, highly driven, impatient, and aggressive, in contrast to _____ people who are more laid back and relaxed and focus on the quality of life.

27. Six types of environmental stressors are:

a. _____

b. _____

c. _____

d. _____

e. _____

f. _____

28. Natural disasters are hazardous in themselves and can also cause _____

_____ to pile atop one another by disrupting community life.

29. High levels of _____ are stressful and can lead to illnesses such as hypertension, neurological and intestinal disorders, and ulcers.

30. High temperatures are connected to _____ behavior.

31. The _____ in auto fumes is known to impair children's intellectual functioning.

32. Higher levels of air pollution are linked to higher _____ rates in cities.

33. _____ major population groups within the United States find high-density living conditions to be uncomfortable, even aversive.

34. _____ _____ is an invisible boundary, a sort of bubble that surrounds you.

35. Personal space appears to serve both _____ and _____ functions.

36. _____ _____ expectations have important influences on our abilities to withstand stress.

37. Kobasa's research found that psychologically hardy individuals were high in

_____, _____, and _____ _____.

38. Psychologically hardy people tend to have an _____ locus of control.

39. Scientific findings on the potential benefits of humor are _____.

40. Being able to _____ a stressor apparently _____ its impact.

63

41.   Examples from everyday life suggest that a sense of _____—a sense of making

choices—fosters healthy adjustment.

42.   People with _____ attitudes tend to be more resilient than others to the effects

of stress.

43.   Five types of social support that may serve to buffer the effects of stressors are:

a.   _____

b.   _____

c.   _____

d.   _____

e.   _____

44.   _____ coping reduces the immediate impact of a stressor, and grants us time to
marshal our resources, but does not deal with the source of the stress.

45.   Four types of defensive coping are:

a.   _____

b.   _____

c.   _____

d.   _____

46.   _____ coping methods for managing stress aim to manipulate the environment

to remove stressors.

47.   Three ways to keep stress at manageable levels include:

a.   _____

b.   _____

c.   _____

48. _____ is a relaxed state in which people's connection with the environment is transformed and worry, planning, and routine concerns are suspended.

49. Research on TM indicates that it produces a _____ response.

50. Edmund Jacobson is noted for developing a relaxation technique known as

_____ _____ _____.

Sample Test

Multiple-Choice Questions

1. The number one reason that college students seek help at college counseling centers is _____.
   a. stress
   b. depression
   c. academic problems
   d. loneliness

2. Byron is feeling very stressed about repeated problems with his college roommates about keeping their apartment clean as well as fears about all of the crime in his neighborhood. The sources of his stress would be best classified as _____.
   a. daily hassles
   b. life changes
   c. uplifts
   d. defense mechanisms

3. Both daily hassles and life changes have been found to be predictors of _____, according to your text.
   a. health problems
   b. psychotic behavior
   c. stunted growth
   d. loneliness

4. People aged 18 to 34 are most likely to attribute chronic pain to _____.
   a. boredom or depression
   b. tension or stress
   c. overwork
   d. their lifestyle

5. Substances derived from fatty acids that are involved in body responses such as inflammation and menstrual cramping are called _____.
   a. endorphins
   b. prostaglandins
   c. analgesics
   d. corticosteroids

6. Endorphins act by _____.
   a. inhibiting the production of prostaglandins
   b. increasing the transmission of pain messages to the brain
   c. locking into receptor sites for chemicals that transmit pain messages to the brain
   d. inhibiting the neurons that would normally transmit pain messages to the brain

7. Which of the following is **NOT** one of the methods described in your text as an effective psychological method for managing pain?
   a. accurate information
   b. distraction and fantasy
   c. hypnosis
   d. flooding

8. Herbert wants to drive his father's car. When he asks, he is told that he is too young (13 years old). The stress he feels as a result of having his refused is called _____.
   a. anxiety
   b. depression
   c. frustration
   d. inadequacy

9. Feeling "darned if you do and darned if you don't" is an example of _____.
   a. frustration
   b. conflict
   c. state anxiety
   d. trait anxiety

10. Tom is on a strict diet when he sees the most delicious-looking double chocolate cheesecake he has ever seen. Part of him really wants to devour the whole cake, but another part of him can't stop thinking about all the calories in the cake. The type of conflict Tom is experiencing is called a(n) _____ conflict.
    a. approach-approach
    b. approach-avoidance
    c. multiple approach-avoidance
    d. avoidance-avoidance

11. The psychologist known for his theories about the impact of irrational beliefs and catastrophizing on people's physical and mental health is _____.
    a. Jacobson
    b. Lazarus
    c. Kobasa
    d. Ellis

12. Each of the following is true of people with a Type A behavior pattern **EXCEPT** _____.
    a. they are more ambitious and more impatient than Type Bs
    b. they believe they must be perfectly competent and achieving in everything they undertake
    c. they demand continual self-improvement
    d. they are more likely than Type Bs to delegate authority when in management positions

13. A sound of 140 dB _____.
    a. is barely audible
    b. is typical of comfortable "background" music
    c. is painfully loud
    d. can rupture the eardrum

14. Which of the following is **NOT** true of high levels of noise?
    a. It is related to a higher risk of developing lymphomas.
    b. It can lead to such illnesses as hypertension.
    c. It can impair daily functioning.
    d. It can decrease feelings of attraction and reduce helping behavior.

15. According to a study in Houston, murders and rapes are most likely to occur when the temperature is in the _____.
    a. 70s
    b. 80s
    c. 90s
    d. 100s

16. People who live in fast-paced cities are _____ likely to smoke and _____ likely to die from coronary heart disease.
    a. less, less
    b. less, more
    c. more, less
    d. more, more

17. Which of the following groups of people maintains the greatest distance between themselves and others?
    a. southern Europeans
    b. Asians
    c. Middle Easterners
    d. North Americans

18. Psychologically hardy people tend to have an _____ locus of control.
    a. external
    b. inconsistent
    c. overactive
    d. internal

19. Which of the following groups of people is least likely to develop infectious diseases, such as colds, when under stress?
   a. extraverts
   b. introverts
   c. people who lack social skills
   d. people who live by themselves

20. Which of the following is an active, or direct, coping technique?
   a. aggression
   b. meditation
   c. withdrawal
   d. substance abuse

True-False Questions

21. Uplifts are the opposite of life changes.   _____

22. Pain is adaptive.   _____

23. Telling oneself that pain is unbearable and that it will never cease increases discomfort.   _____

24. At very hot temperatures, aggressive behavior begins to decline.   _____

25. There is a one-to-one relationship between the amount of stress we experience and outcomes such as physical disorders.   _____

Essay Question

26. Compare and contrast frustration and conflict, identifying the four types of conflict discussed in the text.

Student Activities

Name _____ **Date** _____

3.1 Sources of Stress: Hassles

In this chapter, we learned that stress can be associated with emotional distress, physical illness, poorer performance, and behavioral problems. Among the several sources of stress are the big changes in life, like graduation or marriage, and the daily hassles like broken shoestrings and snarled traffic. The College Life Stress Inventory has us consider some of the major life changes that increase health risks and are associated with stress. In addition to your score on this scale, consider the possible effects of daily hassles by keeping a "hassles diary" for one week.

Follow-Up Questions:

1. Which hassles occur at a frequent rate such as daily or several times daily?

2. For each hassle identified, decide what would be best changed: 1) the hassle or 2) your response. For example, a more scenic route might eliminate the hassle of a difficult commute, while a problem with rainy weather might require a "change in attitude," or more precisely, challenging an irrational idea. Why?

3.2 Where Can You Find "Merry Heart Medicine"?

When author Norman Cousins tried to take some control over his own painful medical condition, in which he was hospitalized for months, he asked friends to bring funny films and videos to the hospital. His choices included Laurel and Hardy and Candid Camera. Where would you turn if you wanted to select humorous material? What are at least five specific sources of comedy material you would use if you were in Cousins' situation?

Follow-Up Questions:

1. If you wanted evidence that your humorous material was having a "medicinal" effect, how could you empirically measure any benefits?

2. What are three kinds of humorous programs you could envision for a pediatric ward at a local hospital? Why would you choose these programs?

3.3 A Moderator of Stress: Hardiness

Sources of stress do not automatically cause stress-related problems. Moderators of stress, which can include our personal strengths, might mean that we can have a healthier and more productive life in spite of life's challenges, or maybe even because of them. As the text mentions, Suzanne Kobasa and others have studied people who have successfully handled much stress without becoming ill. Kobasa and others have listed some of the strengths for moderating stress, which have been paraphrased below to illustrate the concept of hardiness, and to give us a chance to evaluate ourselves. For each strength, write one change that you could **realistically** make for personal improvement, and how (if applicable) you would make that change.

1. Having a clear sense of goals, values, capabilities, and their importance.

2. Active involvement to promote change.

3. Finding personal meaning in stressful life events.

4. Having a sense of control.

5. Having a good support system.

Activity continued on the back

6. Seeking stimulation.

7. Having a stable and even disposition.

8. Having a Type B personality.

Critical Thinking

Could any of the characteristics of hardy people be **results** of health, rather than **causes** of health? Select one characteristic and describe how it might be a result rather than a cause.

Name _____ **Date** _____

3.4 Why Do Married Men Live Longer Than Single Men?

Some of the studies mentioned in the text, which support the relationship between social support and health, are correlational. Consider the observation that married men live longer than single men. What alternative explanations can you offer to the explanation that social support is the **cause** of longer living?

You might begin by thinking of what else is often different about being married and not being married.

Follow-Up Questions:

1. How could you test the alternative you generated?

2. How could men who prefer to remain bachelors gain the benefits of longevity and/or health that married men enjoy?

3. Do you believe that marriage has the same effect for women? Why or why not?

Name _____ **Date** _____

3.5 A Balance Sheet

Pick an issue in your life in which you are, or have been, struggling with what to decide to do about it. Use the following balance sheet, as discussed in your text, to help weigh the "pros" and "cons" of at least one of the alternatives for your decision.

1.   Alternative A

	Positive Anticipation	Negative Anticipation
Tangible gains and losses for me		
Tangible gains and losses for others		
Self-approval or self-disapproval		
Social approval or social disapproval		

Make photocopies of this sheet to fill out and make similar evaluations of other alternatives in your decision.

3.6 Challenging Irrational Thoughts

In this chapter we read about irrational beliefs, and we identified an occasion of some personal distress to analyze by applying Albert Ellis's ABC approach. The current chapter on ways of helping ourselves is described as a do-it-yourself chapter and asks us to take on some very valuable challenges. We can begin by practicing some of the recommendations with hypothetical cases before addressing our own situations. For each example of catastrophizing, write an incompatible and rational rebuttal.

1. "If I flunk this test I'll just die!"

2. "I'll feel stupid if the teacher calls on me today."

3. "I'm too embarrassed to exercise in public."

4. "My parents never gave me a chance to develop any self-esteem."

5. "That @#%^&* driver had no right pulling out in front of me!"

6. "There will never be another love like the one I just lost."

3.7 Controlling Our Own Disturbing Thoughts

We should be ready to take the steps recommended in Meichenbaum's three-step procedure. For this week, keep a diary of any occasions when you feel any discomfort, including fear, anger, frustration, pessimism, anxiety, and so forth. For some of us, a day of experience could keep us busy writing for a week, but a full week is a better representation of our experience. Note cards or slips of paper will serve, as long as we record each step for each occurrence. We will not provide all of the space you might need for a diary, but answer the following questions in the spaces below.

1. How many events during this week were recorded as distressing?

2. Choose six that appear to involve the use of unnecessary, catastrophizing thoughts. For each case, compose more appropriate thoughts as practiced in the above exercise.

   a.

   b.

   c.

   d.

   e.

   f.

3.8 Monitoring Arousal and Relaxation

It is hard to imagine a more positive step we can take in gaining control of our lives than deciding to control stress by learning to lower arousal. This chapter details two very effective and well-researched techniques— meditation and progressive relaxation. Monitoring the effects of these techniques can be interesting and rewarding. The easiest way to verify the arousal-lowering potential of meditation or progressive relaxation is to take one-minute heart rates before and after practice. However, not everyone will detect a change in heart rate. For some people, improvements from relaxation are experienced as slower breathing, less muscle tension, or blood chemistry changes. To see if your heart rate is indicative of changes in your level of arousal, take your pulse for one minute, then engage in one of the recommended techniques detailed in the text, and finish by taking your pulse again for one minute.

1. Your resting pulse prior to meditation or relaxation:

    _____

2. Your pulse immediately after the chosen technique:

    _____

3. For comparison purposes, see how you respond to music. Record your heart's BPM before listening here:

    _____

4. What happens if you vary the musical choices between rowdy and relaxing?

5. If possible, compare yourself with others in your class and record your observations:

Name _____ **Date** _____

3.9 Monitoring Progress in Lowering Arousal

You have read that lowering arousal is worthwhile and will lead to possible improvements in health and performance, so it would be rewarding to verify our progress as we practice meditation and relaxation over days and weeks. One thing that has worked well is to keep a simple arousal diary that records how strong muscle tension is when you first notice it and how strong it remains as you attempt to lower it. Make a note every time you become aware of muscle tension, such as hunching your shoulders during class, or clutching your steering wheel with white knuckles, or wrinkling your forehead while you study or work. Rank your tension on a 10-point scale with 10 equal to the most severe strain possible and 1 equal to a total lack of any tension. Next, try to relax as well as possible and judge the new level of muscle tension on the same 10-point scale. What is commonly reported is 1) to notice more and more unnecessary cases of muscle tension, and 2) to include less severe examples as you become more sensitive to signals about your level of arousal, and 3) to record improvement in the ability to reduce tension to lower levels. Keep a note card or slip of paper in your pocket, purse, or wallet so you can record the two numbers on each occasion. Keep the days separate and at the end of the week answer these questions:

1. Record the total number of times you noticed tension each day.

2. For each day, record the average level of tension which you first noticed.

3. For each day, record the average amount of improvement when you tried to relax.

4. At the end of the project, can you find any changes or improvement in:

    a. Increased recognition of occasions of tension?

    b. Greater sensitivity to even lower levels of unnecessary tension?

    c. Greater reductions in tension after attempting to relax?

5. Explain how this information might be useful to you in helping you cope with stress.

3.10 Handling Hostility and Frustration

In Chapter 11, the text summarizes the rational restructuring procedures described by Albert Ellis. Putting yourself in the shoes of other people and imagining the reasons they may have for their behavior can help you control hostility and frustration when their behavior interferes with your efforts to achieve your own goals. These procedures work! Try this exercise to practice empathizing with others, in order to manage the ill feelings that are sometimes created by their actions.

1. Think of a reasonable justification another driver would possibly give you for pulling out in front of your car from a side street, in a way which would cause you to have to brake quickly to avoid hitting him or her.

2. Think of the reasonable justifications an instructor could have for asking students not to call his or her house the night before tests to confirm information about the assigned reading.

3. Consider the last time someone, whom you were not able to talk to, did something that made you angry. For example, it might have been the way one of your least favorite politicians voted on a bill or measure. Now try to put yourself in their shoes to imagine the justification they would offer for the situation.

4. How can this information be useful to you in future coping with situations like those described above.

4

Psychological Factors and Health

Chapter Outline

Module 4.1: Physical. Emotional, and Cognitive Effects of Stress

Module 4.2: Factors in Health and Illness
Module 4.3: Psychological Factors in Physical Health Problems

Module 4.4: Psychology and Daily Life: Becoming an Active Health Care Consumer

Chapter Overview

Health Psychology. Health psychology studies the relationships between psychological factors, (for example, behavior, emotions, stress, beliefs, and attitudes) and the prevention and treatment of physical health problems.

The General Adaptation Syndrome (GAS). The GAS is a cluster of bodily changes triggered by stressors. The GAS consists of three stages: alarm, resistance, and exhaustion. The bodily responses involve the endocrine system (hormones) and the autonomic nervous system. Corticosteroids help resist stress by fighting inflammation and allergic reactions. Adrenaline arouses the body by activating the sympathetic division of the autonomic nervous system, which is highly active during the alarm and resistance stages of the GAS. Sympathetic activity is characterized by rapid heartbeat and respiration rate, release of stores of sugar, muscle tension, and other responses that deplete the body's supply of energy. The parasympathetic division of the ANS predominates during the exhaustion stage of the GAS and is connected with depression, inactivity, and weakness.

Emotional and Cognitive Effects of Stress. Anxiety tends to occur in response to threatening stressors. Anger usually occurs in response to stressors such as frustration and social provocation. Depression occurs in response to losses, failure, and prolonged stress. High levels of stress are connected with high levels of arousal, which in turn evoke dominant cognitions and behavior patterns and impair problem-solving ability.

The Effects of Stress on the Immune System. Leukocytes (white blood cells) engulf and kill pathogens, worn out body cells, and cancerous cells. The immune system also "remembers" how to battle antigens by marshaling antibodies in the bloodstream. The immune system also facilitates inflammation, which increases the number of white blood cells that are transported to the damaged area. Prolonged or intense stress depresses the functioning of the immune system, in part because it stimulates release of corticosteroids. These steroids counter inflammation and interfere with the formation of antibodies.

The Multifactorial Approach. This view recognizes that many factors, including biological, psychological, sociocultural, and environmental factors, affect our health.

Ethnicity, Gender, Socioeconomic Status, and Physical Health. African Americans live about seven years less than European Americans, largely because of sociocultural and economic factors that are connected with less access to health care and greater likelihood of eating high-fat diets, smoking, and living in unhealthful neighborhoods. Women are less likely than men to have heart attacks in early and middle adulthood due to the protective effects of estrogen. Women outlive men by seven years on average. One reason is that women are more likely than men to consult health professionals about health problems.

Psychology and Headaches. Psychologists have studied how stress contributes to muscle-tension and migraine headaches. Psychologists help people alleviate these kinds of headaches by using psychological techniques, such as biofeedback training, to counter states of bodily tension associated with stress or change patterns of blood flow in the body.

Psychology and Menstrual Problems. Psychologists have participated in research that is exploring the connections among menstrual discomfort, psychological factors (e.g., anxiety, depression, irritability, attitudes toward menstruation), physical symptoms (e.g., bloating, cramping), and changes in the available levels of hormones and neurotransmitters. PMS afflicts many women for a few days prior to menstruation. In most cases, the symptoms are mild to moderate, but they are severe in some women. Psychologists have helped devise strategies women can use to adjust to menstrual and premenstrual discomfort, including not blaming themselves, engaging in pleasant activities, diet, exercise, and assertive attainment of medical assistance, when needed.

Psychology and Coronary Heart Disease. Psychologists have participated in research that shows that risk factors for coronary heart disease include family history; physiological conditions such as hypertension and high levels of serum cholesterol; behavior patterns such as heavy drinking, smoking, eating, fatty foods, and Type A behavior; work overload; chronic tension and fatigue; and physical inactivity. They help people achieve healthier cardiovascular systems by stopping smoking, controlling weight, reducing hypertension, lowering LDL levels, changing Type A behavior, reducing hostility, and exercising.

Psychology and Cancer. Psychologists have participated in research that shows that the risk factors for cancer include family history, smoking, drinking alcohol, eating animal fats, sunbathing, and possibly stress. Making healthy changes in behavior can help reduce the risk of cancer, such as avoiding smoking, having regular medical checkups, controlling alcohol use, adopting a healthy diet, and avoiding sunbathing. Psychologists help cancer patients and their families cope with the disease and maintain a "fighting spirit."

Learning Objectives

After studying this chapter you should be able to:

1. Explain what health psychology is and the types of things it studies.

2. Describe the stages of the general adaptation syndrome and discuss the role of the endocrine system in this process.

3. Identify the various parts of the autonomic nervous system and explain their role in the body's response to stress.

4. Identify the emotional and cognitive responses to stress and explain the effects of those reactions on our mind and body.

5. Describe the functions of the immune system and explain the effects of stress on the immune system.

6. Describe the relationship between life changes and health, as well as the limitations in the research in this area.

7. Explain how ethnicity, gender, and socioeconomic status affects people's reactions to stress and vulnerability to stress-related disorders.

8. Describe the multifactorial model and identify the various factors it examines and their impact on health.

9. Summarize research findings on the relationship between ethnicity and health.

10. Identify the various types of headaches and their symptoms, and discuss how they are related to stress.

11. Discuss the causes and effects of menstrual discomfort, and ways to cope with it.

12. Describe the risk factors for coronary heart disease and the various behavioral measures that can contribute to the prevention and treatment of this disorder.

13. Define Type A behavior, discuss its causes and effects, and describe ways to cope with it.

14. Identify the risk factors for cancer and discuss the various behavioral measures that can contribute to the prevention and treatment of cancer.

15. Summarize research findings on stress and cancer.

16. Identify and briefly describe suggestions for becoming the active manager of your own health care.

Key Terms

health psychology	adrenal medulla	multifactorial model
general adaptation syndrome	hormones	mental disorders
stress response	tend and befriend response	mental illness
Dr. stress	hypertension	muscle-tension headache
alarm stage	resistance stage	migraine headache
alarm reaction	exhaustion stage	serotonin
fight-or flight reaction	diseases of adaptation	neurotransmitters
endocrine system	trait anxiety	prostaglandins
autonomic nervous system	state anxiety	premenstrual syndrome (PMS)
sympathetic nervous system	immune system	gamma-aminobutric acid (GABA)
parasympathetic nervous system	pathogens	coronary heart disease (CHD)
HPA axis	leukocytes	type A personality
hypothalamus	antigens	type D personality
adrenal cortex	antibodies	LDL cholesterol
corticosteroids	inflammation	carcinogenic
ACTH	psychoneuroimmunology	DNA

Key Terms Review

Define each of the following terms:

1. General Adaptation Syndrome: _____

   _____

2. Alarm Reaction: _____

   _____

3. Endocrine System: _____

   _____

4. Autonomic Nervous System: _____

   _____

5. Sympathetic Nervous System: _____

   _____

6. Parasympathetic Nervous System: _____

   _____

7. Resistance Stage: _____

_____

8. Exhaustion Stage: _____

_____

9. Trait Anxiety: _____

_____

10. State Anxiety: _____

_____

11. Immune System: _____

_____

12. Pathogens: _____

_____

13. Leukocytes: _____

_____

14. Antigens: _____

_____

15. Antibodies: _____

_____

16. Inflammation: _____

_____

17. Psychoneuroimmunology: _____

_____

18. Migraine Headaches: _____

_____

19. Multifactorial Model: _____

_____

20. Carcinogenic: _____

_____

Chapter Review

1. _____ psychology studies the relationships between psychological factors and the prevention and treatment of illness.

2. _____ is more than a psychological event and has clear effects on the body.

3. Hans Selye labeled the body's response to stress as the _____ _____ _____. This response can be broken down into three parts: the _____ _____ stage; the _____ stage; and the _____ stage.

4. Walter Cannon's term for the body's innate adaptive response to the presence of danger is the _____ _____ _____ reaction.

5. The _____ system consists of a number of ductless glands that release a number of secretions called _____ which help the body respond to stress by fighting inflammation and allergic reactions.

6. The _____ nervous system has two branches, or divisions, the _____ nervous system, which is most active when the body is expending reserves of energy, and the _____ nervous system, which is most active when the body is restoring its energy reserves.

7. Three hormones that play a role in the alarm reaction are _____, which fight inflammation and cause the liver to release stores of sugar, and _____ and _____ which arouse the body.

8. During the resistance stage of the GAS, levels of endocrine and sympathetic activity

   are _____ than in the alarm stage.

9. Continued stress during the exhaustion stage may lead to diseases of _____.

10. When under stress, many women exhibit a _____ and _____ response

    which may be due to the effects of the pituitary hormone _____.

11. Three types of negative emotional responses to stress that can motivate us to behave
    in maladaptive ways are:

    a. _____

    b. _____

    c. _____

12. Two types of anxiety are _____ anxiety, a personality variable, and

    _____ anxiety, a temporary condition of arousal triggered by external events.

13. Hostility differs from anger in that it is an _____ trait.

14. On a biological level depression is characterized by dominance of the _____
    nervous system.

15. The immune system is the body's line of defense against _____ and defective

    _____.

16. White blood cells, called _____, routinely engulf and kill _____, by

    recognizing _____ and producing _____ which bind to foreign

    substances in the body and mark them for destruction.

17. Inflammation is a function of the _____ system.

18. When physical injury occurs, blood vessels in the area first _____, then

    _____.

19. The relationship between psychological factors and the immune system is studied by

    the field of _____.

20. One of the reasons that stress eventually exhausts us is that it stimulates the production of _____, which suppress functioning of the _____ system.

21. Four limitations on the connections between daily hassles, life changes, and health problems are:

    a. _____

    b. _____

    c. _____

    d. _____

22. The _____ model recognizes that there is no single, simple answer to questions such as why people become ill.

23. Practicing _____ behaviors can save lives.

24. The life expectancy of African Americans is _____ years shorter than that of European Americans.

25. Nearly _____ of the men and _____ of the women with AIDS are African American or Latino and Latina American.

26. _____ Americans have the highest risk of dying from heart disease due to hypertension than any population group in the United States.

27. _____ Americans have higher rates of cancer than any other racial or ethnic group in the United States.

28. African American women are _____ likely than European American women to contract breast cancer, and when they do, it is at a(n) _____ age and they are _____ likely to die from it.

29. Women are less likely than men to have coronary heart disease at younger ages because they may be "protected" by high levels of _____ until menopause.

30. Men's life expectancy is _____ years shorter, on average, than women's.

31. People with higher socioeconomic status have _____ health and lead

    _____ lives, which may be due in large part to better _____.

32. _____ are the most common stress-related physical ailments.

33. Two types of headaches are _____ _____ headaches, the most frequent

    kind, and _____ headaches, which result from changes in blood supply to the

    head.

34. _____ headaches come on gradually and are characterized by a dull, steady

    pain on both sides of the head, whereas _____ have a sudden onset and are
    identified by a severe throbbing pain on one side of the head.

35. Migraine headaches, may in part be affected by imbalances in the neurotransmitter

    _____.

36. _____ percent of women experience some discomfort prior to or during
    menstruation.

37. The prevailing view today is that premenstrual syndrome has a primarily _____

    basis.

38. Women with menstrual problems seem to be extremely sensitive to the hormones

    _____ and _____. They also show imbalances in neurotransmitters such

    as _____ and _____.

39. Your text describes eleven ways to handle menstrual discomfort. Five of them are:

    a. _____

    b. _____

    c. _____

    d. _____

    e. _____

40. _____ _____ disease is the leading cause of death in the United States.

41. Six major risk factors for cardiovascular disease are:

a. _____

b. _____

c. _____

d. _____

e. _____

f. _____

42. Five behavior modifications one can make to reduce the risk of developing cardiovascular disease are:

a. _____

b. _____

c. _____

d. _____

e. _____

43. Five exercises to combat the sense of time urgency common to Type A behavior are:

a. _____

b. _____

c. _____

d. _____

e. _____

44. Five methods for alleviating hostility are:

a. _____

b. _____

c. _____

d. _____

e. _____

45. The term _____ refers to a number of disorders that involve the development of mutant cells that reproduce rapidly and rob the body of nutrients.

46. Overall, nearly two of three deaths from cancer in the United States are linked to two modifiable behaviors: _____ and _____.

47. Six things we can do to reduce our risk of dying of cancer are:

a. _____

b. _____

c. _____

d. _____

e. _____

f. _____

48. Four things you should do when communicating with your physician are:

a. _____

b. _____

c. _____

d. _____

49. Five steps you can take to protect yourself against mismanaged health care are:

a. _____

b. _____

c. _____

d. _____

e. _____

Sample Test

Multiple-Choice Questions

1. _____ psychologists study the way stress affects the body, especially the immune system.
   a. Clinical
   b. Experimental
   c. Forensic
   d. Health

2. According to Hans Selye, the body's response to stress is _____.
   a. cognitive dissonance
   b. the Stockholm syndrome
   c. the phi phenomenon
   d. the general adaptation syndrome

3. According to your text, the "fight or flight" reaction is the same as the _____.
   a. alarm reaction stage
   b. exhaustion stage
   c. resistance stage
   d. refractory reaction stage

4. A person who finds herself impatient and fidgeting while stuck in traffic or waiting in line is activating the _____.
   a. sympathetic nervous system
   b. parasympathetic nervous system
   c. afferent nervous system
   d. efferent nervous system

5. The structure in the brain that is crucial to the alarm reaction stage is the _____.
   a. thalamus
   b. hypothalamus
   c. reticular formation
   d. caudate nucleus

6. If the "fight or flight" reaction mobilizes the body and the stressor is not removed, we enter the _____ stage of the general adaptation syndrome.
   a. alarm reaction
   b. exhaustion
   c. resistance
   d. refractory

7. Jonathon experiences persistent feelings of dread and foreboding. He is chronically worried and concerned. He has _____.
   a. the general adaptation syndrome
   b. state anxiety
   c. the Stockholm syndrome
   d. trait anxiety

8. Biologically, depression is characterized by _____.
    a. neither sympathetic nor parasympathetic arousal
    b. sympathetic, but not parasympathetic arousal
    c. parasympathetic, but not sympathetic arousal
    d. both sympathetic and parasympathetic arousal

9. Anxiety tends to motivate _____.
    a. escape behavior   c. withdrawal
    b. aggressive behavior   d. assertive behavior

10. When our bodily arousal becomes too high, we tend to focus on _____.
    a. the task at hand   c. our body's responses
    b. distracting stimuli   d. other people around us

11. The immune system remembers how to battle antigens from previous infections through the use of
    _____.
    a. endorphins   c. antibodies
    b. neurotransmitters   d. hemoglobin

12. Researchers have found that suppression of the immune system has _____.
    a. negligible effects when steroids are secreted intermittently or persistently
    b. negligible effects when steroids are secreted intermittently but can impair immune system
        functioning when steroids are secreted persistently
    c. negligible effects when steroids are secreted persistently but can impair immune system
        functioning when steroids are secreted intermittently
    d. effects that can impair immune system functioning when steroids are secreted intermittently or
        persistently

13. The life expectancy for African Americans is about _____ that of Europeans Americans.
    a. 12 years shorter than   c. 3 years shorter than
    b. 7 years shorter than   d. the same as

14. African Americans are more likely than European Americans to suffer from each of the following
    disorders **EXCEPT** _____.
    a. breast cancer   c. AIDS
    b. hypertension   d. heart attacks

15. People with lower SES are _____ likely to exercise and _____ likely to smoke.
    a. less, less   c. less, more
    b. more, less   d. more, more

16. Jeremiah has a dull, steady pain on both sides of his head. He also feels a tightness or pressure in his
    head and scalp. His headache came on gradually and is best described as a _____ headache.
    a. muscle-tension   c. migraine
    b. sinus   d. cluster

17. Evidence on PMS suggests each of the following **EXCEPT** _____.
    a. women with severe PMS have different levels of estrogen and progesterone than women with
        mild symptoms or none
    b. women with PMS may have unusual high sensitivity to estrogen and progesterone
    c. PMS appears to be linked to imbalances in some neurotransmitters
    d. dietary control can help some women lessen PMS symptoms

18. Of the following, researchers believe that _____ may be the most powerful predictor of coronary
    heart disease.
    a. smoking   c. chronic anger
    b. obesity   d. high-fat diet

19. Dan wants to reduce his risk for coronary heart disease. He should do each of the following **EXCEPT**
_____.

    a.   stop smoking   c.   reduce hypertension
    b.   control his weight   d.   reduce Type B behavior

20. Health care consumers who wait until they get sick to seek health care or learn about care options are called _____ consumers.

    a.   primary   c.   tertiary
    b.   passive   d.   reactionary

True-False Questions

21. Trait anxiety involves predominantly sympathetic arousal whereas state anxiety involves primarily parasympathetic arousal.   _____

22. Inflammation results from a breakdown in the functioning of the immune system.   _____

23. African Americans experience different treatment than European Americans by medical practitioners.   _____

24. Most women are severely impaired by premenstrual syndrome.   _____

25. People can inherit a disposition toward cancer.   _____

Essay Question

26. Discuss the causes of menstrual problems, their effects, and ways to cope with them.

Student Activities

Name _____ **Date** _____

4.1 How Much Do We Value Health?

Ask yourself and as many others as you care to, the following questions to obtain some idea of our values about health. Before you finish, consider what additional questions you could ask.

1. If you could achieve your ideal in only one of the following respects, while only achieving mediocrity in the others, which would you choose?

    a. Perfect health
    b. Perfect psychological well-being
    c. Perfect financial success
    d. Perfect career success
    e. Perfect spiritual success

    Why did you choose this one over the other ones?

2. If a new drug were to be made legally available that increased happiness by ten percent, but reduced the length of life, how many years would you be willing to forfeit to use the drug? How did you decide upon this number? What if the drug were illegal?

Activity continued on other side

3. If you could sell years of your life to people willing to buy them, would you sell any? Why or why not? If you would sell some, how many would you sell and for how much money?

Name _____ **Date** _____

4.2 Health-Related Attitudes and Habits

Some good health habits are easier to acquire than others. Just as some bad health habits are more difficult to eliminate than others. Make a list of some of your current health-related attitudes and behaviors. When you have completed the list, answer the following questions:

1.   Which of your health-related attitudes or behaviors is causing you the most stress or discomfort? Why?

2.   What might you do to change this attitude or behavior? Identify at least three possible changes you could make.

3.   What is the most difficult health-related habit for you to acquire and why is it such a problem for you?

Activity continued on other side

4. What are at least two health-related attitudes or habits you would like to acquire and what can you do to help yourself acquire them?

Name _____ **Date** _____

4.3 The Physiology of Stress

As we learn about the autonomic nervous system and its role in our response to stress, we can create a demonstration of the response of two involuntary reactions, one in our heart rate, and one in our rate of perspiration. Changes in heart rate and perspiration are two of the physiological changes observed in stress research and also in so-called "lie detection" testing. If you can do these with a friend or classmate, you will be able to create a "balance order" of effects.

1. Alone, or together, take your resting heart rate and record the number of beats for one minute (BPM).

    Your BPM   Friend's BPM

    _____   _____

2. To create a mild, temporary stressor, cough hard three times in a row. Your partner, if included, can skip the coughing this time for comparison.

    Your 2nd BPM   Friend's 2nd BPM

    _____   _____

3. If applicable, change roles with your friend, and let the friend cough hard three times in a row while you relax. Then immediately count the heart rates after he or she coughs.

    Your 3rd BPM   Friend's 3rd BPM

    _____   _____

4. After your heart rate(s) return to their original level, both of you cough hard three times and count BPMs until they recover to within two beats of the original level. How long does it take to recover?

    Minutes for you   Minutes for your friend

    _____   _____

5. You can create a similar demonstration showing the response of the skin to a stressor. In bright light, or outside on a sunny day, look at the pad of your index finger. As you turn or tilt your finger, you will probably see it sparkle from the oils and sweat on it. These can be seen even better with slight magnification. If you wipe the finger on a cloth, the sparkle will be removed. How long does it take to return to this sparkling state if you cough as above? How long does it take if you just wait?

Activity continued on the back

Follow-Up Questions

1. Who responds stronger to the coughing?

2. How could you measure the recovery from the coughing?

3. What branch of the autonomic nervous system have you just witnessed?

4. According to the text, what other physical changes took place in response to the coughing and how could they be measured?

5. What stage or stages of the General Adaptation Syndrome have you demonstrated?

Name _____ Date _____

4.4 Demonstrating the Stress/Health Relationship

If you want to examine the effects of stress on health, you could ask people to record their physical ailments long before and shortly before a stressor such as final examinations. To actually do so would require that you investigate your school's human research guidelines and follow them to protect the rights and well-being of the subjects. Even if you do not attempt any actual data collection, you can design a research proposal. You will have to decide such issues as how many subjects, how health complaints can be recorded, which times recording takes place, and, if possible, how control subjects can be used to help verify any effects of stress.

1. Where can you recruit subjects and how many do you believe you will need?

2. How can your subjects' physical complaints be assessed?

3. When can you test the subjects to illustrate any effects of stress?

Activity continued on other side

4. What kinds of differences, and how much in the way of differences, are necessary to verify stress effects?

5

Developing Healthier Behaviors

Chapter Outline

Module 5.1: Nutrition: The Stuff of Life

Module 5.2: Fitness: Run (at Least Walk) for Your Life

Module 5.3: Sleep: A Time for Renewal

Module 5.4: Substance Abuse and Dependence: When Drug Use Causes Harm

Module 5.5: Psychology in Daily Life: Finding Healthful Alternatives to Harmful Substances

Chapter Overview

Ingredients of a Healthful Diet. People need to consume a balanced diet that provides sufficient quantities of proteins, carbohydrates, fats, vitamins, and minerals. But we tend to eat too much protein and fats. Complex carbohydrates (starches) are better sources of nutrients than simple carbohydrates (sugars). Consumption of high levels of dietary cholesterol and saturated fat, along with obesity, heightens risk of cardiovascular disorders.

Obesity. Obesity is a complex health problem that involves biological factors, such as heredity, amount of adipose tissue (body fat), and metabolic rate (the rate at which the individual converts calories to energy), as well as psychological factors, such as stress and use of food to alleviate negative emotions.

Major Eating Disorders. The major eating disorders are anorexia nervosa, and bulimia nervosa. Anorexia is characterized by refusal to eat and maintenance of an unhealthy low body weight. Bulimia is characterized by cycles of binge eating and purging. women are more likely than men to develop these disorders. Psychodynamic theorists propose that young women who are conflicted about their developing sexuality and womanhood may refuse to eat in order to maintain a childlike appearance. However, other theorists emphasize the role of cultural idealization of the slender female—and the pressure that such idealization places on young women—as the major contributor.

Exercise. Aerobic exercise involves activities in which there is a sustained increase in the consumption of oxygen, such as working out on a treadmill or jogging. Anaerobic exercise, by contrast, involves short bursts of muscle activity, such as lifting weights. Both types of exercise have healthful benefits. Regular exercise helps us maintain a healthy weight by directly burning calories and by building muscle mass (muscle tissue burns more calories than fats). Regular exercise also reduces the risks of cardiovascular disease and osteoporosis. Evidence indicates that exercise can help relieve depression, decrease anxiety and hostility, and boost self-esteem.

Sleep. Sleep apparently serves a restorative function, a memory consolidation function, and a survival function.

Insomnia. Insomnia is connected with stress, physical and psychological disorders, and states of bodily tension. We can also set the stage for insomnia by worrying whether we will be able to get to sleep, or get enough sleep, to meet our daily responsibilities.

Substance Abuse and Dependence. Substance abuse is use of a substance that persists even though it impairs one's social or occupational functioning or general health. Substance dependence has behavioral and physiological aspects. It may be characterized by a lack of control over the use of a substance and by the development of tolerance, withdrawal symptoms, or both.

Causes of Substance Abuse and Dependence. People usually try drugs out of curiosity or because of peer pressure, but drug use comes to be reinforced directly by anxiety reduction or by feelings of euphoria or other desirable effects. Once people become physiologically dependent on a drug, they continue to use it to avert the development of unpleasant withdrawal symptoms. People may have genetic predispositions to become physiologically dependent on certain substances.

Alcohol. Alcohol is a depressant drug that induces states of relaxation by slowing the activity of the central nervous system. It can lead to physiological dependence and may cause death in overdoses. Alcohol lowers inhibitions, makes it difficult to weight the consequences of our actions, and provides an excuse for failure or for undesirable behavior. A drink a day seems to be healthful, but most professionals do not recommend drinking because of concern that the individual may develop a problem drinking habit. Heavy drinking is connected with liver damage and other health problems.

Opioids. The opioids morphine and heroin are depressants that relieve pain, but they are also bought on the street because of the euphoric "rush" they provide. Opioid use can lead to physiological dependence.

Sedatives. Barbiturates and a similar drug, methaqualone, are depressants. Though barbiturates have some medical uses, they can lead rapidly to physiological and psychological dependence and can be abused as street drugs.

Nicotine. Nicotine is an addictive stimulant found in tobacco that can paradoxically help people relax. Cigarette smoking is a major contributor to heart disease and cancer, and to other health problems.

Amphetamines. Stimulants are substances that act by increasing activity of the central nervous system. Amphetamines are stimulants that produce feelings of euphoria when taken in high doses. But high doses may also cause restlessness, insomnia, psychotic symptoms, and a "crash" upon withdrawal. Amphetamines and a related stimulant, Ritalin, are commonly used to treat hyperactive children.

Cocaine. Psychologically speaking, the stimulant cocaine provides feelings of euphoria and bolsters self-confidence. Physiologically, it causes sudden rises in blood pressure and constricts blood vessels. Overdoses can lead to restlessness, insomnia, psychotic reactions, and cardiorespiratory collapse.

LSD. LSD is a hallucinogenic drug that produces vivid hallucinations. Some LSD users have "flashbacks" to earlier experiences.

Marijuana. Marijuana's active ingredients, including THC, often produce relaxation, heightened and distorted perceptions, feelings of empathy, and reports of new insights. Mild hallucinations may occur. Marijuana use elevates the heart rate, impairs perceptual motor skills, and may damage the developing brain. The smoke also brings cancer-causing compounds into the body.

Learning Objectives

After studying this chapter your students should be able to:

1. Identify the essential food elements and discuss how nutritional patterns influence our health.

2. Describe the various factors that contribute to obesity.

3. Identify and describe the various psychological methods for controlling your weight.

4. Compare and contrast anorexia nervosa and bulimia nervosa in terms of their sufferers, symptoms, and effects.

5. Compare the various theoretical views regarding the causes of eating disorders such as anorexia nervosa.

6. Discuss the differences between aerobic and anaerobic exercise and explain the physical and psychological effects of exercise on health.

7. Discuss the functions of sleep and how sleeping patterns influence our health.

8. Explain why psychologists are opposed to using sleeping pills to help people get to sleep, and describe various psychological methods for coping with insomnia.

9. Compare and contrast substance abuse and substance dependence. Make sure to explain what tolerance and abstinence syndrome are as part of your discussion.

10. Summarize the various viewpoints regarding the causal factors in substance abuse and dependence.

11. Discuss the effects of alcohol and the problems associated with its abuse.

12. Identify the various opioids, discuss their effects, and describe the problems associated with their use.

13. Discuss the effects of the sedatives, and describe the problems associated with their use.

14. Discuss the effects of nicotine and the health problems associated with smoking, including passive smoking.

15. Identify some of the amphetamines, discuss their effects, and describe the problems associated with their use.

16. Discuss the effects of ecstasy and health problems associated with its use.

17. Discuss the effects of cocaine and explain the problems associated with its use.

18. Discuss the effects of marijuana, LSD, and other hallucinogens and describe the problems associated with their use.

19. Discuss the effects of marijuana and describe the problems associated with its use.

20. Identify and briefly describe at least five self-control strategies for modifying the ABCs of substance abuse.

21. Identify and briefly describe at least five drug-free alternatives for coping with occasional depression, stress, or boredom.

Key Terms

nutrition	anorexia nervosa	binge drinking
nutrients	bulimia nervosa	opioids
proteins	prepubescence	narcotic
amino acids	aerobic exercise	barbiturates
carbohydrates	anaerobic exercise	stimulants
dietary fiber	fitness	nicotine
fats	high-density lipoproteins (HDLs)	passive smoking
vitamin	insomnia	amphetamines
anti-oxidants	substance abuse	ecstasy
free radicals	substance dependence	cocaine
osteoporosis	tolerance	hallucinogenic drugs
obesity	alcoholism	psychedelic
body mass index	delirium tremens	hallucinations
calories	disorientation	LSD
fat cells	depressants	flashbacks
adipose tissue	central nervous system (CNS)	hashish

Key Terms Review

Define each of the following terms:

1. Nutrients: _____

_____

2. Free Radicals: _____

_____

3. Osteoporosis: _____

_____

4. Calories: _____

_____

5. High Density Lipopropteins (HDLs): _____

_____

6. Anorexia Nervosa: _____

_____

7. Bulimia Nervosa: _____

_____

8. Aerobic Exercise: _____

_____

9. Fitness: _____

_____

10. Depressants: _____

_____

11. Stimulants: _____

_____

12. Substance Abuse: _____

_____

13. Tolerance: _____

_____

14. Substance Dependence: _____

_____

15. Delirium Tremens: _____

_____

16. Hallucinations: _____

_____

17. Ecstasy: _____

_____

18. Opioids: _____

_____

19. Barbiturates: _____

_____

20. Flashbacks: _____

_____

Chapter Review

1. Foods provide _____, which furnish energy and the building blocks of muscle, bone, and other tissue.

2. Essential nutrients include _____, _____, _____, _____, and _____.

3. Proteins are _____ acids that serve as _____, _____, and _____.

4. The most popular sources of protein are _____, _____, _____, _____, and _____ products.

5. _____ are the major sources of energy in our diet.

6.   _____ are simple carbohydrates, whereas _____ are complex

      carbohydrates that provide vitamins, minerals, and a steadier flow of energy.

7.   Fats provide _____, nourish the _____, and store _____.

8.   Vitamins are essential _____ compounds that need to be eaten regularly.

9.   Vitamins like A, C, and E are _____; that is, they deactivate substances in some

      foods (called _____ _____) that may contribute to the development of

      cancer.

10.   Vitamins found in _____ and _____, appear to reduce the risk of cancer.

11.   Numerous biological factors are involved in obesity, including _____,

      _____ tissue, and _____.

12.   Obese people and formerly obese people tend to have more _____ cells than

      people of normal weight.

13.   _____ and _____ factors, as well as _____ play a key role in

      obesity.

14.   _____ is now the normative pattern for young women in the United States.

15.   Two types of eating disorders are _____ _____, which is characterized

      by maintenance of abnormally low body weight and intense fear of weight gain, and

      _____ _____, which is characterized by recurrent episodes of binge

      eating followed by purging.

16.   Eating disorders largely afflict women during _____ and _____
      adulthood.

17.   Anorexia and bulimia are frequently found together with clinical _____.

18.   Many young women with eating disorders have issues of _____ and

      _____.

19. Two types of exercise are _____ exercise, which does not require sustained increases in oxygen consumption, and _____ exercise, which does require sustained increases in oxygen consumption.

20. The major physiological benefit of aerobic exercise is _____ .

21. Exercise raises _____ rate and burns more _____ than we burn in a resting state.

22. Aerobic exercise _____ levels of "good" cholesterol and _____ hypertension.

23. Exercise alleviates feelings of _____ , and can help _____ our mental health.

24. Most people should aim for about _____ a day of moderate physical activity.

25. Most people need between _____ and _____ hours of sleep to feel fully rested.

26. When deprived of sleep for several nights, psychological functioning such as

_____ , _____ , and _____ deteriorate notably.

27. Our most common method of fighting insomnia is _____

_____ .

28. Five methods for coping with insomnia are:

a. _____

b. _____

c. _____

d. _____

e. _____

29.   **Matching:** Match the terms on the left with the appropriate descriptors or definitions on the right.

_____ a. Substance abuse

_____ b. Substance dependence

_____ c. Tolerance

_____ d. Withdrawal syndrome

_____ e. Delirium tremens

_____ f. Disorientation

1. persistent use of a drug despite efforts to cut down, marked tolerance, and withdrawal symptoms

2. a condition characterized by sweating, restlessness, and hallucinations

3. continued use of a drug despite knowledge that it is linked to social, occupational, physical, or psychological problems

4. gross confusion

5. increasingly higher doses of a drug are needed to achieve similar effects

6. symptoms resulting from the sudden decrease in the usage of an addictive drug

30.   There is some evidence that some people may be born with a genetic _____ toward physiological dependence on certain substances, such as alcohol, opioids, cocaine, and nicotine.

31.   _____ is the all-purpose medicine you can buy without a prescription.

32.   Many college officials view _____ _____ as the major drug problem on campus.

33.   Men mainly metabolize alcohol in the _____, and women mainly metabolize alcohol in the _____.

34.   Women who drink heavily are _____ men to develop alcoholism.

35.   _____ _____ is the most widely used program to treat alcoholism.

36.   Among alcoholics, deficiencies in the neurotransmitter _____ may account for strong cravings for alcohol.

37.   Opioids are a group of _____ drugs that include _____ and _____.

38.   Heroin was developed in Germany as a cure for physiological dependence on _____.

39.   Methadone is used to treat physiological dependence on _____.

40. Barbiturates have been used for relief of _____ and treatment of _____.

41. Because of additive effects, it is dangerous to mix alcohol with other _____.

42. The stimulant in tobacco products is _____.

43. Nicotine is a _____ addictive drug to which addiction develops _____.

44. Nicotine _____ the appetite and _____ metabolic rate.

45. Nearly _____ Americans die each year from smoking-related illnesses.

46. Each cigarette smoked steals about _____ minutes from the smoker's life.

47. It is apparently the _____ in cigarette smoke that lead(s) to lung cancer.

48. _____ smoking is connected with respiratory illnesses, asthma, and other health problems.

49. Amphetamines include _____, _____, _____, and a related stimulant called _____.

50. The most abused amphetamine is _____.

51. Heavy use of methamphetamine is linked to _____ and _____ problems, and possible _____ damage.

52. _____ is a chemical cousin of amphetamine that can produce psychotic features and even be deadly in high doses.

53. Cocaine produces _____, curbs _____, deadens _____, and bolsters self-_____.

54. Cocaine is a _____ addictive drug that gives rise to a severe _____ syndrome.

55. Cocaine is a highly _____ drug that when overdosed may lead to respiratory and cardiovascular _____.

56. Cocaine _____ the coronary arteries, _____ the blood, and _____ the heart rate.

57. One of the prominent advocates of cocaine, at least initially, was _____, who used it for awhile to fight depression.

58. **Matching:** Match the drug, or class of drugs, on the left with the appropriate descriptor on the right.

_____ a.	Opioids	1.	an addictive sedative used to relieve anxiety or induce sleep
_____ b.	Nicotine	2.	a class of stimulants used to produce a rush or euphoria in high doses and often used to stay awake or to lose weight
_____ c.	Methadone		
_____ d.	Barbiturate	3.	a class of drugs that produce hallucinations and sometimes relaxation or euphoria
_____ e.	Ecstasy	4.	a drug that produces vivid hallucinations and claims to "expand awareness"
_____ f.	Cocaine		
_____ g.	Hallucinogen	5.	a group of addictive drugs that provide a euphoric rush but depress the nervous system and are used medicinally for the control of pain
_____ h.	Marijuana		
_____ i.	LSD	6.	a synthetic drug, chemically related to amphetamine, that produces mild euphoric and hallucinogenic effects
_____ j.	Amphetamines	7.	a substance that helps people relax, can elevate mood, can produce mild hallucinations, and has been linked to amotivational syndrome and may raise risk of lung cancer

8. a stimulant that causes the release of adrenaline resulting in a mental "kick" but is excreted rapidly in stressful periods requiring larger doses to maintain its effects

9. an artificial drug used to allow heroin addicts to abstain from heroin without experiencing withdrawal

10. a powerful stimulant that provides feelings of euphoria and bolsters self-confidence

59. Hallucinogenic drugs include _____, _____, _____, and

_____.

60. Regular use of hallucinogenic drugs may lead to _____ and _____

dependence, but probably not _____ dependence.

61. Marijuana helps some people relax and can _____ mood, but it can sometimes

produce mild _____.

62. In the 19th century, marijuana was used to treat _____ and minor _____.

63.   _____ is the most widely used illicit drug in the United States.

64.   Marijuana use may result in impaired _____ ability and _____

        functioning, and raises the risk of developing _____.

Sample Test

Multiple-Choice Questions

1. Each of the following is a type of essential nutrient **EXCEPT** _____.
    a. calories
    b. carbohydrates
    c. fats
    d. minerals

2. Starches should account for _____ percent of the diet.
    a. 10-20
    b. 30-40
    c. 50-60
    d. 70-80

3. Americans eat enough extra calories each day to feed a nation of _____ people.
    a. 20 million
    b. 40 million
    c. 60 million
    d. 80 million

4. A person with a high-fat-to-muscle ratio will metabolize _____ than a person of the same weight with a lower fat-to-muscle ratio.
    a. food more slowly than
    b. protein more rapidly but fats and starches more slowly
    c. fats and starches more rapidly but protein more slowly
    d. food more rapidly

5. In his efforts to lower his calorie intake, Julius practices meditation when feeling tense rather than turning to food, and refuses to bury disturbing feelings in a box of cookies or a carton of ice cream. His efforts are examples of _____.
    a. controlling internal stimuli
    b. controlling external stimuli
    c. competing responses
    d. chain breaking

6. Mona refuses to maintain a healthy body weight. She has an intense fear of being overweight, absence of menstruation, and a distorted body image. She is suffering from _____.
    a. bipolar disorder
    b. menarche
    c. anorexia nervosa
    d. bulimia nervosa

7. Jill enjoys jogging, bicycle riding, and cross-country skiing. All of these activities are _____.
    a. aerobic
    b. anaerobic
    c. anabolic
    d. isometric

8. Research suggests that exercise alleviates _____.
    a. narcolepsy
    b. hyperactivity
    c. depression
    d. symptoms of schizophrenia

9. Each of the following statements is true **EXCEPT** _____.
    a. the amount of sleep we need seems to be in part genetically determined
    b. people tend to need more sleep during periods of change and stress
    c. most students cannot successfully pull all-nighters
    d. sleep deprivation negatively affects attention, learning, and memory

10. The most commonly reported form of sleep disorder is _____.
   a. insomnia
   c. sleep apnea
   b. narcolepsy
   d. cataplexy

11. Elrod knows that his drinking is destroying his family and threatening his job, but he continues to drink heavily. In fact, his drinking is increasing and he is spending more and more time obtaining and drinking alcohol. The few times he has tried to quit he has suffered severe anxiety, tremors, and rapid pulse. Elrod's symptoms are characteristic of _____.
   a. casual drug usage
   c. substance dependence
   b. substance abuse
   d. substance intoxication

12. Elrod is so drunk that he is totally confused, has lost his sense of time and place, and cannot recognize who anybody is. His symptoms are classic symptoms of _____.
   a. disequilibrium
   c. tolerance
   b. disorientation
   d. physical dependence (addiction)

13. The social-cognitive explanation of substance abuse is that _____.
   a. people commonly try drugs based on the recommendation or observation of others
   b. drugs biologically numb people so that nothing bothers them
   c. some people are born with a genetic predisposition toward physiological dependence on various drugs such as alcohol or nicotine
   d. drugs help people control or express unconscious needs and impulses

14. Children of alcoholics may inherit a _____ sensitivity to its rewarding effects and a _____ tolerance of its negative effects.
   a. lower, lower
   c. lower, greater
   b. greater, lower
   d. greater, greater

15. No drug has meant so much to so many and been so abused as _____.
   a. alcohol
   c. Valium
   b. marijuana
   d. cocaine

16. Opioids are a class of _____ drugs.
   a. stimulant
   c. antipsychotic
   b. hallucinogenic
   d. narcotic

17. Amphetamines are _____.
   a. analgesics
   c. stimulants
   b. depressants
   d. hallucinogens

18. Cocaine was first used as a _____.
   a. cure for heroin addiction
   c. dietary supplement
   b. local anesthetic
   d. pain killer

19. Regular use of hallucinogens may lead to _____.
   a. tolerance and physiological dependence
   b. psychological and physiological dependence, but no tolerance
   c. tolerance and psychological dependence
   d. tolerance, but no psychological or physiological dependence

20. In the last century, _____ was available without prescription and was used almost as aspirin is used today for headaches and other minor aches and pains.
   a. heroin
   c. marijuana
   b. mescaline
   d. hashish

True-False Questions

21.   Many people with anorexia are obsessed with food.   _____

22.   Fitness is entirely a matter of strength.   _____

23.   Trying to get to sleep may keep you up at night.   _____

24.   The majority of American college students engage in binge drinking.   _____

25.   Cocaine dilates blood vessels in the brain, temporarily enhancing learning and memory.   _____

Essay Question

26.   Summarize the various viewpoints regarding the causal factors in substance abuse and dependence.

Student Activities

Name _____ **Date** _____

5.1 Personal Attitudes Toward Some Health-Related Issues

While considering the health-related problems below, which do you think would be the most difficult to experience? What would be next, and so forth? Rank from 1 to 5, the worst to the least troubling:

1. Type A behavior pattern _____

2. Inactive lifestyle _____

3. Obesity _____

4. Insomnia _____

5. Heart disease _____

Follow-Up Questions:

1. Considering these problems, which one is the object of the most ridicule? What defense could be offered for bashing these people?

2. Which of the problems do you think is the most difficult to correct? Why?

Activity continued on the back

3. How can one change from a Type A behavior pattern to more of a Type B behavior pattern? What social or psychological obstacles are likely to interfere with this change?

4. How much do you weigh, and what is your ideal weight? How much do you believe your ideal weight has been shaped by media influences, and, to the extent that they have, why have you let these influences determine your ideal weight?

5. How much sleep is ideal and how much do you prefer? How does it compare to how much sleep you are actually getting? What effect is it having on your daily energy levels and performance?

You will learn a great deal about health and health-related issues in this chapter. When you finish, you may find that you need to reconsider some of your answers. As always, you could ask others to reconsider their ideas about the above questions.

Name _____ **Date** _____

5.2 New Weight Guidelines

We can often turn to the government and other institutions for good information about nutrition, weight, and health. It might be interesting to compare your ideal weight from question 4 in activity 5.1 with a set of tables for healthy weight from the U. S. Departments of Agriculture and Health and Human Services. In comparison to the most recent tables and guidelines, these are more forgiving and allow a wider range of weights at each height. The source is the *1990 Dietary Guidelines for Americans.*

Height	Weight (in Lbs.)	
	19 to 34 years	35 years and over
5'0"	97-128	108-138
5'1"	101-132	111-143
5'2"	104-137	115-148
5'3"	107-141	119-152
5'4"	111-146	122-157
5'5"	114-150	126-162
5'6"	118-155	130-167
5'7"	121-160	134-172
5'8"	125-164	138-178
5'9"	129-169	142-183
5'10"	132-174	146-188
5'11"	136-179	151-194
6'0"	140-184	155-200
6'1"	144-189	159-205
6'2"	148-195	164-210

How close are you to the recommended weight range for your height?

Name _____ **Date** _____

5.3 Testing Our Aerobic Fitness

The text offers many reasons to exercise and quite a few guidelines for beginning and maintaining an aerobic training program. You might find the following test a challenging and rewarding way to chart your progress. Please observe the standard health precautions discussed in Chapter 5 before attempting this test if you are not already exercising, you smoke, have a family history of heart disease, are overweight, or are over 40. Time yourself and perhaps a friend or date if you care to, for a 1.5-mile run/walk. Your aerobic fitness rating can then be compared to the standards in the chart below (for all ages 13 and over).

Aerobic Fitness of Males and Females Estimated from 1.5-Mile Run*

	High (in minutes)	Low (in minutes)	Average (in minutes)
Males	9:29	12:39	11:29
Females	13:38	18:50	16:57
Sailing Team	9:54	11:49	10:43

*Source: Sharkey (no date)

You can use the 1.5-mile run to assess your status and your progress. You could also choose to repeat and time almost any similar task to measure progress. You do not have to compare yourself to any other people or a set of arbitrary standards to be motivated.

5.4 Sleep: The Gentle Tyrant or Benign Dictator?

Samuel Johnson called sleep the gentle tyrant because we cannot resist it, but we could also call sleep a benign dictator because it serves the body and mind as a clock that helps to organize the hundreds of functions that cycle through the 24-hour period. Sleep is only one of the clocks for controlling patterns that influence almost everything about us, including our moods, our intelligence, and most bodily functions. Without these clocks we might experience permanent jet lag. They seem to interact and help each other organize so we are generally at our best during the day.

One of the other clocks for controlling our body and mind is our core temperature, which is higher during our wake time and lower when we sleep. Even if we stay up all night, our temperatures still drop to their lowest levels at night and begin rising as our normal wake-up time approaches. Those functions that use core temperature for their timing go on as normal. Not so those functions that use sleep as a timer for control. Such desynchronization is largely responsible for discomfort and poor performance following a sleepless night. Usually one or two nights of sleep restores synchronization, and we feel better.

Occasionally specialists are asked to help people who have slept so poorly or inconsistently that their patterns and body clocks are confused. We often rely on oral temperature records to let us know where these people stand. Typically, if we take our temperature with an oral thermometer first thing in the morning, it will be several tenths of a degree cooler than just a few hours later. Then, in the late evening, as the day wanes, the pattern reverses and our temperature drops as our sleep time approaches. Sleep medicine specialists can use this pattern to study jet lag, depression, and other problems that seem to be highly related to the coordination of the patterns. For example, many depressed people show little or no pattern of core temperature changes.

You may find it interesting to graph your oral temperatures over the course of several days to verify this pattern, and also to see if it tends to correlate with your tendencies to be a morning person, otherwise known as a "Lark," or an evening person, known as an "Owl," or something in-between (see activity 5.5). Morning temperatures tend to rise faster for Larks and more slowly for Owls. Knowing our own pattern can help us choose class times or design our own schedules.

With an oral thermometer, sample your temperature several times each day for one week. Plot the temperatures on the following graph. Estimate the curving lines that run through the points and best fit your data. You will find a prepared graph on the back of this page.

Activity continued on the back

Daily Oral Temperatures

```
        -
        -
        -
        -
        -
100.0-----------------------------------------------------------------------
        -
        -
        -
        -
 99.0-----------------------------------------------------------------------
        -
        -
        -
        -
 98.0-----------------------------------------------------------------------
        -
        -
        -
        -
 97.0-----------------------------------------------------------------------
        -
        -
        -
        -
 96.0-----------------------------------------------------------------------
      6AM  8AM  10AM  12PM  2PM  4PM  6PM  8PM  10PM  12AM  2AM  4AM
```

Time of Day

5.5 Are You a "Lark" or an "Owl"?

Some of us hit the floor running when we get up in the morning. We usually eat breakfast, prefer morning classes, and do not care to stay up too late "past our bedtime" without some very good reason. This is the pattern of "Larks," or morning people. Others of us hate getting up in the morning, avoid breakfast, and do not need an excuse to stay up late, even to watch a television show that has little attraction. This is the pattern of "Owls," or evening people. Still more of us fit neither extreme case, and fall somewhere in between. Use the questions below to create a better idea of your patterns.

1. Estimate the number of breakfasts you skip each week (0-7):

2. Estimate how often you sleep in each week (0-7):

3. Estimate how often you stay up past your best sleep time each week (0-7):

4. Estimate what time you feel and respond your very best (AM/PM):

Total the scores on questions 1–3: Total = _____

The higher your score, the more you are like an "owl" in your waking/sleeping pattern. Conversely, the lower your score, the more you are like a "lark."

Name _____ **Date** _____

5.6 Taming the Tyrant

Even gentle tyrants are at times unable to get their way, and so many people suffer a range of sleep-related difficulties. In addition to insomnia, as discussed in Chapter 5, some people sleep too long, some suffer from pattern disruption caused by shift work, and some people even create their own difficulties by keeping irregular sleep schedules. If we want to feel our best during the day and sleep better at night, we are told that it is best to maintain regular sleep patterns. To assess the regularity of your sleep, or lack of it, keep the following simple diary. You may want to do this exercise at the same time you keep track of your daily oral temperature (activity 5.4).

Date	Wake-Up Time	Sleep Start Time

Follow-Up Questions:

1. How much do you vary your sleep start? Various studies indicate that more than two hours' variation daily can have detrimental effects on daytime performance.

2. Do you sleep in after late nights? Research suggests that this will also decrease daytime abilities.

Activity continued on the back

3. Did you experience any "Sunday night insomnia"? If we stay up later on weekends, we may delay our biological clocks and create problems, possibly including "Monday blues." It is best to keep to our regular patterns as much as possible by waking at our usual times even when we stay up late. While there is little trouble if we lose some sleep, there can be a problem if we disrupt our schedules.

Name _____ **Date** _____

5.7 Personal Attitudes Toward Some Drug-Related Issues

While considering the drug-related problems discussed in the text, which of the following do you think would cause the most difficult psychological and physical health problems? What would be next, and so forth? Rank from 1 to 5, the worst to the least troubling:

1. Alcoholism   _____

2. Addiction to nicotine   _____

3. Addiction to heroin   _____

4. Chronic marijuana use   _____

5. Addiction to crack or cocaine   _____

Follow-Up Questions:

1. Why do you consider your "1" choice to be the most troubling and your "5" choice to be the least troubling?

2. Considering these problems, which person is likely to be the object of the most ridicule? What defense could be offered for these people?

3. Which of the problems do you think is the most difficult to correct? Why?

5.8 Questioning Ourselves, Part I

Name _____ **Date** _____

1. If drugs were to become available that could improve life in some ways but cause life to be shorter, what choices would you make regarding your use of such drugs? How many years of your life, if any, would you give up to experience a 25 percent improvement in:

    a. Intelligence   _____ years

    b. Attractiveness   _____ years

    c. Physical strength   _____ years

    d. Sexual enjoyment   _____ years

    e. Popularity   _____ years

Which, if any, were you willing to give up the most years of life for? Why?

Which, if any, were you least willing to give up any years for? Why?

What if there were a "magic" potion that could give you unlimited political power, military control, social status, or knowledge of how the universe works? Would you be willing to shorten your life for any of these? Why or why not?

5.9 Questioning Ourselves, Part II

Name _____ **Date** _____

1. Two Seattle cocktail waiters were fired because they did not want to serve a strawberry daiquiri to a pregnant woman (*Newsweek,* 1991). It raises an issue that could quickly divide opinions. Would you favor laws that would prevent or restrict pregnant women from smoking, drinking alcohol, or abusing drugs? What would be your most important argument for such laws? On the other hand, what would be the most powerful argument against such laws?

   For:

   Against:

2. If you were throwing a party, would you serve alcohol to a pregnant woman? Justify your response.

3. When do you say when? How many alcoholic beverages at the **most** would you want to see the following people consume in one evening?

   a. Your date   _____

   b. Your designated driver   _____

Activity continued on the back

c. Your best friend   _____

d. Your minister   _____

e. The president of the United States _____

f. Your boss   _____

g. Your grandparent(s)   grandma _____   grandpa _____

h. Your parent(s)   mother   _____   father   _____

i. Your sibling   brother _____   sister   _____

j. Yourself   _____

5. Except for the designated driver, who should not drink any alcohol? How do you explain any differences in your answers? Are any sexist or ageist attitudes or stereotypes influencing your judgments?

6. What answers would you expect other people to give to these questions?

For an interesting variation of this exercise, answer these questions again as if they referred to smoking, using marijuana, or using some other illegal drug. How are your answers different this time than they were before? Why?

5.10 Social Approval of Alcohol Abuse

At some point in our lives we decide what our approach to alcohol should be. One influence we can document is peer pressure. If friends and roommates frequently voice approval of "getting wasted," "getting bombed," or "getting ripped," etc., it would be hard to avoid the conclusion that alcohol should be used as a drug, rather than a beverage. Try this exercise for one week:

1. How many times does someone speak of intoxication as if it is desirable or acceptable and how often is it spoken of in disapproving ways?

2. What words or phrases are used as synonyms for intoxication?

3. How many times did you catch yourself speaking of alcohol the same way?

4. How do you react to the desirable as opposed to the undesirable references? Is there a difference? Why or why not?

Activity continued on the back

5. Where do you draw the line between use and abuse of alcohol? How did you decide upon where to draw the line? In other words, what are your reasons for drawing the line where you drew it?

5.11 Binge Drinking

A major concern in recent years for college, and high school, administrators is "binge drinking." Each year several adolescents and young adults die, hundreds more are hospitalized, and countless numbers made sick from bouts of binge drinking.

1. How many of your friends binge drink occasionally? Regularly? Constantly?

2. What have been the immediate and long-term effects, if any, of this drinking on their health and behavior?

3. What reason can you give for your friends binge drinking?

4. How many times, if any, have you been pressured by your friends to binge drink with them?

Activity continued on the back

5. How did you feel about it and how have you reacted to this pressure?

6. If you have engaged in binge drinking, or have been tempted to binge drink, what factors were key in your drinking or in your being tempted to drink?

7. If you have never engaged in binge drinking, or have been tempted to binge drink and refused to do it, what factors were key in your decision not to do it?

5.12 Does Smoking and Secondary Smoke Affect Heart Rate?

People who are allergic to or bothered by secondary cigarette smoke may not want to participate in this activity except at a distance. If you smoke or know someone who smokes, you may be able to see one of the physiological effects of nicotine first-hand. You would want to be tactful in requesting the cooperation of someone so the request is not interpreted as a challenge.

1. Take a base rate of the smoker's heart rate after a typical amount of time has passed since the last cigarette —at least an hour or so. The pulse can be monitored at the wrist or neck for one minute.

    Record here _____

2. Now, if you intend to remain close enough to be affected by the secondary smoke of the smoker, take your own heart rate before asking the smoker to light up.

    Record your heart rate here _____

3. Allow the smoker to smoke one cigarette and monitor the heart rate at the end of five minutes, even if he or she is still smoking.

    Record the smoker's second heart rate here _____

4. Record your second heart rate here _____

5. What have you been able to demonstrate?

Activity continued on the back

6. Please explain your feelings, pro or con, about smokers' rights.

7. Now you may wish to compare your notes with your classmates.

Name _____ **Date** _____

5.13 Should Marijuana Be Legalized?

Ever since the 1960s, a national debate has continued as to whether or not marijuana should be legalized. What do you think?

Reasons for legalization: Give at least three reasons why you think marijuana should be legalized.

    a.

    b.

    c.

Reasons to keep it illegal: Give at least three reasons why you think marijuana should not be legalized.

    a.

    b.

    c.

Consequences (good or bad) of legalization of marijuana: List at least three positive or negative consequences you believe would result from the legalization of marijuana.

    a.

    b.

    c.

5.14 Should Trans-Fats Be Banned?

A recent trend in the United States has been a movement by some schools and communities to remove fatty and sugary foods from cafeteria menus and replace them with healthier choices. An extension of that trend has been the effort in a few cities to ban certain high-fat foods, the use of trans-fatty acids (which are often used in margarines and in cooking foods such as French fries, etc.) in cooking foods in restaurants. some people view this as political correctness taken too far, and an invasion of people's personal rights to choose what they eat for themselves. Other see this as a necessary first step toward ending the growing "obesity epidemic in the United States. How do you feel?

1. Should schools removed unhealthy foods from cafeteria menus and replace them with healthier choices? Why or why not?

2. Should cities be able to ban fatty foods from restaurant menus, with the threat of criminal charges being filed against chefs or restaurant owners who violate these rules? Why or why not?

3. Should people be able to sue companies like McDonald's for becoming obese, or developing other health-related problems after years of eating their food? Why or why not?

6

The Self in a Social World

Chapter Outline

Module 6.1: The Self: The Core of Your Psychological Being

Module 6.2: The Self-Concept, Self-Esteem, and Self-Identity

Module 6.3: Perception of Others

Module 6.4: Prejudice and Discrimination

Module 6.5: Attribution Theory and Personal Adjustment

Module 6.6: Psychology in Daily Life: Enhancing Self-Esteem

Chapter Overview

The Self. The self is the core or center of your psychological being. It is an organized and consistent way of perceiving yourself as a unique being—an "I." The self also involves your perceptions of the ways in which you relate to the world. The self has physical, social, and personal aspects. Our social selves are the masks and social roles we don to meet the requirements of our situations. Our personal selves are our private inner identities.

Names. Names are linked to expectations by parents and society at large. People with common names are usually rated more favorably, but people with unusual names often accomplish more. We have given names, but the names we choose to go by—often nicknames—can say much about how we view ourselves.

Values. Our values give rise to our personal goals and tend to place limits on the means we shall use to reach them. We are more subject to social influences when we do not have personal values or our values are in flux.

Self-Concept. Your self-concept is your impression of yourself. It includes your perception of the traits (fairness, competence, sociability, and so on) you possess to the degree to which you deem these traits to be important in defining yourself.

Self-Esteem. Self-esteem begins to develop as the reflected appraisal of how we regarded by important figures in our lives, especially parents. Children who are cherished by their parents, and receive their approval and support, usually come to see themselves as being worthy of love. Research suggests that the children of strict parents are more likely than the children of permissive parents to develop high self-esteem. Although self-esteem can be a relatively stable element of personality, it can also vary depending on external events—such as test grades or other people's acceptance—and our emotional reaction to them.

The Ideal Self. The ideal self is our concept of what we ought to be. The closer your self-description is in keeping with your ideal self, the higher your self-esteem is likely to be.

Self-Identity. Self-identity is your sense of who you are and what you stand for.

Identity Statuses. Identity statuses are categories that describe an individual's level of self-identity. Marcia identified four identity statuses: identity achievement, identity foreclosure, identity moratorium, and identity diffusion. The status of identity achievement describes people who have resolved an identity crisis and are committed to a relatively stable set of beliefs or a course of action. Identity foreclosure describes people who have adopted a commitment to a set of beliefs or a course of action without undergoing an identity crisis. Identity moratorium describes people who are in the throes of an identity crisis; they are undergoing an intense examination of alternatives. Identity diffusion describes people who have neither arrived at a commitment as to who they are and what they stand for nor experienced a crisis.

Ethnicity, Gender, and Identity. People from ethnic minority groups often need to come to terms with conflicting values—those that characterize their particular ethnic background and those that characterize the dominant (European American, middle class) culture in the United States. Erikson's views of identity development were intended to apply mainly to males because they focus on embracing a philosophy of life and commitment to a career at a time when most women remained in the home. Today, however, identity achievement in terms of a career is as important to women as to men in our society.

Social Perception. Through the process of social perception, we come to form impressions of other people and develop attitudes about people and social issues.

First Impressions. First impressions obtain their importance because of the primacy effect. That is, we tend to infer traits from behavior. If people act considerately at first, they are conceptualized as considerate people and future behavior is interpreted according to that view of them.

Body Language. People's body language provides important information about their thoughts and feelings which can help us adjust in social situations. For example, when people lean toward us they are usually showing interest in us.

Prejudice. Prejudice is a preconceived attitude toward a group that typically leads people to evaluate members of that group in negative terms.

Discrimination. Discrimination is negative behavior that results from prejudice. It includes denial of access to jobs and housing.

Stereotypes. Stereotypes are fixed conventional ideas about groups of people, such as stereotypes that Italian-Americans are hot-tempered and Chinese-Americans are deferential.

Origins of Prejudice and Discrimination. Sources of prejudice include dissimilarity (or assumptions of dissimilarity), social conflict, social learning, the relative ease of processing information according to stereotypes, and social categorization ("us" versus "them").

Attribution. The attribution process involves the ways in which people infer the motives and traits of themselves and others. In dispositional attributions, we attribute people's behavior to internal factors such as their personality traits and personal decisions. In situational attributions, we attribute people's behavior to external circumstances or forces.

Attributional Bias. According to the actor-observer effect, we tend to attribute the behavior of others to internal, dispositional factors. However, we tend to attribute our own behavior to external, situational factors. The so-called fundamental attribution error is the tendency to attribute too much of other people's behavior to dispositional factors. The self-serving bias refers to the finding that we tend to attribute our successes to internal, stable factors and our failures to external, unstable factors.

Learning Objectives

After studying this chapter your students should be able to:

1. Identify the various types of schemas and explain how they influence our perceptions of others.

2. Describe the various parts of the self and discuss how, together, these parts meld together to form the "self."

3. Summarize the research on the relationship between names and personality.

4. Explain what values are and why they are important to self-development.

5. Compare and contrast the self-concept, the ideal self, and self-esteem, and explain how each contributes to our overall self-perception.

6. Identify and briefly explain each of Marcia's four possible identity statuses, and briefly describe the effects of human diversity on identity formation.

7. Compare and contrast the primacy and recency effects, and explain how important these effects are in our relationships with others in the long run.

8. Explain what body language is and why it is important.

9. Compare and contrast prejudice and discrimination, and identify at least five sources of prejudice.

10. Identify and briefly describe at least four methods of coping with prejudice and discrimination.

11. Identify the various types of attributions and discuss the attribution process in terms of the fundamental attribution error, the actor-observer effect, and the self-serving bias.

12. Identify and briefly describe five ways one can boost one's self-esteem.

Key Terms

schema	self-esteem	prejudice
role schema	ideal self	discrimination
person schema	identity crisis	stereotypes
self-schema	identify achievement	attribution
self	identity foreclosure	attribution process
physical self	identity moratorium	dispositional attribution
social self	identity diffusion	situational attribution
personal self	social perception	fundamental attribution error
ethics	primacy effect	actor-observer effect
self-concept	recency effect	self-serving bias

Key Terms Review

Define each of the following terms:

1. Schema: _____

_____

2. Person Schema: _____

_____

3. Self: _____

_____

4. Ethics: _____

_____

5. Self-Concept: _____

_____

6. Self-Esteem: _____

_____

7. Ideal Self: _____

_____

8. Identity Achievement: _____

_____

9. Identity Diffusion: _____

_____

10. Primacy Effect: _____

_____

11. Recency Effect: _____

_____

12. Prejudice: _____

_____

13. Discrimination: _____

_____

14. Stereotypes: _____

_____

15. Attribution: _____

_____

16. Dispositional Attribution: _____

_____

17. Situational Attribution: _____

_____

18. Fundamental Attribution Error: _____

_____

19. Actor-Observer Effect: _____

_____

20. Self-Serving Bias: _____

_____

Chapter Review

1.   We all carry different kinds of schemas such as _____ schemas, about how

people in certain roles (husbands, wives, bosses, teachers) are expected to behave,

_____ schemas, about how particular individuals are expected to behave, and

_____ schemas, the generalizations, beliefs, and feelings we have about

ourselves.

2.   We process information about the self and others through our _____.

3.   The three parts of the self are the _____ self, the _____ self, and the

_____ self.

4.   African-American girls are likely to be _____ with their physical appearance

than are European-American girls, and African Americans overall tend to have

_____ self-esteem than Euro Americans.

5.   Your name, your values, and your self-concept are all aspects of your _____
self.

6.   Our names and nicknames can reflect our _____ toward ourselves.

7.   The importance we place on objects and things, called _____, is closely related

to our standards of conduct or behavior, called _____.

8.   Our values are most likely to be in flux during _____.

9.   Your impression of yourself is your _____ _____.

10. The self-concept includes one's self-_____ and one's _____ self.

11. Self-approval, or one's favorable opinion of oneself, is called _____.

12. Parents of boys with higher self-esteem are _____ demanding and are

_____ involved in their lives.

13. One's concept of what one **ought** to be is called one's _____.

14. Your self-esteem typically reflects the difference between your _____ self and

your self-_____.

15. Self-esteem is _____ correlated with psychological and physical health.

16. According to Erikson, your self-_____ is your sense of who you are and what
you stand for.

17. Erik Erikson believed that a crisis of self-identity is a _____ part of
development and can be a _____ experience.

18. **Matching:** Match the following terms with their definitions.

a. _____ Identity achievement

b. _____ Identity foreclosure

c. _____ Identity moratorium

d. _____ Identity diffusion

1. Individuals who have adopted a commitment to a set of beliefs or a course of action without undergoing an identity crisis.

2. Individuals who are in the throes of an identity crisis.

3. Individuals who have neither arrived at a commitment as to who they are and what they stand for nor experienced a crisis.

4. Individuals who have resolved an identity crisis and committed to a relatively stable set of beliefs or a course of action.

19. Among college students, the lowest incidence of identity diffusion is in the area of

_____ _____.

20. Identity formation is more _____ for adolescents from ethnic minority groups.

21. The tendency to evaluate others in terms of first impressions is called the _____

effect, whereas the tendency to evaluate others in terms of the most recent impression

is called the _____ effect.

22. At least five ways to manage first impressions are:

    a. _____

    b. _____

    c. _____

    d. _____

    e. _____

23. When people _____ us, and lean _____ us, we may assume that they like us or are interested in us.

24. When other people look us squarely in the eye, we may assume that they are being _____ or _____ with us. Avoidance of eye contact may suggest _____ or _____.

25. Hard stares are interpreted as _____ or signs of _____.

26. Three ways you can use information about body language to foster adjustment in social relationships are:

    a. _____

    b. _____

    c. _____

27. Racism, sexism, and ageism are all examples of _____, which often results in biased treatment toward minorities, women, or older persons, known as _____.

28. Discrimination is frequently based on _____.

29. Five sources of prejudice are:

    a. _____

    b. _____

    c. _____

d. _____

e. _____

30. Five methods of coping with prejudice and discrimination are:

a. _____

b. _____

c. _____

d. _____

e. _____

31. A belief concerning why people behave in a certain way is called a(n) _____.

32. The process by which people draw inferences about the motives and traits of others is the _____ process.

33. An assumption that a person's behavior results from internal causes is called a _____ attribution, whereas an assumption that a person's behavior results from external sources is called a _____ attribution.

34. **Matching:** Match the following terms on the right with their corresponding definitions on the left.

_____ a.	The tendency to attribute our own behavior to external factors but to attribute the behavior of others to internal factors	1. Dispositional attribution
_____ b.	An assumption that a person's behavior is motivated by external forces	2. Fundamental attribution error
_____ c.	The tendency to view one's success as stemming from internal factors and one's failures from external factors	3. Situational attribution
_____ d.	An assumption that a person's behavior is motivated by internal forces	4. Self-serving bias
_____ e.	The tendency to assume that others act primarily because of internal causes even when there is evidence that their behavior is due to external factors	5. The actor-observer effect

35. The self-serving bias is more common in _____ cultures.

36.   Five methods of improving self-esteem are:

a.   _____

b.   _____

c.   _____

d.   _____

e.   _____

Sample Test

Multiple-Choice Questions

1.   Social roles and masks _____.
a.   are merely deceptions and lies in most cases
b.   are usually an effort to hide our real personalities due to feelings of inadequacy or inferiority
c.   have been found to be rarely, if ever, useful in helping people function socially
d.   are typically genuine efforts to meet the requirements of a situation

2.   In Mark Twain's ***The Prince and the Pauper***, court officials choosing between two boys whose appearance and behaviors are identical seek out the one whose _____ is that of the prince.
a.   inner identity   c.   ideal self
b.   social self   d.   value system

3.   Which of the following is **NOT** true of names?
a.   names and nicknames can reflect our attitudes toward ourselves
b.   names often reflect parental expectations of what their children are to become
c.   different names give rise to different expectations of people by others
d.   unusual names seem linked to popularity in childhood and adolescence

4.   Our "oughts" and "shoulds" are found primarily in our _____.
a.   self-concept   c.   self-serving bias
b.   self-efficacy expectancies   d.   ideal self

5.   According to your text, self-esteem _____.
a.   is innate
b.   is your perception of yourself
c.   begins with parental love and approval
d.   develops primarily during adolescence

6.   According to your text, parents of boys with high self-esteem were likely to be _____.
a.   extremely lenient; rarely, if ever, disciplining their sons
b.   generally lenient, but harsh when they did decide to discipline their sons
c.   strict, but not harsh or cruel
d.   rigid and harsh when dealing with most disciplinary situations

7.	According to your text, parents of boys with low self-esteem were likely to be _____.
	a.	extremely lenient; rarely, if ever, disciplining their sons
	b.	generally lenient, but harsh when they did decide to discipline their sons
	c.	strict, but not harsh or cruel
	d.	rigid and harsh in dealing with most disciplinary situations

8.	Which of the following is **NOT** one of the four identity statuses identified by Marcia?
	a.	identity achievement	c.	identity diffusion
	b.	identity crisis	d.	identity foreclosure

9.	Mary is confused. She is intensely examining various alternatives on issues that are important to her and her future. Should she get married or not, go to graduate school or get a full-time job, or become active in the local environmental group? She is best described as having an identity status of

	_____.
	a.	identity foreclosure	c.	identity achievement
	b.	identity moratorium	d.	identity diffusion

10.	The tendency to evaluate others in terms of first impressions is called the _____.
	a.	primacy effect	c.	fundamental attribution error
	b.	recency effect	d.	actor-observer effect

11.	When people like us, they are likely to _____.
	a.	lean forward and face us	c.	cross their arms
	b.	lean back and toy with their hair	d.	lean back and face us

12.	_____ touch other people when they are interacting with them.
	a.	Men are more likely than women to
	b.	Men and women are equally likely to
	c.	Neither men nor women are likely to
	d.	Women are more likely than men to

13.	In high school, "staring contests" among adolescent males are seen as _____.
	a.	tests of visual acuity	c.	tests of muscle control
	b.	assertions of dominance	d.	measures of trust

14.	Prejudices about a group of people that can lead us to process information about members of these groups in a biased fashion are called _____.
	a.	discrimination	c.	response sets
	b.	subjugation	d.	stereotypes

15.	Which of the following is **NOT** a proven source of prejudice?
	a.	biological inferiority	c.	social conflict
	b.	attitudinal differences	d.	social categorization

16.	Explaining someone's behavior in terms of internal causes, such as attitudes or beliefs, is called

	_____.
	a.	the fundamental attribution error	c.	situational attribution
	b.	dispositional attribution	d.	psychogenic attribution

17.	Cindy tells Jim that she fired him because she was ordered to by her own bosses. Her explanation for firing Jim is based on _____.
	a.	the fundamental attribution error	c.	situational attribution
	b.	dispositional attribution	d.	psychogenic attribution

18. After just saying how the world is full of "insensitive jerks" who deliberately hurt people, Joe excuses his own rude behavior because he was late and "had a lot of problems" to deal with. Joe's comments reflect _____.
  a. the fundamental attribution error
  b. the actor-observer effect
  c. a psychogenic attribution
  d. the self-serving bias

19. Depressed people are more likely than other people to attribute their failures to _____.
  a. situational factors
  b. chance or luck
  c. fate or destiny
  d. internal factors

20. Focusing on the parts of the body that we can change rather than the parts that cannot be changed falls under which method of raising self-esteem?
  a. self-improvement
  b. challenging the realism of your ideal self
  c. substituting real, attainable goals for unattainable goals
  d. building self-efficacy expectations

True-False Questions

21. Person schemas are formed by first impressions. _____

22. European-American girls tend to have higher self-esteem than African-American girls. _____

23. Social roles and masks are usually deceptions and lies. _____

24. Waitresses who touch their patrons while making change receive higher tips. _____

25. Prejudice is a negative form of behavior that results from discrimination. _____

Essay Question

26. Describe the various parts of the self and discuss how these parts meld together to form the "self."

Student Activities

Name _____ **Date** _____

6.1 Testing Our Perceptions

If there is a consistency in the theories of Freud, Erikson, Rogers, and Maslow, it may be the idea that adjustment depends on the accuracy of the perception of reality. It would seem that accurate perception would increase the likelihood of correct choices, reduce or eliminate anxieties from unnecessary worry, provide feedback for change, and so on and so on. In this chapter, Nevid and Rathus portray the virtues of accurate social perception. If only we could see others more accurately without prejudice! If only others could see us the same way!

Select a classmate, or roommate, for this exercise which tests your perceptiveness. It will be a tough test so be prepared to encounter your limitations.

Ask a friend to recall or answer as well as possible and write down:

1. The last two magazines read and circle the one he or she liked best.

2. The last two movies seen and circle the one he or she liked best.

3. Two television shows watched regularly and the one he or she prefers.

4. Would the person quit school or work if he or she won a $5,000,000 lottery? Why?

5. Would the person sacrifice his or her life to save anyone in the world? Why or why not?

6. Did he or she vote in the last election?

7. Would the person choose the sex of his or her first child?

Activity continued on the back

You can make up and ask many more such questions. Now tell your subject what you think his or her answer will be on the first question and your rationale for it. Proceed through all the questions to test your accuracy. Maybe you would be willing to let your friend try the same thing with you as a target.

Follow-Up Questions:

1. What, if any, are the bases for predicting people's responses in advance?

2. What leads you to make correct predictions?

3. What leads you to make incorrect predictions?

Name _____ Date _____

6.2 Testing the Accuracy of Social Perceptions

As part of a class discussion, generate a 'master list' of labels people typically use to describe each other (i.e. "shy," "aggressive," "outgoing," "smart," "friendly," etc.).

Which labels in the list would you assign to yourself and your classmates? Can you correctly guess each other's assignments? Students have often found this exercise to be one of the most revealing and interesting activities in this course.

1. Each person has access to the master list which everyone just created, which might be on the blackboard or some other handy place.

2. Assign a label to yourself from the list created by the class. Do not tell others what label you have chosen.

3. Each person then prepares two response sheets. On the first sheet write down the names of everyone in the class and beside each name assign a stereotype from the master list you think best fits them (be gentle!). On the second sheet, write only your name.

4. Pass the second sheet around the room systematically so each person can record the label or stereotype they chose for the named individual in question 3. When everyone has responded, each paper is returned to the person named at the top of the page.

5. Students then reveal the label they originally chose to describe themselves. They can then check the accuracy of their label assignments against other students' perceptions of themselves.

Follow-Up Questions:

1. Do people perceive you the way you thought they would? If not, in what way were their perceptions different?

2. How do you feel about the way that others perceived you? Has it made you think about changing some aspect of your public "persona"? If so, what would you change and how would you do it?

3. How accurate were *your* perceptions? What percentage of your labels did your classmates assign themselves?

4. If your perceptions were incorrect, in what way were they incorrect, and what could you do to increase their accuracy?

5. Look again at the text discussion regarding how to cope with prejudice and discrimination. Is it possible that this activity could alter the way we discriminate?

Name _____ **Date** _____

6.3 Perceiving How Others Dress to Impress

Does your school require you to wear a uniform? Probably not, but it may be possible for students to choose some rather uniform ways to dress, which may be their attempt to make a statement about what they want us to think about them. How do you believe that people use their clothing, hairstyles, and even facial expressions to help themselves achieve an identity?

This activity asks you to sit in the student union or another suitable location and catalog the different social identities you perceive others are trying to project. You might categorize some as Greek, some as Athletes, some as Art Students, and so on. List your proposed labels here:

Questions:

1. How can you do this without being negative? For example, are any of the labels you use derogatory, such as "nerds," "frat rats," or "animals"? How can you avoid labels such as this?

2. Beside each label write the degree of confidence you have in assigning people you see in this category as a percentage from 0 to 100 percent. How does this idea alter the way you see this task?

3. With classmates, create a single list of labels that will be useful for the next project. Assign a number to each label as a code. How many labels have you created?

6.4 Exploring Your Identity

1. Identify your four greatest personal strengths:

   a. _____

   b. _____

   c. _____

   d. _____

2. Identify your four greatest personal weaknesses or areas of difficulty:

   a. _____

   b. _____

   c. _____

   d. _____

3. What do you currently see as the biggest challenge in your life:

4. If you could change one thing about yourself, what would that be:

Activity continued on the back

5. Do you believe you were put here for a specific purpose? If not, why not? If so, what do you believe that purpose to be?

6. What are the three most important goals for you in your life?

   a. _____

   b. _____

   c. _____

7. Which of the four identity statuses described by Marcia do you feel you are in? Why?

7

Social Influence: Being Influenced By—and Influencing—Others

Chapter Outline

Chapter Overview

Routes of Persuasion.   The central route involves the careful weighing of the content of messages. The peripheral route involves persuasion through cues that are peripheral to the content of the message.

Factors in Persuasion. Emotional appeals are more effective with most people than are logical presentations. Repeated messages are usually more effective than messages presented once. People tend to be persuaded by celebrities, experts, and people who seem to be similar to themselves. People are more likely to be persuaded when they are in a good mood. People with low sales resistance tend to have low self-esteem and to worry about the impression they will make if they say no.

The Foot-in-the-Door Technique. With the foot-in-the-door technique, salespeople encourage customers to accede to minor requests to prime them to agree with larger requests later on.

Low-balling. Low-balling is a sales method in which the customer is persuaded to make a commitment on favorable terms, but the salesperson then says that he or she must revise the terms.

The Bait-and-Switch Technique. The customer is baited by an offer of merchandise at an extremely low price. But the merchandise appears to be of inferior quality or missing desirable features. The salesperson then pulls the switch by offering higher-quality but also more expensive merchandise.

Obedience. Milgram found that the great majority of participants in his research would deliver a strong electric shock to an innocent party when instructed to do so by an experimenter. Possible reasons why people will commit atrocities include propaganda (degrading the victims), socialization, lack of social comparison, perception of the authority figure as being legitimate, inaccessibility of one's personal values, and lack of buffers.

Conformity. Conformity is changing one's behavior to adhere to social norms, such as facing forward in elevators, or wearing what "people like us" are wearing. Factors that enhance the likelihood of conformity include belonging to a collectivist culture, desire to be liked by others, low self-esteem, shyness, and lack of personal expertise in the situation.

Deindividuation. Deindividuation is a state of reduced self-awareness and lowered concern for social evaluation. Factors that foster deindividuation include anonymity, diffusion of responsibility, high levels of arousal, and focus on group norms rather than on one's own values. As members of crowds, many people engage in behavior they would find unacceptable if they were acting alone.

Altruism. Altruism is a selfless concern for the welfare of others, which is characterized by helping others. People are more likely to help others when they are in a good mood, are empathic, believe that an emergency exists, assume the responsibility to act, know what to do, and are acquainted with those in need. When we are members of groups or crowds, we may ignore people in trouble because of diffusion of responsibility. We may be less likely to help when we feel that others are available to offer help, when we don't perceive a clear need for help, when we don't feel capable of helping, or when we fear being harmed ourselves.

Learning Objectives

After studying this chapter your students should be able to:

1.   Define "social influence", explain the ELM model and discuss the "routes" involved in the social influence process.

2.   Identify and briefly discuss the factors involved in making a message persuasive.

3.   Identify and briefly discuss the factors involved in making a communicator persuasive.

4.   Discuss how the context of a message influences its persuasiveness and briefly describe the audience factors involved in the persuasiveness of a message.

5. Explain the "foot-in-the-door" technique, lowballing, and the bait and switch technique. Give an example of each and discuss methods of coping with these techniques.

6. Describe what happened in the Milgram studies on obedience and identify the factors thought to be responsible.

7. Identify and briefly describe the seven factors that may foster blind obedience to perceived authority.

8. Define conformity and social norms and briefly discuss the factors that influence conformity.

9. Explain why people behave differently in groups than they do as individuals.

10. Explain what altruism is, and why it is not always as selfless as it may seem.

11. Explain what the bystander effect is and the various factors that determine or influence helping behavior.

12. Compare and contrast assertive, passive, and aggressive behavior. Also, briefly explain the four methods discussed in your text for becoming a more assertive person.

13. Discuss the nature of shyness, how people can learn to be "successfully shy," and the reasons why becoming a volunteer can help people overcome shyness.

Key Terms

social influence	obedience	bystander effect
elaboration likelihood model (ELM)	conform	assertiveness
emotional appeals	social norms	irrational beliefs
foot-in-the-door technique	deindividuation	modeling
low-balling	diffusion of responsibility	behavioral rehearsal
bait-and-switch	altruism	

Key Terms Review

Define each of the following terms:

1. Social Influence: _____

_____

2. Elaboration Likelihood Model (ELM): _____

_____

3. Emotional Appeals: _____

_____

4. Foot-in-the-Door Technique: _____

_____

5. Low-balling: _____

_____

6. Bait-and Switch: _____

_____

7. Obedience: _____

_____

8. Conform: _____

_____

9. Social Norms: _____

_____

10. Deindividuation: _____

_____

11. Diffusion of Responsibility: _____

_____

12. Altruism: _____

_____

13. Bystander Effect: _____

_____

14. Assertiveness: _____

_____

15. Irrational Beliefs: _____

_____

16. Modeling: _____

_____

17. Behavioral Rehearsal: _____

_____

Chapter Review

1. Social _____ is the area of social psychology that studies the way in which people alter the thoughts, feelings, and behaviors of other people.

2. The _____ _____ model focus on two different routes by which persuasion works.

3. Petty and others point out that persuasive messages use two routes, the _____ route and the _____ route, to change people's opinions and behavior.

4. When elaboration likelihood is high, persuasion is most likely to take place through the _____ route. When it is low, persuasion is most likely to take place through the _____ route.

5. Repeated exposure to people and things tends to _____ their appeal.

6. Four techniques for increasing the likelihood that a message will be persuasive are:

a. _____

b. _____

c. _____

d. _____

7. Five personal characteristics that make a person's message more persuasive are

_____, _____, _____, _____, and _____ to the audience.

8. Elements of the immediate _____, such as music, increase the likelihood of persuasion.

9. Persuasive messages are most likely to be accepted when the person is in a

_____ mood.

10. People with _____ self-esteem and _____ social anxiety are least likely to resist social pressure.

11. Three common sales techniques designed to persuade you to buy something you may

not really want are the _____-_____-_____-_____

technique, the _____ technique and the _____-_____-_____

technique.

12. We are _____ creatures, influenced by the _____ with which we interact

in our daily lives.

13. Atrocities are made possible through the _____ of people who are more

concerned about the _____ of their supervisors than about their own

_____.

14. In the Milgram studies, subjects were told that they were taking part in a study on

_____.

15. Of those who took part in Milgram's original "learning" study, _____ percent delivered the full 450-volt shock.

16. Seven reasons why people obey the commands of others, even when asked to commit immoral acts, are:

a. _____

b. _____

c. _____

d. _____

e. _____

f. _____

g. _____

17. We are said to _____ when we change our behavior on order to adhere to social norms.

18. Conformity was studied by _____.

19. Personal factors that prompt conformity to social norms are belonging to a

_____ society, desire to be _____ by the group, _____ self-esteem,

social _____, and lack of _____ with the task. Situational factors include

group _____ and social _____.

20. The likelihood of conformity increases rapidly until group size is about _____ members, then it levels off.

21. People often behave the way they do in a mob, because they experience _____.

22. Four factors that contribute to a state of deindividuation are:

a. _____

b. _____

c. _____

d. _____

23. Altruism is a form of _____ behavior.

24. The Kitty Genovese case is a classic example of the _____ _____.

25. Five factors that increase the chances that bystanders will come to the aid of people in distress are:

a. _____

b. _____

c. _____

d. _____

e. _____

26. People are more likely to help people who are _____ to themselves, and if they are _____ dressed.

27. Women are most likely to be helped if they are _____ and _____.

28. Behavior that is expressive of genuine feelings and maintains social rights is called _____ behavior. This compares to submissive, passive _____ behavior in which one's feelings are not expressed, and _____ behavior in which one expresses feelings in a way that does not respect the rights of others.

29. Four techniques which can be helpful in an attempt to become more assertive are:

a. _____

b. _____

c. _____

d. _____

30. A techniques which can help you remain assertive in the face of someone who is resisting your efforts to stand up for your rights is the _____-_____ technique.

Sample Test

Multiple-Choice Questions

1. According to the elaboration likelihood model, if viewers of a political debate are well-informed and interested in the issues, they are most likely to be _____.
   a. persuaded by neither the central nor the peripheral route
   b. persuaded primarily by the central route
   c. persuaded by the peripheral route
   d. equally persuaded by both the central and peripheral routes

2. When exposed to ads warning about the negative effects of sun tanning, students _____.
   a. ignored both ads that warned of cancer risks and ads that warned of risks to students' appearance
   b. were more affected by ads that warned of cancer risks than ads that warned of risks to students' appearance
   c. were more affected by ads that warned of risks to students' appearance than by ads that warned of cancer risks
   d. were strongly and equally affected by ads that warned of cancer risks and of risks to students' appearance

3. Studies on mood and persuasion indicate that _____.
   a. people's moods are not related to their susceptibility to a persuasive message
   b. people are more likely to be affected by a persuasive message when they are physically aroused
   c. people are more likely to be affected by a persuasive message when they are in a bad mood
   d. people are more likely to be affected by a persuasive message when they are in a good mood

4. Which of the following people are **MOST** likely to resist social pressure?
   a. people with high self-esteem and low social anxiety
   b. people with high self-esteem and high social anxiety
   c. people with low self-esteem and high social anxiety
   d. people with low self-esteem and low social anxiety

5. A person calls you on the phone and asks you to take a "few minutes" to complete a survey. Once you agree to this, the salesperson then asks if you would also agree to listen to a sales pitch for their product. When you agree to this, the salesperson then aggressively tries to sell you the product AND all the expensive attachments that go with it. This approach is a classic example of the _____ technique.
   a. lowballing   c. foot-in-the-door
   b. repeated exposure   d. "bandwagon"

6. Each of the following is true of atrocities **EXCEPT** _____.
   a. they reflect the inherently selfish and evil nature of capitalistic societies
   b. victims are often portrayed as being criminals
   c. victims are often depicted by propaganda as being subhuman
   d. they are often made possible by the compliance of people more concerned about the approval of their supervisors than their own morality

7. If you volunteered for Milgram's study, you would have been appointed "by chance" as _____.
   a. a learner   c. a referee
   b. an observer   d. a teacher

8. Milgram found that of the different groups he studied, _____.
   a. males from the general community gave the highest levels of electric shocks
   b. Yale undergraduates gave the highest levels of electric shocks
   c. women gave the highest levels of electric shocks
   d. all three groups gave relatively equal levels of electric shocks

181

9. Milgram's research alerted us to the real and present danger of the tendency of people to _____.
   a. inflict overly severe punishment out of pure anger and frustration
   b. obey authority figures, even when it involves immoral actions
   c. lose control of their innate aggressive tendencies, once those tendencies are released
   d. use deception to get away with activities in which they shouldn't be engaged

10. The researcher known for his studies on conformity to group pressure was _____.
    a. Asch
    b. Zimbardo
    c. Milgram
    d. Sharif

11. Research on situational factors and conformity indicates that the probability of conformity, even to incorrect group judgments, grows most rapidly as a group increases to _____ members.
    a. three
    b. five
    c. seven
    d. nine

12. When there is diffusion of responsibility for individual behavior, crowd members tend to act _____.
    a. more cautiously than they would act as individuals
    b. more introspectively than they would act as individuals
    c. about the same as they would act as individuals
    d. more aggressively than they would act as individuals

13. The Kitty Genovese case is one of the most well-known examples of the _____.
    a. elaboration-likelihood model
    b. "bandwagon" effect
    c. bystander effect
    d. Stockholm syndrome

14. A bystander is most likely to help if he or she is _____.
    a. the only person around
    b. one of a small group of people nearby
    c. part of a large crowd of people who know each other
    d. part of a large crowd of people who are strangers to each other

15. Which of the following people is most likely to engage in altruistic behavior?
    a. A male in a good mood who believes an emergency exists and is very different from the person needing help.
    b. A male in a bad mood who believes an emergency exists and is very similar to the person needing help.
    c. A female in a good mood who believes an emergency exists and is very similar to the person needing help.
    d. A female in a good mood who does not believe an emergency exists and is very similar to the person needing help.

16. Which of the following people, when in need, is **MOST** likely to be helped by a male?
    a. an older, unattractive female
    b. a younger, attractive female
    c. an older male
    d. a younger male

17. According to your text, assertive people use the power of _____ to achieve desired ends.
    a. physical intimidation
    b. psychological coercion
    c. social influence
    d. silent self-control

18. A student fails a math test, and upon receiving his "F" he immediately jumps up in front of the class and accuses the teacher of being a lousy teacher and giving an unfair test. His behavior is best described as _____.
    a. passive
    b. assertive
    c. submissive
    d. aggressive

19. Joan goes to a therapist to learn how to become more assertive. The therapist makes Joan try out her new assertive behaviors by practicing them in front of a mirror by herself. The therapeutic technique being used by Joan's therapist is called _____.
   a. behavioral rehearsal
   b. role-playing
   c. modeling
   d. fogging

20. According to your text, one of the best ways to make connections with others and overcome self-focused tendencies is to _____.
   a. develop a hobby
   b. learn to perform on stage
   c. have children
   d. become a volunteer

True-False Questions

21. It is easier to say no, and stick to it, the first time a request is made, not later. _____

22. Most of the participants in Milgram's study showed no signs of stress when they administered punishment to "learners." _____

23. Crowd members tend to behave less aggressively than they would as individuals. _____

24. Men are more likely than women to be empathic. _____

25. Expressing your genuine beliefs may lead to some immediate social disapproval. _____

Essay Question

26. Compare and contrast assertive, passive, and aggressive behavior. Also, Briefly explain the four methods discussed in your text for becoming a more assertive person.

Student Activities

Name _____ **Date** _____

7.1 Who's Listening?

No one has ever lost money by underestimating the intelligence of the American people.

P. T. Barnum

I am confident that Mr. Barnum didn't have us in mind when he was estimating people's gullibility. But researchers repeatedly question how mindfully we handle attempts to influence us. Consider what you would predict people would do in response to these experimental conditions set forth by Harvard's Ellen Langer and her research group.

Imagine you have positioned yourself at a library table very near the photocopy machine. Each time someone starts to use the machine and **before** he or she puts money in it, you approach with one of three requests to use the machine without waiting. Estimate what percent of people will comply with each type of request:

1. "Excuse me, I have five pages. May I use the Xerox machine?"

    Compliance estimate = _____ %

2. "Excuse me, I have five pages. May I use the Xerox machine because I have to make copies?"

    Compliance estimate = _____ %

3. "Excuse me, I have five pages. May I use the Xerox machine, because I am in a rush?"

    Compliance estimate = _____ %

Follow-Up Questions:

1. What reasons would you give for any differences in your predictions?

Activity continued on the back

2. What real value is there in the reason given for request number 2?

3. Now try to explain the results Langer reported for approaches 1, 2, and 3 respectively: 60, 93, and 94 percent.

4. What do Langer's results say about people's attempts to organize incoming information?

5. The researchers also tested the same requests except they changed the number of pages from 5 to 20. These requests resulted in compliance rates of 24, 24, and 42 percent. How do you explain the differences from the first set of results, including a general decline in compliance, and the similar results for approaches 1 and 2? Langer has used the concepts "mindlessness" and "mindfulness" to account for these outcome differences. How do you think she used them?

7.2 A Simple Question

Compared to Britain and other nations, people in the U.S.A. watch more TV and, on the average, sets are switched on for seven hours a day. This would expose some of us to a considerable amount of effort to influence us through advertising.

For this activity please watch your favorite commercial TV show this week. (Sorry about the hard assignment, but it will be a good lesson.) While watching, use a watch, clock, or calendar to keep track of the total time devoted to advertising and take some notes on your favorite ad. If you are not quite fast enough to catch it all, you might watch for the ad again. It is bound to be repeated, especially if it is interesting and well done. You will be able to identify some of the strategies used in the ad to persuade the audience by analyzing the characteristics of the communicator, the central and peripheral routes of the message, and the audience.

1. Is the communicator an expert, attractive, familiar, or similar to the intended listener? Why do you think he or she was chosen?

2. It is not uncommon for people strong in some of these qualities to be weak in others, and yet still be chosen. For example, ex-athletes often represent brands of beer, and actresses explain why it is good to use buffered aspirin. Since they are not experts, why are they chosen?

3. Would the use of music, dance, song, beautiful people or scenery (all known as production values) take advantage of the central or the peripheral route of influencing discussed in Chapter 4? What route was used in the ad you have chosen to analyze? How do you think it affected the ad's persuasiveness? Why?

Activity continued on the back

4. What information used the central route? How memorable or effective was this information? Why?

5. What audience do you think this ad is aimed at? Can you characterize the intended audience as to age, gender, and motivation to be mindful? What other audiences do you think this ad could be targeted toward, if any? Why?

6. Would you evaluate the ad as successful or not? Why or why not?

7. In general, which influences you more? The communicator, the central message, or the peripheral messages? Why?

Name _____ **Date** _____

7.3 Another Simple Question

For this activity please watch your favorite commercial TV show this week. (Sorry about another difficult assignment, but it will also be a good lesson.) While watching, use a watch, clock, or calendar to keep track of the total time devoted to advertising and take some notes on your *least* favorite ad. If you are not quite fast enough to catch it all, you might watch for the ad again. It is bound to be repeated, and you are bound to notice it, especially if it is annoying to you. You will be able to identify some of the strategies used in the ad to persuade the audience by analyzing the characteristics of the communicator, the central and peripheral routes of the message, and the audience.

1. Is the communicator an expert, attractive, familiar, or similar to the intended listener? Why do you think he or she was chosen, and could they have chosen someone better? If so, who, and why would your choice have been better than theirs?

2. What information in the ad used the central or the peripheral route? How do you think it could have been better used to affect the ad's persuasiveness? Why?

3. What audience do you think this ad is aimed at? Can you characterize the intended audience as to age, gender, and motivation to be mindful? What other audiences do you think this ad could be targeted toward, if any? Why?

Activity continued on the back

4. What biases, positive or negative, do you have about the product being advertised in this ad. Do you think any negative biases about the product or the spokesperson in the ad could have affected your reaction to the ad? If so, how? And what could the ad have done differently to help prevent your biases from interfering with the persuasiveness of the message it wanted you to accept?

5. Some advertisements are used even when market research indicates that a large percentage of the public finds the ad annoying. This is because the same research indicates that the more annoying some ads are, the more likely it is that viewers will buy that product when they shop, despite the annoying qualities of the ad. Why do you think this happens? Has this ever happened to you? If so, what was the ad and the product being advertised?

Name _____ **Date** _____

7.4 What Would You Predict?

1. Consider for a moment the next presidential election. What would influence you to become highly involved in the campaign of your choice for president? List your ideas here:

2. Now suppose you want to persuade someone who does not know whom he or she wants to support to help you with the very big job of handing out leaflets for your candidate in public places on campus and elsewhere. Which techniques in the chapter can you use to influence this person to help? Why would he or she help?

3. Predict your helper's attitude toward your favorite candidate if: you only thank the helper for the help he or she gave you, or you pay more than the usual amount students can earn in such jobs. Under which condition do you think your helper's attitude would change more? Why?

7.5 Will We Be Willing to Help?

We are disturbed by the Kitty Genovese story, and probably ask ourselves what we would do in similar situations. After the discussions of helping behavior in Chapter 7, we realize that circumstances and even our mood may influence our willingness to help or remain a bystander. If we chose to be more helpful, we can consider ideas already discussed earlier in the text, and organize our thoughts to increase helping. Consider your answer to these questions:

1. How do you create a schema of yourself as a helper? What would be your ideal?

2. How do you practice being helpful? What are some common opportunities to use? What are some opportunities you could create for yourself, with a little effort?

3. Are you comfortable that you can assert yourself when the occasion warrants it? Why or why not? If the answer is no, what changes can you make so that eventually the answer will be yes?

4. Social psychologists, who have led the work on helping research, are prone to investigate the situational variables that affect behavior—that's why it's called social psychology. While they may not emphasize enduring traits of persons as factors, we can speculate what traits might be worth investigating. What traits do you think would be worth studying? Why?

Name _____ **Date** _____

7.6 Are Our Attitudes Being Manipulated by Madison Avenue?

It appears to me to be a very clever advertising campaign when I see a beer pegged as the choice of **real** mountain men. The ads are replete with implied similes about appreciating the "wildlife," and carrying six-packs instead of six-shooters. Of course, we could not have expected advertisers to be so truthful as to include the possibilities of beer bellies, belches, and hangovers. Instead, we are exposed to promises that the good life is a function of our beverage choice, with popularity and sex as bonuses if we choose wisely. To begin questioning the possible influence advertising could have, we might start with our own experience.

1. During this week, keep a diary of all alcohol and tobacco ads you encounter. Record the products and the total number of ads. You are likely to encounter ads in newspapers, television, radio, billboards, and points of purchase in stores. How many did you record total? For each specific item?

2. Would you include T-shirts, sponsorship of sports or music events, and insignias on equipment as ads also? Why or why not?

3. Which ones were the most effective? Why?

4. Which ones were the least effective? Why?

Activity continued on the back

5. Also record some information about the actors and models in the ads with particular attention to such details as their age, gender, appearance, and behavior. Other information includes to whom the ads are addressed (the target audience), what implicit rewards are promised for using the product, and what kinds of behavior are encouraged by the ads. What conclusions can you draw from what you have seen, giving specific reasons to support your conclusions?

8

Psychological Disorders

Chapter Outline

Chapter Overview

Psychological Disorders. Psychological disorders are characterized by such criteria as unusual behavior, socially unacceptable behavior, faulty perception of reality, personal distress, dangerous behavior, or self-defeating behavior.

Classification of Disorders. The most widely used classification scheme is found in the *Diagnostic and Statistical Manual* (DSM) of the American Psychiatric Association. The DSM groups disorders on the basis of observable symptoms or features and uses a multiaxial model to provide a more complete diagnostic evaluation.

Adjustment Disorders. Adjustment disorders are maladaptive reactions to one or more identified stressors that occur shortly after exposure to the stressor(s) and cause signs of distress beyond that which would normally be expected or impaired functioning. Adjustment disorders are usually resolved when the stressor is removed or the person learns to cope with it.

Anxiety Disorders. Anxiety disorders are characterized by motor tension, feelings of dread, and overarousal of the sympathetic branch of the autonomic nervous system. These disorders include irrational, excessive fears, or phobias; panic disorder, characterized by sudden attacks in which people typically fear that they may be losing control, going crazy, or having a heart attack; generalized anxiety disorder, a generalized pattern of worrisome, anxious behavior and heightened bodily arousal; obsessive-compulsive disorder, in which people are troubled by intrusive thoughts or impulses to repeat some behavioral ritual; and the posttraumatic stress disorder and acute stress disorder, which involve maladaptive reactions to a traumatic event.

The psychodynamic perspective views anxiety disorders in terms of underlying psychological conflicts. Learning theorists view phobias as conditioned fears. Cognitive theorists focus on ways in which people interpret threats. Some people may also be genetically predisposed to acquire certain kinds of fears. Biochemical factors—which could be inherited—may create a predisposition toward anxiety disorders. One such factor is faulty regulation of neurotransmitters.

Dissociative Disorders. Dissociative disorders are characterized by sudden, temporary changes in consciousness or self-identity. They include dissociative amnesia, in which personal memories are forgotten; dissociative fugue, which involves forgetting plus fleeing and adopting a new identity; dissociative identity disorder (multiple personality), in which a person behaves as if more than one personality occupies his or her body; and depersonalization, which is characterized by feelings that one is not real, or that one is standing outside oneself.

Many psychologists suggest that dissociative disorders help people keep disturbing memories or ideas out of mind. Childhood abuse or trauma figures prominently in the case histories of many people with dissociative disorders.

Somatoform Disorders. People with somatoform disorders exhibit or complain of physical problems, although no medical evidence of such problems can be found. In conversion disorder, a person loses a physical function or capability without any apparent medical cause. The person may show la belle indifference (indifference to the symptom), which is suggestive that the symptom serves a psychological purpose. In hypochondriasis, people have exaggerated fears about the significance of their physical complaints and fail to be reassured when their doctors tell them their fears are groundless.

These disorders were once called "hysterical neuroses" and expected to be found more among young women. However, they are also found among men and may reflect tendencies to focus on physical symptoms than underlying fears and conflicts. They may also reflect ways of avoiding painful or anxiety-evoking situations. Distorted cognitions also play a role.

Mood Disorders. Mood disorders involve disturbances in expressed emotions. Major depression is characterized by persistent feelings of sadness, loss of interest, feelings of worthlessness or guilt, inability to concentrate, and physical features that may include disturbances in the regulation of eating and sleeping. Even hallucinations and delusions may be present. Bipolar disorder is characterized by dramatic swings in mood between elation and depression and back. Manic episodes may involve pressured speech, and rapid flight of ideas.

Women are more likely than men to be depressed. This may reflect biological influences, but women typically also experience greater stress than men in our culture—including the stress that accompanies carrying a greater proportion of household and childcare responsibilities..

Research emphasizes possible roles for learned helplessness, attributional styles, and underutilization of serotonin in depression. People who are depressed are more likely than other people to make internal, stable, and global attributions for failures. Genetic factors involving regulation of neurotransmitters may also be involved in mood disorders, Moreover, people with severe depression often respond to drugs that increase the availability of serotonin.

Schizophrenia. Schizophrenia is a most severe and persistent psychological disorder that is characterized by disturbances of thought and language, such as loosening of associations and delusions; in perception and attention, as found in hallucinations; in motor activity, as shown by a stupor or by excited behavior; in mood, as in flat or inappropriate emotional responses, and in social interaction, as in social withdrawal. The major types of schizophrenia are paranoid, disorganized, catatonic. Paranoid schizophrenia is characterized largely by systematic delusions; disorganized schizophrenia by incoherence; and catatonic schizophrenia by motor impairment.

According to the multifactorial model, genetic vulnerability to schizophrenia may interact with other factors, such as stress, complications during pregnancy and childbirth, and quality of parenting, to cause the disorder to develop. According to the dopamine theory of schizophrenia, people with schizophrenia use more dopamine than other people do, perhaps because an overabundance of dopamine receptors in the brain.

Personality Disorders. Personality disorders are inflexible, maladaptive behavior patterns that impair personal or social functioning and cause distress for the individual or others. The defining trait of paranoid personality disorder is suspiciousness. People with schizotypal personality disorders show oddities of thought, perception, and behavior. Social withdrawal is the major characteristic of schizoid personality disorder. People with antisocial personality disorders persistently violate the rights of others and are in conflict with the law. They show little or no guilt or shame over their misdeeds and are largely undeterred by punishment. People with avoidant personality disorder tend to avoid entering relationships for fear of rejection and criticism.

Psychodynamic theory connected many personality disorders with hypothesized Oedipal problems. Genetic factors may be involved in some personality disorders. Antisocial personality disorder may develop from a combination of factors, including genetic vulnerability and harsh or neglectful parenting in childhood.

Learning Objectives

After studying this chapter your students should be able to:

1. Explain what psychological disorders are and identify the various criteria used to decide if someone should be labeled as "disordered."

2. Explain what the DSM is, what it is used for, and what each of its axes does.

3. Explain what adjustment disorders are and identify and describe the various adjustment disorders.

4. Explain what anxiety disorders are and identify and describe the various anxiety disorders.

5. Summarize the various theoretical perspectives on anxiety disorders.

6. Explain what dissociative disorders are and identify and describe the various dissociative disorders.

7. Summarize the various theoretical perspectives on dissociative disorders.

8. Explain what somatoform disorders are and identify and describe the various somatoform disorders.

9. Explain what mood disorders are and identify and describe the various mood disorders.

10. Summarize research findings on the differences among men and women in rates of depression.

11. Summarize the various theoretical perspectives on mood disorders.

12. Explain what schizophrenia is and identify and describe the three major subtypes of schizophrenia.

13. Summarize the various theoretical perspectives on schizophrenia.

14. Explain what personality disorders are and identify and describe the various types of personality disorders.

15. Summarize the various theoretical views on personality disorders.

16. Describe who is most likely (statistically) to commit suicide, and identify at least three myths about suicide and explain why each one of them is incorrect.

17. Identify and briefly describe at least five things you can do if someone tells you that he or she is considering suicide.

Key Terms

hallucinations
ideas of persecution
Diagnostic and Statistical Manual
adjustment disorder
anxiety disorders
specific phobia
claustrophobia
acrophobia
social phobia
social anxiety disorder
agoraphobia
panic disorder
generalized anxiety disorder
obsessive-compulsive disorder
obsession
compulsion
posttraumatic stress disorder
acute stress disorder
gamma-aminobutric acid (GABA)
benzodiazepines

dissociative disorders
dissociative identity disorder
somatoform disorders
dissociative amnesia
dissociative fugue
dissociative identity disorder
depersonalization disorder
conversion disorder
la belle indifférence
hypochondriasis
mood disorders
major depression
psychotic
bipolar disorder
manic
rapid flight of ideas
schizophrenia
learned helplessness
attributional styles
delusions

stupor
paranoid schizophrenia
disorganized schizophrenia
catatonic schizophrenia
waxy flexibility
mutism
concordance rate
diathesis
personality disorders
paranoid personality disorder
schizoid personality disorder
schizotypal personality disorder
borderline personality disorder
histrionic personality disorder
narcissistic personality disorder
antisocial personality disorder
avoidant personality disorder
dependent personality disorder
obsessive-compulsive personality
    disorder

Key Terms Review

Define each of the following terms:

1. Dissociative Identity Disorder: _____

   _____

2. Personality Disorders: _____

   _____

3. Hallucinations: _____

   _____

4. Ideas of Persecution: _____

   _____

5. Adjustment Disorder: _____

   _____

6. Panic Disorder: _____

   _____

7. Generalized Anxiety Disorder: _____

   _____

8. Obsession: _____

   _____

9. Compulsion: _____

   _____

10. Manic: _____

    _____

11. Dissociative Disorders: _____

    _____

12. Delusions: _____

_____

13. Rapid Flight of Ideas: _____

_____

14. Learned Helplessness: _____

_____

15. Attributional Style: _____

_____

16. Psychotic: _____

_____

17. Diathesis: _____

_____

18. Stupor: _____

_____

19. Waxy Flexibility: _____

_____

20. Mutism: _____

_____

Chapter Review

1. _____ people affected by psychological disorders do not receive adequate mental health care.

2. Psychological disorders are _____ or _____ processes that are connected with various kinds of distress or impaired functioning.

3. Six criteria for determining whether someone has a psychological disorder are:

    a. _____

    b. _____

    c. _____

    d. _____

    e. _____

    f. _____

4. The most widely used classification scheme for psychological disorders is the

    _____ and _____ _____.

5. **Matching:** Match the Axis from the DSM on the left with its appropriate descriptor on the right.

    _____ a. Axis I   1. Psychosocial and environmental problems

    _____ b. Axis II   2. Global assessment of functioning

    _____ c. Axis III   3. General medical conditions

    _____ d. Axis IV   4. Clinical syndromes

    _____ e. Axis V   5. Personality disorders

6. About _____ of American adults suffer from a psychological disorder at some point in their lifetimes.

7. _____ disorders are maladaptive reactions to identified stressors, and are

    considered to be among the _____ psychological disorders.

8. Anxiety has _____, _____, and _____ features.

9. Six types of anxiety disorders are:

    a. _____

    b. _____

    c. _____

    d. _____

e. _____

f. _____

10. Phobias can be broken down into three major types: _____ phobias, which involve excessive fears of specific objects or situations; _____ phobias, which involve persistent fears of scrutiny by others; and _____, which involves fears of being in open spaces or places from which it might be difficult to escape.

11. In panic disorder, the anxiety is _____, as opposed to generalized anxiety disorder, in which it appears to be _____ _____.

12. An _____ is a recurring thought or image that seems irrational or beyond control, whereas a _____ is a seemingly irresistible urge to engage in an act.

13. Posttraumatic stress disorder differs from acute stress disorder in that it occurs _____ after the traumatic event and tends to _____.

14. Psychological disorders are _____ problems that defy _____ explanations.

15. In anxiety disorders, faulty regulation of the neurotransmitters _____ and _____ may be involved, and receptor sites in the brain may not be sensitive enough to _____, a neurotransmitter that may help calm anxiety reactions.

16. In dissociative disorders, there is a separation of the mental processes that make the person feel _____.

17. Multiple personality disorder is now known as _____ _____ disorder.

18. People with _____ disorders may present a physical problem that defies any medical explanation.

19. Four major dissociative disorders are:

a. _____

b. _____

c. _____

d. _____

20. **Matching:** Match the psychological disorder on the left with its appropriate description on the right.

_____ a. Dissociative amnesia

_____ b. Dissociative fugue

_____ c. Dissociative identity disorder

_____ d. Depersonalization disorder

_____ e. Phobia

_____ f. Panic disorder

_____ g. Generalized anxiety disorder

_____ h. Obsessive-compulsive disorder

_____ i. Posttraumatic stress disorder

_____ j. Acute stress disorder

1. persistent or recurrent feelings that one is not real or is detached from one's own experience or body

2. recurring irrational and uncontrollable thoughts that lead to irresistible urges to engage in ritualistic behaviors

3. a person experiences amnesia and flees to a new location and establishes a new lifestyle

4. recurrent attacks of extreme anxiety in the absence of any known or obvious source

5. a disorder which follows an emotionally distressing event characterized by intense fear, avoidance of stimuli associated with the event, and reliving of the event

6. loss of memory or self-identity

7. two or more identities, each with distinct traits and memories, exist simultaneously within the same person

8. irrational fear of specific objects, people or situations

9. feelings of dread and foreboding and sympathetic arousal of at least one month's duration

10. symptoms involving reliving of an event, and intense fear and anxiety develop within four weeks of the event but do not persist for more than four weeks

21. According to psychodynamic theory, people with dissociative disorders use massive _____ to prevent them from recognizing improper impulses.

22. Two types of somatoform disorders are _____ disorder, in which unconscious conflicts are turned into physical symptoms, and _____, which is marked by the persistent belief that one has a medical disorder despite the lack of medical findings.

23. Lack of concern over their severe symptoms shown by people suffering from

conversion disorder is called _____ _____ _____.

24. The use of the term "hysteria" stemmed from the ancient belief that it was a sort of

female trouble caused by a wandering _____.

25. Two types of mood disorders are _____ _____ and _____

_____.

26. Major _____ is the "common cold" of psychological problems.

27. Women are about _____ more likely than men to be diagnosed with depression,
a difference that begins in adolescence,

28. Men are more likely to cope with depression by _____ themselves from their

feelings, while women are more likely to _____ about their feelings.

29. Manic-depression is now called _____ disorder.

30. Researchers have found a link between creative genius and _____ and

_____ disorder.

31. Freud viewed depression as _____ turned inward.

32. Learning researchers have found links between depression and _____

_____.

33. Research has shown that people who are depressed are likely to attribute their failures

to _____, _____, and _____ factors.

34. Genetic research has linked susceptibility to depression with imbalances of the

neurotransmitter _____.

35. Schizophrenia is a _____ and _____ disorder that touches just about
every aspect of a person's life.

36. Schizophrenia is characterized by a break with reality that may take the form of

    _____ (hearing or seeing things that are not there) and _____ (fixed, false beliefs).

37. People with schizophrenia have problems in _____, _____, and

    _____.

38. Three types of delusions are delusions of _____, delusions of _____, and

    delusions of _____.

39. Three types of schizophrenia are the _____ type, which is characterized by

    disorganized delusions and vivid hallucinations, the _____ type, which is

    characterized by striking impairment in motor activity, and the _____ type,
    which is characterized by delusions, usually of persecution, and by vivid
    hallucinations.

40. Schizophrenic persons constitute about _____ percent of the general

    population, but children with an identical twin with schizophrenia have about a

    _____ percent chance of developing the disorder.

41. Schizophrenia occurs _____ in men than in women. In men, it occurs

    _____ and in _____ severe forms.

42. Most investigators today believe that schizophrenia is a _____ disorder

    involving the neurotransmitter _____, among other factors.

43. _____ disorders are characterized by enduring patterns of inflexible and

    maladaptive behaviors that impair personal and social functioning.

44. **Matching:** Match the personality disorder on the left with the appropriate description on the right.

_____ a. Avoidant personality disorder

_____ b. Paranoid personality disorder

_____ c. Schizotypal personality disorder

_____ d. Schizoid personality disorder

_____ e. Antisocial personality disorder

1. characterized by social withdrawal and indifference

2. characterized by persistent suspiciousness

3. characterized by oddities of thought, perception, and behavior

4. characterized by frequent conflict with society undeterred by punishment and with little or no guilt, remorse, or anxiety

5. characterized by unwillingness to enter into relationships without assurance of acceptance because of fears of rejection

45. **Matching:** Match the personality disorder on the left with the appropriate description on the right.

_____ a. Borderline personality disorder

_____ b. Histrionic personality disorder

_____ c. Narcissistic personality disorder

_____ d. Dependent personality disorder

_____ e. Obsessive-compulsive personality disorder

1. characterized by failure to develop a stable self-image, and wild mood swings

2. characterized by an inflated or grandiose self-image and extreme needs for admiration

3. characterized by excessive reliance upon others and difficulties making decisions

4. characterized by excessive needs for attention to detail and demands for orderliness

5. characterized by overly dramatic and emotional behavior and excessive needs to be the center of attention

46. People with antisocial personality disorder have abnormalities in the _____

cortex of the brain.

47. Most suicides are linked to _____ and _____ disorder.

48. Suicide attempts are more frequent following _____ life events, especially

events that involve loss of _____ _____.

49. Three common, but untrue, myths about suicide are:

a. _____

b. _____

c. _____

50. Five things you can do to help someone who has threatened suicide while talking to you are:

a. _____

b. _____

c. _____

d. _____

e. _____

Sample Test

Multiple-Choice Questions

1. Type A behavior, overeating, chronic gambling, alcoholism, and cigarette smoking are all examples of _____.
   a. self-defeating behavior
   b. faulty perception of reality
   c. personal distress
   d. dangerous behavior

2. The current edition of the DSM employs _____ axes.
   a. two
   b. three
   c. four
   d. five

3. A clinician's rating of a client's level of functioning and his or her highest level of functioning before the onset of a psychological disorder would be found in _____ of the DSM-IV-TR.
   a. Axis I
   b. Axis II
   c. Axis IV
   d. Axis V

4. A maladaptive reaction to an identified stressor resulting in impairment in school or occupational functioning or in social activities or relationships is called _____.
   a. a personality disorder
   b. an affective disorder
   c. an adjustment disorder
   d. a dissociative disorder

5. Which of the following is **NOT** an anxiety disorder?
   a. phobia
   b. generalized anxiety disorder
   c. obsessive-compulsive disorder
   d. conversion disorder

6. Shelly has intense speech anxiety and stage fright. She is suffering from _____.
   a. agoraphobia
   b. a simple phobia
   c. a social phobia
   d. panic disorder

7. Every few days, with little or no warning, Jake is overwhelmed by intense fear, shortness of breath, a pounding heart, and heavy sweating. He often feels like he is suffocating, having a heart attack, or going crazy. He can never identify a reason for having these attacks but they leave him worried and exhausted. His attacks are best described as _____.
   a. generalized anxiety disorder
   b. panic disorder
   c. phobia
   d. acute stress disorder

8. A young mother is terrorized by the recurring fear that her children have been run over by a car on their way home from school. She cannot block out this fear even though her children do not cross any streets and never had any accidents involving a car. Her irrational fear is best described as _____.
   a. an obsession
   b. a phobia
   c. a delusion
   d. acute stress disorder

9. According to the psychodynamic perspective, phobias _____.
   a. are conditioned fears that were acquired in early childhood
   b. are acquired through observational learning in childhood
   c. result from genetically inherited predispositions and a highly sensitive nervous system
   d. symbolize conflicts originating in childhood

10. The benzodiazepines are a class of drugs that _____.
    a. relieve depression
    b. reduce anxiety
    c. increase attention-span
    d. eliminate free radicals

11. A disorder in which a person suffers memory loss and also flees to a new locale and takes up a new life with a new identity is called _____.
    a. depersonalization
    b. psychogenic amnesia
    c. dissociative fugue
    d. conversion disorder

12. Bob constantly feels as if he is operating on "automatic pilot," or as if he is in a dream. His feelings are typical of someone with _____.
    a. psychogenic fugue
    b. depersonalization disorder
    c. conversion disorder
    d. dissociative identity disorder

13. A disorder in which there is a major change in or loss of physical functioning, although there are no medical findings to support the loss of functioning, is called _____.
    a. a personality disorder
    b. an acute stress disorder
    c. a conversion disorder
    d. hypochondriasis

14. Freud's classic case of "Anna O.," in which a woman with a large family developed paralysis, despite the fact that no physical causes could be detected, is an example of _____.
    a. conversion disorder
    b. a reaction formation
    c. hypochondriasis
    d. acute stress disorder

15. The most common psychological problem people face is _____.
    a. depression
    b. schizophrenia
    c. phobia
    d. generalized anxiety

16. Mildred goes to her therapist to get treatment for her severe depression. He says that her depression is due to her having an external locus of control. His beliefs mirror the _____ explanation of depression.
    a. psychodynamic
    b. behavioral
    c. social-cognitive
    d. biological

17. Sensory imagery in the absence of external stimulation, such as hearing voices no one else can hear or seeing things no one else can see, is called _____.
   a. a hallucination
   b. an obsession
   c. a delusion
   d. a compulsion

18. Ned's behavior is marked by impairment of motor activity, stupor, and "waxy flexibility." He is most likely suffering from _____.
   a. conversion schizophrenia
   b. disorganized schizophrenia
   c. paranoid schizophrenia
   d. catatonic schizophrenia

19. Enduring patterns of inflexible and maladaptive behavior that impair personal functioning and are a source of distress to others are called _____.
   a. affective disorders
   b. personality disorders
   c. somatoform disorders
   d. dissociative disorders

20. Researchers have found links between creative genius and _____.
   a. mood disorders
   b. dissociative disorders
   c. schizophrenia
   d. personality disorders

True-False Questions

21. Some psychiatrists believe that the disorders described by the DSM are not really disorders at all.   _____

22. Acute stress disorder lasts longer than posttraumatic stress disorder.   _____

23. Creativity has been linked to mood disorders.   _____

24. Schizophrenic persons appear to produce more dopamine in their brains than others.   _____

25. Most people who threaten suicide are just looking for attention and will not actually carry out the threat.   _____

Essay Question

26. Explain what anxiety disorders are and identify and describe the various anxiety disorders.

Student Activities

Name _____ **Date** _____

8.1 What Is Abnormal?

When legal cases such as John Hinckley's involve pleas of "not guilty by reason of insanity," it is common to read that the defense was able to find expert witnesses who testified the defendant was "insane," while the prosecution was also able to call expert witnesses who testified the defendant was "sane." Who is right? Much of the problem is created by the difficulty of defining insanity. The same problem occurs when we try to define abnormal. It is easy to recognize the extreme cases, but often difficult to decide the cases in between, which are the majority. Consider the text's criteria of psychological disorder and think of a case that satisfies the definition, yet would not be likely to be called abnormal. For example, wearing bow ties or beehive hair styles may be unusual, which is the first criterion, but will not cause a diagnosis of "psychological disorder."

1. Identify an **unusual behavior** that is not an example of a psychological disorder. Why is it not a disorder?

2. Identify an **unacceptable behavior** that is not an example of a psychological disorder. Why is it not a disorder?

3. What **faulty perception of reality** is not an example of a psychological disorder? Why is it not a disorder?

4. When might **severe personal distress** fail to be considered an example of a psychological disorder? Why is it not a disorder?

5. Name a **self-defeating behavior** that would not be an example of a psychological disorder. Why is it not a disorder?

Activity continued on the back

6. Name a behavior that is **dangerous** but not considered an example of a psychological disorder. Why is it not a disorder?

7. For a real challenge, identify a behavior that is all of the above, or as much of the above as possible, but is not regarded as a psychological disorder.

8. Now write an alternative definition of psychological disorder. (If you can manage this, you might become famous!)

9. Which theoretical model of psychological disorders would your definition best fit? Why?

Name _____ **Date** _____

8.2 Checking Our Attitudes Toward People With Psychological Disorders

Suppose the government leased the apartments or home next door to your residence and converted them into use for the following people. Which types of handicaps or disorders, if any, would create the most discomfort for you? Rank each from 1 to 4, with 1 representing the most alarming, and 4 representing the least alarming.

_____ Persons with mental retardation   _____ Recovering illegal drug users

_____ Schizophrenics   _____ Convicted pedophiles or other sexual predators

_____ Recovering alcoholics   _____ Adolescents with anti-social personality disorder

_____ Convicted violent criminals   _____ Convicted non-violent criminals

1. What would be your worst fears in each case above?

    a.

    b.

    c.

    d.

    e.

    f.

    g.

    h.

2. Ask others the same questions and record their responses here:

    1.

    2.

    3.

    4.

Activity continued on the back

3. Have you any evidence that prejudices exist against the people who are labeled psychologically disordered? If so, what is it?

4. Why do you believe that prejudices exist against people who are labeled as being psychologically disordered?

5. What are three things you believe can be done to help alleviate prejudices against the psychologically disordered?

6. What ill effects could prejudices cause the psychologically handicapped?

8.3 You Make the Diagnosis

Diagnosis is not always as easy as it looks, and diagnosticians can easily disagree about a label if certain features of a person's problems are more prominent at some times and not at other times, or if behaviors associated with one disorder can be associated with a different disorder as well. For instance, people can cry when they are sad, but people can also cry when they are happy. Some people may have symptoms of multiple disorders and then the problems becomes, which one is causing them most distress and needs to be addressed first?

Diagnose the following cases:

Case 1. Sam is a military dictator who surrounds himself with multiple rings of security due to fears of plots to assassinate him. He has body "doubles" who precede him to any scheduled appointments. He sleeps in a different, random location each night, and has guards randomly assigned to 'taste-test' his food in case his personal chefs are involved in a plot to kill him. He regular purges his political rivals and military commanders to 'weed out' those potentially disloyal to him, and has killed or arrested thousands in the process. He feels no guilt over his actions, as he claims his victims 'got what they deserved' and he had the right to 'get them before they got him.' Additionally, he names everything in the country after himself, and has huge posters of himself everywhere. He surrounds himself with 'worshippers,' constantly glorifies himself at others' expense, and constantly criticizes or demeans anyone who is potentially as intelligent or skillful as he is. How would you label this person? Why?

Case 2. Bonnie, age 53, complains of constantly feeling down and has little or no energy. She feels she can't do anything right and will never be happy. She cries at 'the drop of a hat' over almost anything. Other than visits to her doctor, she is reclusive and rarely goes anywhere. She has always worried about illness, has an extensive list of perceived health problems, and is a regular visitor to on-line sites like "web M.D," where she tries to diagnose the symptoms that she claims her physicians have ignored. She is convinced that she has an undiagnosed life-threatening disorder that will kill her if she can't find a treatment for it, despite repeated reassurances from her doctors that there is nothing physically wrong with her. If it wasn't for the attention she gets from her adult children, who drop whatever they are doing to take care of her when she gets 'sick,' she doesn't feel she would be able to survive at all. How would you diagnose Bonnie? Why?

8.4 A Second Look at Bonnie's Case

Good diagnosticians want to look for a phenomenon known as **secondary gain**. Secondary gain occurs when the disorder results in rewards. An example in the text described the inability to fly missions when some bomber pilots developed a type of conversion disorder, including night blindness. You may remember that memory failures in dissociative disorders were linked to avoidance of painful thoughts, and thus can also illustrate secondary gain.

1. Can you detect any possible secondary gain for Bonnie? If so, what is it?

2. In your opinion, what is the merit in hypothesizing that secondary gain plays any role in the problems Bonnie is experiencing?

3. How could you test to see whether secondary gain is involved or not?

4. Is it necessary to assume that secondary gain is the only principle that is needed to explain Bonnie's difficulties? Why or why not?

8.5 Finding Help for Someone Considering Suicide

After reading the discussion of suicide, you probably found the suggestions for helping someone who is contemplating suicide quite valuable. In a real crisis it might be difficult to comply quickly with some of the recommendations, including finding professional help. Answer these questions and you can be steps ahead in a real crisis.

1. What is the phone number of a "hotline" (other than 911) you can call?

2. How long did it take you to answer question number one? What problems did you run into? If you gathered the results for your class, the emergency service that administers the hotline might appreciate learning your results.

Activity continued on the back

3. Does your school have a counseling center or any service that can respond to emergencies, including potential suicide? Does this service have data on the frequency of emergency phone calls? Is it a 24-hour service? How would someone in crisis typically access this service?

9

Therapies: Ways of Helping

Chapter Outline

Module 9.9 Psychology in Daily Life: Coping with Emotional Responses to Stress—Anxiety, Anger, Depression

Chapter Overview

Psychotherapy.   Psychotherapy is a systematic interaction between a therapist and a client that applies psychological principles to affect the client's thoughts, feelings, or behavior in order to help the client overcome psychological disorders, adjust to problems in living, or develop as an individual.

Traditional Psychoanalysis. The goals of psychoanalysis are to provide self-insight into unconscious conflicts and replace defensive behavior with coping behavior. The major techniques used are free association, dream analysis, and interpretation of the transference. For example, a psychoanalyst may help clients gain insight into the ways in which they are transferring feelings toward their parents onto a spouse or even onto the analyst.

Modern Psychodynamic Approaches. These are briefer and more directive, and the therapist and client usually sit face-to-face.

Client-Centered Therapy.   Client-centered therapy was developed by Carl Rogers. It uses nondirective methods to help clients overcome obstacles to self-actualization. The therapist shows unconditional positive regard, empathic understanding, and genuineness.

Gestalt Therapy. Gestalt therapy was originated by Fritz Perls. It is a highly directive method that aims to help people integrate conflicting parts of their personality. He aimed to make clients aware of conflict, accept its reality, and make choices despite fear.

Behavior Therapy. Behavior therapy relies on learning principles (for example, conditioning and observational learning) to help clients develop adaptive behavior patterns and eliminate maladaptive ones. Behavior therapy methods include flooding, gradual exposure, systematic desensitization, and modeling. Flooding exposes a person to high levels of fear-evoking stimuli without aversive consequences until fear is extinguished. In gradual exposure, the person progresses through a series of exposure encounters with increasingly fearful stimuli. Systematic desensitization reduces fears by gradually exposing clients to fear-evoking stimuli while they remain relaxed. Modeling encourages clients to imitate another person (the model) in approaching fear-evoking stimuli.

Aversive Conditioning.   This is a behavior-therapy method for discouraging undesirable behavior by repeatedly pairing the stimuli associated with self-defeating goals (for example, alcohol, cigarette smoke) with aversive stimuli so that the undesirable stimuli evoke an aversive response.

Operant Conditioning.   These are behavior therapy methods that foster adaptive behavior through applying principles of reinforcement. Examples include token economies, social skills training, and biofeedback training.

Aaron Beck's Cognitive Therapy. Aaron Beck notes that clients develop emotional problems such as depression because of cognitive errors that lead them to minimize accomplishments and catastrophize failures. He found that depressed people experience cognitive distortions such as the cognitive triad; that is, they expect the worst of themselves, the world at large, and the future. Beck teaches clients how to dispute cognitive errors.

Albert Ellis's Rational-Emotive-Therapy. Albert Ellis originated rational-emotive behavior therapy, which holds that people's beliefs about events, not only the events themselves, shape people's responses to them. Ellis points out how irrational beliefs, such as the belief that we must have social approval, can worsen problems.

Group Therapy. Group therapy is more economical than individual therapy. Moreover, group members benefit from the social support and experiences of other members. However, some clients cannot disclose their problems in the group setting or risk group disapproval. They need individual attention.

Couples Therapy. In couples therapy, a couple is treated together in the attempt to help them improve their communication skills and manage conflicts more effectively.

Family Therapy. In family therapy, one or more families make up the group. Family therapy undertaken from the "systems approach" modifies family interactions to enhance the growth of individuals in the family and the family as a whole.

Does Psychotherapy Work? Yes, statistical analyses using the technique of meta-analysis provide impressive evidence for the effectiveness of psychotherapy. Evidence from controlled research trials also supports the therapeutic benefits of particular forms of therapy (called empirically supported treatments) for particular disorders.

In conducting research on psychotherapy, investigators face such problems as difficulties in randomly assigning participants to different methods of therapy, problems with measurement of outcome, and problems in sorting out the effects of nonspecific therapeutic factors, such as instillation of hope, from the specific effects of particular methods of therapy.

Psychotherapy and Human Diversity. Therapists need to be sensitive to cultural differences. For example, they should understand how people from ethnic minority groups which have been subject to oppression and prejudice may be distrustful of European American therapists. Therapy methods and goals may also conflict with a client's own cultural values. Feminist therapy attempts to increase awareness of sociocultural issues that contribute to women's problems and challenges the tradition of male dominance. Many professionals believe that psychotherapy should not attempt to change a gay male or lesbian's sexual orientation, but should help that person adjust to social and cultural pressures to be heterosexual.

Drug Therapy. Antianxiety drugs help quell anxiety, but tolerance and dependence may develop over time. Antipsychotic drugs help many people with schizophrenia by blocking the action of dopamine receptors. Antidepressants often help people with severe depression, apparently by raising levels of serotonin in the brain. Lithium often helps stabilize mood swings in people with bipolar disorder.

Electroconvulsive Therapy (ECT). In ECT an electrical current is passed through the temples, inducing a seizure and frequently relieving severe depression. ECT is controversial because of its side effects, such as memory loss and because of the highly intrusive nature of the procedure.

Psychosurgery. Psychosurgery is a yet more controversial (and rarely if ever practiced) technique for controlling severely disturbed behavior through surgery on the brain.

The Effectiveness of Biomedical Therapies. There is controversy as to whether psychotherapy or drug therapy should be used with people with anxiety disorders or depression. Drugs do not teach people how to solve problems and build relationships. Having said that, antidepressants may be advisable when psychotherapy does not help people with depression. Furthermore, ECT appears to be helpful in some cases of severe depression in which neither psychotherapy nor drug therapy (antidepressants) is of help. Antipsychotic drugs can help control more flagrant symptoms of schizophrenia. Psychosurgery is all but discontinued because of the questions about its effectiveness and the occurrence of serious side effects.

Learning Objectives

After studying this chapter your students should be able to:

1. Explain what psychotherapy is, describing its essential features.

2. Describe the goals and methods of psychoanalysis, and explain how modern psychodynamic approaches differ from traditional psychoanalysis.

3. Explain what client-centered therapy is, what its methods are, and discuss the qualities of a client-centered therapist.

4. Explain what Gestalt therapy is, describing its essential features and techniques.

5. Describe the goals and methods of behavior therapy, and briefly describe at least three behavior therapy methods for reducing fears.

6. Identify and briefly describe at least 5 steps you can take to ensure that you receive appropriate care when you are seeking help from mental health professionals.

7. Compare and contrast aversive conditioning and operant conditioning, identifying several specific types of operant conditioning in your discussion.

8. Explain what biofeedback training is, how it works, and what it is used for.

9. Describe the goals and methods of Beck's cognitive therapy.

10. Describe the philosophy, goals, and methods of Ellis's rational emotive behavior therapy.

11. Compare and contrast individual therapy with group therapy, and briefly describe at least two types of group therapy.

12. Summarize the advantages and disadvantages of internet counseling.

13. Summarize the research on the efficacy of psychotherapy, and explain the problems associated with conducting this type of research.

14. Discuss the issues involved in the practice of psychotherapy with clients from ethnic minority groups.

15. Explain what feminist therapy is, and why it developed.

16. Discuss the issues unique to therapy for gay males and lesbians.

17. Identify three biomedical approaches to therapy, explaining how they work and any problems associated with them.

18. Describe how best to cope with anxieties and fears.

19. Describe how best to cope with anger.

20. Describe how best to cope with depression.

Key Terms

psychotherapy
psychoanalysis
free association
resistance
interpretation
transference
dream analysis
wish fulfillment
phallic symbols
manifest content
latent content
ego analysis
existentialism
client-centered therapy
Gestalt therapy
frames of reference
nondirective
unconditional positive regard

empathic understanding
genuineness
gestalt
behavior therapy
behavior modification
flooding
gradual exposure
systematic desensitization
counterconditioned
hierarchy
modeling
aversive conditioning
rapid smoking
token economy
social skills training
biofeedback training (BFT)
cognitive therapy
rational-emotive behavior therapy

group therapy
family therapy
meta-analysis
nonspecific factors
therapeutic alliance
ESTs
biomedical therapy
psychotropic drugs
rebound anxiety
antipsychotic drugs
antidepressants
MAO inhibitors
tricyclic antidepressants
SSRIs
lithium
electroconvulsive therapy
psychosurgery
prefrontal lobotomy

Key Terms Review

Define each of the following terms:

1. Psychotherapy: _____

_____

2. Psychoanalysis: _____

_____

3. Free Association: _____

_____

4. Resistance: _____

_____

5. Transference: _____

_____

6. Ego Analysis: _____

    _____

7. Unconditional Positive Regard: _____

    _____

8. Frames of Reference: _____

    _____

9. Gestalt Therapy: _____

    _____

10. Systematic Desensitization _____

    _____

11. Counterconditioned: _____

    _____

12. Token Economy: _____

    _____

13. Aversive conditioning: _____

    _____

14. Modeling: _____

    _____

15. Nonspecific Factors: _____

    _____

16. Therapeutic Alliance: _____

    _____

17. Rebound Anxiety: _____

    _____

18. Antidepressants: _____

    _____

19. Electroconvulsive Therapy: _____

    _____

20. Psychosurgery: _____

    _____

Chapter Review

1. Four essential elements of psychotherapy are:

   a. _____

   b. _____

   c. _____

   d. _____

2. _____ is the clinical method devised by Sigmund Freud which seeks to allow to

   provide _____ into the conflicts at the root of the clients' problems.

3. Freud first used _____ to allow clients to focus on repressed conflicts, but later

   turned to the more gradual process of _____ _____, the uncensored

   uttering of all thoughts that come to mind.

4. Freud believed that patients often related to him in ways similar to how they related

   to their own parents through a process he called _____.

5. For Freud, unconscious urges tend to be expressed in dreams as a form of

   _____ _____.

6. In psychodynamic theory, dreams contain both _____, or shown, content and

    _____, or hidden, content.

7. Modern psychodynamic therapy is _____ and _____ intense than
    traditional psychoanalysis.

8. In modern psychodynamic therapy, there is usually more focus on the _____ as

    the "executive" of personality and less emphasis on the _____.

9. Psychodynamic therapies focus on _____ conflicts and _____ processes,

    whereas humanistic-existential therapists focus on the _____- _____-

    _____.

10. Carl Rogers developed _____-_____ therapy, which encourages people

    to rely on their own values and _____ _____ _____.

11. According to Rogers, psychological problems arise from roadblocks placed in the

    path of _____-_____.

12. Three qualities shown by the client-centered therapist are:

    a. _____

    b. _____

    c. _____

13. Gestalt therapy aims to help people _____

    _____

14. Three Gestalt therapy techniques are:

    a. _____

    b. _____

    c. _____

15. A Gestalt therapy technique in which people engage in verbal confrontations between opposing wishes and conflicting parts of their personality is called _____.

16. Psychodynamic and humanistic-existential forms of therapy focus on what people _____ and _____, whereas behavior therapists focus on what people _____.

17. Behavior therapists rely heavily on principles of _____ and _____ conditioning, as well as _____ learning.

18. Four methods behavior therapists use for reducing fears are _____, _____ _____, _____ _____, and _____.

19. Systematic desensitization assumes that maladaptive behaviors are _____ and, therefore, can be eliminated through _____.

20. Modeling relies on _____ learning to change behavior.

21. The use of rapid smoking to cure cigarette smoking is a form of _____ conditioning.

22. Three operant conditioning methods for managing behavior problems are:

    a. _____

    b. _____

    c. _____

23. _____ therapy focuses on changing the beliefs, attitudes, and automatic thinking that create and compound clients' problems.

24. Most behavior therapists today directly incorporate _____ methods into their treatment approach.

25. According to Beck's "cognitive triad," depressed people expect the worst of _____, the _____ at large, and the _____.

26. Ellis's rational-emotive behavior therapy methods are _____ and _____.

27. Ellis's approach straddles _____ and _____ therapies.

28. **Matching:** Match each of the following therapies with the person who is most closely associated with it

_____	a. psychoanalysis	1. Aaron Beck
_____	b. client-centered therapy	2. Fritz Perls
_____	c. Gestalt therapy	3. Carl Rogers
_____	d. cognitive therapy	4. Albert Ellis
_____	e. rational emotive behavior therapy	5. Sigmund Freud

29. _____ therapists draw upon the principles and techniques of multiple approaches to therapy.

30. Six advantages to group therapy include:

a. _____

b. _____

c. _____

d. _____

e. _____

f. _____

31. Couple therapy helps couples enhance their relationship by improving their

_____ skills and helping them manage _____.

32. In the _____ approach, family interaction is studied and modified to enhance

the growth of individual family members and of the family unit as a whole.

33. Family therapists usually assume that the identified patient is a _____ for other problems within and among family members.

34. Research on the effectiveness of therapy has relied heavily on a technique termed

_____-_____.

35. Several recent meta-analyses have found that psychotherapy is generally

_____, and usually, the _____ therapy, the better.

36. Investigators believe that specific techniques may explain about _____ the amount of therapeutic change as nonspecific factors.

37. _____ _____ therapies have been shown, in carefully controlled research, to be effective in treating particular problems

38. To be effective with ethnic minority groups, clinicians need to develop _____ competence.

39. In addressing the psychological problems of African American clients, therapists

often need to help them cope with the effects of _____ and _____.

40. Three things clinicians can do to bridge the gap between them and their Latino and Latina American clients are:

a. _____

b. _____

c. _____

41. Efforts to help Native Americans should focus on strengthening their cultural

_____, _____, and _____.

42. Feminist psychotherapy challenges the validity of _____-_____

stereotypes and the tradition of _____ dominance.

43. The great majority of gay males and lesbians are _____ with their sexual

orientation and seek therapy because of conflicts that arise from social

_____ and _____.

44. Psychotherapy is most effective when therapists attend to and respect people's

_____ as well as _____ differences.

45. Three types of biological therapies are _____, _____ therapy, and

_____.

46. _____ drugs are prescription drugs that are widely used to help relieve to control symptoms associated with mental disorders, such as anxiety disorders, mood disorders, and schizophrenia.

47. Antianxiety drugs are also known as _____ tranquilizers, whereas antipsychotic drugs are known as _____ tranquilizers.

48. _____ is the most common side-effect of antianxiety drugs, sometimes followed by _____ anxiety when use of the drugs is discontinued..

49. Four classes of drugs used in chemotherapy for psychological disorders are:

   a. _____

   b. _____

   c. _____

   d. _____

50. Neuroleptics refer to _____ drugs.

51. Three types of antidepressant drugs are:

   a. _____

   b. _____

   c. _____

52. _____ is used to treat bipolar disorder.

53. Electroconvulsive therapy is used mainly for people with severe _____.

54. The best known, but now discredited, psychosurgery technique is the _____ _____.

55. Antipsychotic drugs can produce a severe and apparently irreversible type of movement disorder called _____ _____.

56. Psychiatric drugs provide patients with _____ relief, but do not teach patients new _____ or ways of _____ with their difficulties.

57. Five methods of coping with anger are:

a. _____

b. _____

c. _____

d. _____

e. _____

58. Three methods for lifting your mood are:

a. _____

b. _____

c. _____

Sample Test

Multiple-Choice Questions

1. Elwood goes to his therapist to get treatment for his severe depression. His therapist has him lie on a couch in a slightly darkened room and talk about anything that comes to mind. This process of discussing whatever comes to mind is called _____.
   a. transference
   b. free association
   c. catharsis
   d. reaction formation

2. In psychoanalysis, the tendency to block free expression of impulses and primitive ideas is called _____.
   a. catharsis
   b. regression
   c. sublimation
   d. resistance

3. Freud believed that dreams were made up of unconscious urges that were expressed as a form of _____.
   a. free association
   b. catharsis
   c. transference
   d. wish fulfillment

4. Because of the focus of modern psychoanalysis, many modern psychoanalysts are called _____.
   a. ego analysts
   b. dream analysts
   c. humanists
   d. Gestalt therapists

5. Client-centered therapy is _____, and Gestalt therapy is _____.
   a. nondirective, nondirective
   b. directive, nondirective
   c. nondirective, directive
   d. directive, directive

6. Behavior therapists are similar to humanistic-existential therapists in that they both tend to _____.
   a. focus on the present
   b. focus on the role of conditioning in shaping behavior
   c. emphasize the importance of re-integrating disowned parts of the self
   d. be nondirective

7. Elwood goes to his therapist to get treatment for a phobia. His therapist uses a method for reducing phobic responses that associates images of fear-inducing objects or situations with deep muscle relaxation. This technique is called _____.
   a. operant conditioning   c. systematic desensitization
   b. aversive conditioning   d. self-control

8. Token economies are a form of _____.
   a. operant conditioning   c. systematic desensitization
   b. aversive conditioning   d. classical conditioning

9. As part of his therapy, Elwood has a device strapped to his arm that beeps when his muscle tension goes down. He is taught to gain more conscious control of the tension in his body by learning to make changes that make the device on his arm beep constantly. This technique is a form of _____.
   a. functional analysis   c. systematic desensitization
   b. biofeedback training   d. successive approximations

10. The psychologist who originated the idea of the "cognitive triad" and its relationship to depression is _____.
    a. Freud   c. Beck
    b. Rogers   d. Ellis

11. Elwood goes to his therapist to get treatment for his severe depression. His therapist actively urges him to explore a number of "irrational beliefs" that appear to be contributing to his depression. The therapist then points out *how* the beliefs are contributing to Elwood's depression and helps him replace those beliefs with more rational alternatives. This technique is **MOST** like that of _____.
    a. Beck   c. Lazarus
    b. Perls   d. Ellis

12. Which of the following is **NOT** a benefit to group therapy?
    a. It allows a therapist to treat several clients at once.
    b. Group members who improve their adjustment provide hope for other members.
    c. Clients can draw upon a wide pool of knowledge and experiences to solve problems.
    d. It is faster than individual psychotherapy.

13. Family therapists often find that family members cannot tolerate differences in other family members because of _____.
    a. their needs for conformity
    b. their needs to dominate others
    c. their desires to "help" the other family members
    d. their own low self-esteem

14. According to the studies cited in your text, psychotherapy is effective _____ percent of the time.
    a. 15-20   c. 55-60
    b. 35-40   d. 75-80

15. Asians often express psychological complaints in terms of _____.
    a. emotional anguish   c. physical symptoms
    b. stoic platitudes   d. aggressive behavior

16. Drug therapy, electroconvulsive shock therapy, and psychosurgery are all examples of _____.
    a. biological therapies
    b. illegal therapies
    c. behavioral therapies
    d. Gestalt therapies

17. Phenothiazines and clozapine are examples of _____.
    a. antianxiety drugs
    b. antipsychotic drugs
    c. antidepressant drugs
    d. stimulants

18. Antidepressant drugs have been found to also be effective in the treatment of each of the following disorders **EXCEPT** _____.
    a. conversion disorder
    b. eating disorders
    c. obsessive-compulsive disorder
    d. social phobia

19. ECT is almost exclusively used in the treatment of _____.
    a. minor depression
    b. schizophrenia
    c. epilepsy
    d. major depression

20. Each of the following is a true of internet counseling **EXCEPT** _____.
    a. online consulting may encourage people to seek help who have hesitated out of shyness or embarrassment.
    b. online consulting may make people feel more comfortable about receiving help and become a first step toward meeting a therapist in person
    c. online therapy may provide badly needed services for those living in remote or inaccessible areas
    d. online therapists are better able to provide intensive services that clients need during times of emotional; crisis

True-False Questions

21. Gestalt therapy is the application of principles of learning to promote desired behavioral changes.   _____

22. Flooding is based on extinction.   _____

23. Aversive conditioning has been used with great success because it has almost no negative side-effects.   _____

24. Research into the effectiveness of therapy has not been encouraging.   _____

25. The American Psychiatric Association does not consider a gay male or lesbian sexual orientation to be a psychological disorder.   _____

Essay Question

26. Identify three biological approaches to therapy, explaining how they work and any problems associated with them.

Student Activities

Name _____ **Date** _____

9.1 Asking Ourselves

After reading this chapter on therapies, you probably will have some opinions about psychotherapies. If you have not read the chapter yet, look at the first question and keep it in mind as you read.

1. If you or someone you know were looking for a psychotherapist, which system or type of therapy would you choose or recommend and why?

2. Now consult the yellow pages of your local phone directory under the two headings "psychologists" and "psychiatrists" (the latter are often listed under physicians). Which schools of psychotherapy are represented, and is your choice included?

Activity continued on back

3. Without asking, write down how you believe your adjustment instructor would answer question number 1 above. Why do you believe this to be true? Even if your instructor has no preference, he or she might be interested in knowing what kind of impression you have.

9.2 As Simple as ABC

Based on the discussion of Albert Ellis's Rational Emotive Behavior Therapy, try to interpret the following situation and offer some hypothetical assistance. A student-acquaintance informs you that he or she has failed an important exam in a required math class and is depressed and considers the situation in that class hopeless.

1. What is "A," the activating event?

2. What seems to be the "C," or consequences in this case?

3. Which irrational belief(s), or "B," could be applicable in this example?

4. What arguments would you propose to dispute these irrational beliefs?

Activity Continued on back

5. What was the last event that upset you?

6. What feelings and thoughts did that event cause?

7. Which irrational belief or beliefs could account for your responses?

8. How would Albert Ellis challenge the ABC's in your example?

9.3 Constructing the Anxiety Item Hierarchy

To conduct systematic desensitization, clients help their therapists to arrange disturbing stimuli in an order of increasing challenge known as an anxiety item hierarchy. For this exercise, choose a topic, behavior, or situation you associate with fear or anxiety. It does not need to be something that results in feelings of phobic proportions. For example, it could be competing in a race, telling the boss she or he made a mistake, looking over the edge of "Lover's Leap," or taking lessons in scuba. Some people find that the construction of the hierarchy alone can reduce some of their apprehension.

1. Identify one item for a hierarchy that could be the first and least disturbing item. For example, related to the challenges discussed above, first items could be registering one week before the race, telling the boss the mail has arrived, standing 100 feet from the edge of Lover's Leap, or calling the scuba school to inquire about the cost of lessons.

2. Now identify the most distressing situation you can imagine for the challenge you have chosen. Again, for example: a competitor says "You don't belong in the race," the boss yells "You're fired," you lean over the edge of the cliff, or you find no air coming to the mouthpiece.

Activity Continued on back

3. Now for your challenge, arrange eight to eighteen stimuli in-between the two you have chosen, trying your best to make the perceived difference between each item about equal. If you have chosen a complex situation to cope with, it may take more than 20 items in your hierarchy, so don't hesitate to write more.

Name _____ **Date** _____

9.4 Identifying Caffeine Consumption

Among the self-control techniques outlined in this chapter is the functional analysis of behavior. By recording information about problem behaviors, including the stimuli that encourage the behavior, and the situation in which the behavior occurs, we may see change occur in reaction to functional analysis, or at least gain ideas about the steps that could lead to successful intervention. For our project we can focus on consumption of caffeine. Prepare a note card so you can record caffeine consumption, including all caffeinated beverages and over-the-counter medications you use, the time, location, and rewards for use. Remember the colas, Dr. Pepper, Mountain Dew, chocolate, some analgesics, and some cold preparations are likely candidates for inclusion. You may find possible rewards include stimulation, socialization, prevention of headaches, or you may chalk it up to simple "habit." Can you record any adverse consequences you experience caused by caffeine, such as sleeplessness, nervousness, headaches, stomach complaints, and so on?

Follow-Up Questions:

1. What situations prompt you to use caffeine?

2. What effects, if any, have you noticed if you fail to get your average daily dosage of caffeine? How have you dealt with those effects?

Activity Continued on back

3. What is the average number of doses of caffeine taken per day? How does this compare to numbers reported by classmates?

4. What self-control strategies could help reduce your caffeine consumption based on your functional analysis?

10

Gender Roles and Gender Differences

Chapter Outline

Module 10.1: Gender Roles and Stereotypes: What Does It Mean to Be Masculine or Feminine?

Module 10.2: Gender Differences: Vive La Différence or Vive La Similarité?

Module 10.3: Gender-Typing: On Becoming a Woman or a Man

Module 10.4: Psychology in Daily Life: Coping with the Costs of Gender Polarization

Chapter Overview

Stereotypes. A stereotype is a fixed conventional idea about a group that can give rise to prejudice and discrimination. A gender stereotype is a fixed, conventional idea about how men and women ought to behave.

Cultural Beliefs and Gender Roles. Women are typically perceived as nurturing, gentle, dependent, warm, emotional, kind, helpful, patient and submissive. Men are typically stereotypes as independent, competitive, tough, logical, self-reliant, dominant, and protective.

Gender Polarization. Gender polarization is the tendency to see males and females as opposites. This polarization is linked to the traditional view of men as breadwinners and women as homemakers. People see the feminine gender role as warm, dependent, submissive, and interested in the arts. They see the masculine gender role as independent, competitive, protective, and competent at business, math, and science.

Psychological Androgyny. Throughout history it has been widely assumed that the more masculine a person is, the less feminine he or she is, and vice versa. However, many psychologists look upon masculinity and femininity as independent dimensions. The construct of psychological androgyny characterizes people who possess both stereotypically masculine and feminine traits.

Psychologically androgynous individuals can apparently summon up both "masculine" and "feminine" traits to express their talents and desires and to meet the demands of their situations. Psychologically androgynous people show high "identity" and "intimacy"—using concepts of Erik Erikson. They show both independence and nurturance, depending on the situation. They have higher self-esteem and greater ability to bounce back from failure. Wives of psychologically androgynous husbands are happier than wives of husbands who adhere to a strict stereotypical masculine gender role.

Cognitive Gender Differences. Boys have traditionally excelled in math and spatial relations skills, whereas girls have had the edge in language skills. However, these differences are small and growing narrower.

Gender Differences in Social Behavior. Females are typically more extroverted and nurturant than males. Males are typically more tough-minded and aggressive than females. Men tend to express more interest than women in casual sex and having multiple sex partners.

Biological Views on Gender-Typing. Biological views of gender typing focus on the roles of evolution, genetics, and prenatal influences in predisposing men and women to gender-linked behavior patterns. According to evolutionary psychologists, gender differences were fashioned by natural selection in response to problems in adaptation that were repeatedly encountered by humans over thousands of generations. Testosterone in the brains of male fetuses may be connected with the ability to manage spatial relations tasks. Testosterone is also connected with aggressiveness.

Psychological Views on Gender Typing. According to psychodynamic theory, gender typing stems from resolution of the conflicts of the phallic stage. However, children assume gender roles at much earlier ages than the theory would suggest. Social-cognitive theory explains gender-typing in terms of observational learning, identification, and socialization. Gender-schema theory proposes that children use the gender schema of their society to organize their self-perceptions, and that they then evaluate themselves in relation to the schema.

Learning Objectives

After studying this chapter your students should be able to:

1. Explain what gender roles, gender-role stereotypes are, and gender polarization are. Describe the characteristics typical of the traditional masculine and feminine gender roles in the United States.

2. Compare and contrast the concepts of "Machismo" and "marianismo." What effects do they have on males and females in Hispanic culture, and how have they been affected by the process of acculturation?

3. Explain what psychological androgyny is and how it is different from other personality styles. Discuss how androgyny contributes to healthy adjustment and personal development.

4. Discuss the various gender-based differences in cognitive functioning and explain why these differences need to be viewed cautiously.

5. Identify and describe the various gender differences in sexuality, aggression, and communication.

6. Define gender typing and explain what gender identity disorder is. Also, discuss how biological influences may affect gender typing.

7. Compare and contrast the psychodynamic, social-cognitive, and gender-schema views of gender typing.

8. Summarize research findings on whether men are naturally more aggressive than women.

9. Define gender polarization and discuss the various personal, educational, and job-related costs of gender-role stereotyping.

Key Terms

gender roles	psychological androgyny	gender identity disorder (GID)
gender stereotype	undifferentiated	evolutionary psychology
stereotype	relational aggression	identification
machismo	gender typing	socialization
marianismo	gender identity	gender-schema theory
acculturation	sexual orientation	gender polarization

Key Terms Review

Define each of the following terms:

1. Gender Roles: _____

   _____

2. Gender Stereotype: _____

   _____

3. Stereotype: _____

   _____

4. Machismo: _____

   _____

5. Marianismo: _____

   _____

6. Acculturation: _____

   _____

7. Psychological Androgyny: _____

_____

8. Undifferentiated: _____

_____

9. Relational Aggression: _____

_____

10. Gender Typing: _____

_____

11. Gender Identity: _____

_____

12. Sexual Orientation: _____

_____

13. Gender Identity Disorder (GID): _____

_____

14. Evolutionary Psychology: _____

_____

15. Identification: _____

_____

16. Socialization: _____

_____

17. Gender-Schema Theory: _____

_____

18. Gender Polarization: _____

_____

Chapter Review

1. Complex clusters of ways in which men and women are expected to behave within a culture are called _____ _____.

2. Generalized beliefs about how men and women are supposed to be are _____ _____.

3. In our society, people tend to see the _____ as warm, emotional, dependent, and submissive, and the _____ as independent, competitive, tough, and protective.

4. Cross-cultural research has found that gender-role stereotypes are _____.

5. _____ is a cultural stereotype that defines masculinity in terms of being strong, virile, and dominant, while _____ is a cultural stereotype that defines femininity in terms of the virtuous woman who "suffers in silence."

6. While most people see masculinity and femininity as _____ poles of one continuum, many psychologists look at them as _____ dimensions.

7. People who show high levels of independence, aggressiveness, and dominance are seen as _____. Those who show high levels of warmth, nurturance, and expressiveness are seen as _____. Those who show high levels of both dominance and nurturance are said to be _____, and those who show low levels of both are _____.

8. In terms of Erikson's concepts of ego identity and intimacy, _____ college students are most likely to show "high identity" and "high intimacy."

9. Antill's study of marital happiness found that husbands' levels of happiness were linked to their wives' _____, and wives' levels of happiness were linked to their husbands' _____.

10. "Masculine" traits such as _____ and _____ contribute to high

self-esteem in both genders.

11. It is now believed that males' greater knowledge of world affairs and skill in science and industry is largely due to:

_____.

12. Males and females are _____ in general intelligence.

13. It appears that girls are somewhat superior to boys in _____ ability, whereas

boys seem to be somewhat superior in _____-_____ abilities.

14. Regarding gender differences in cognitive abilities, researchers note that:

a. _____

b. _____

c. _____

15. Men's friendships with other men tend to be _____ and _____ supportive than women's friendships with other women.

16. Researchers have found that men are _____.

17. Women interact at _____ distances than men do, and seek to keep _____

space between themselves and strangers of the other gender than men do.

18. In our culture, _____ are more interested in casual sex and having more than

one sex partner, and _____ are more interested in combining sex with a

romantic relationship.

19. _____ engage in more physical and overt aggression, and _____ more often engage in relational aggression.

20. Girls are more likely to express _____ by excluding others from friendship groups or starting rumors.

21. Your perception of yourself as male or female is your _____ _____.

22. Adults with gender identity disorder are sometimes called _____ or

_____ individuals.

23. Researchers have found gender differences in the _____ and _____ of the brain.

24. The brain hemispheres may be more _____ in males than in females.

25. Women's brains may be organized to keep _____ cues in mind, whereas men's

brains may reflect a more _____ approach

26. _____ hormones may "masculinize" or "feminize" the brain by creating

predispositions that are consistent with some gender-role stereotypes.

27. The two most prominent psychological perspectives on gender-typing today are

_____-_____ theory and _____-_____ theory.

28. According to psychodynamic theory, gender roles are acquired through a process of

_____.

29. Freud believed that gender identity remains flexible until the resolution of the

_____ at the

age of 5 or 6.

30. According to social-cognitive theory, _____ learning, _____, and

_____ all play a role in the acquisition of gender roles and gender-role

stereotypes

31. Girls frequently learn to respond to social provocations by feeling _____.

Boys, however, are often encouraged to _____ back.

32. _____-_____ theory holds that children use gender as one way of

organizing their perceptions of the world.

33. Children have usually developed a sense of being male or being female by the age of

_____.

34. Physical aggression is associated with higher levels of _____ in men and

higher levels of _____ in women.

35. Gender-types differences in behavior are best understood by the interaction of

_____ factors and _____ factors.

36. Far _____ American boys than girls have reading problems, in part because

reading is considered a _____ activity in the United States.

37. Four reasons why boys are more likely than girls to feel at home with math are:

a. _____

b. _____

c. _____

d. _____

38. Women's wages average _____ than men's, and women are _____ likely
to be promoted into high-level managerial positions.

39. Compared to women who identify with more flexible gender roles, women who adopt
traditional feminine gender roles:

a. _____

b. _____

c. _____

d. _____

e. _____

40. Compared to men who identify with more flexible gender roles, men who adopt traditional masculine gender roles:

a. _____

b. _____

c. _____

d. _____

e. _____

Sample Test

Multiple-Choice Questions

1. The possession of stereotypic traits and behavior patterns of both genders is called _____.
   a. psychological androgyny
   b. empathy
   c. psychological transsexualism
   d. psychological heterosexuality

2. Today, many behavior scientists have argued that masculinity and femininity are _____.
   a. independent personality dimensions
   b. part of the same personality dimension
   c. opposite poles on one continuum
   d. indefinable

3. Undifferentiated women tend to be viewed _____ positively than other women and are _____ satisfied with their marriages than are other women.
   a. less, less
   b. more, less
   c. less, more
   d. more, more

4. A person with which of the following personal characteristics is likely to be **MOST** well-adjusted?
   a. stereotypically masculine
   b. stereotypically feminine
   c. undifferentiated
   d. psychologically androgynous

5. According to the Antill study of marital happiness, the happiest couples were women whose husbands had _____ levels of femininity and men whose wives had _____ levels of femininity.
   a. low, low
   b. low, high
   c. high, low
   d. high, high

6. Researchers have argued that the self-esteem benefits of androgyny stem mainly from the _____.
   a. greater tolerance for and acceptance of homosexuality in recent years
   b. presence of traditionally female traits in both men and women
   c. presence of traditionally male traits in both men and women
   d. presence of a combination of masculine and feminine traits in men and women

7. Assessment of intelligence has _____.
   a. shown that males have higher overall levels of cognitive ability than females
   b. shown that males are more logical and analytical than females
   c. found no overall differences in cognitive abilities between males and females
   d. found that females are more sociable and suggestible than males

8. In math, the differences in test performance between males and females are _____.
   a. small, but growing
   b. large and growing
   c. small and narrowing
   d. large, but narrowing

9. Compared to men, women, in terms of social behavior, tend to be _____ cooperative and _____ competitive.
   a. less, less
   b. less, more
   c. more, less
   d. more, more

10. Research indicates that boys are _____ likely than girls to engage in physical aggression and _____ likely than girls to engage in relational aggression.
    a. less, less
    b. less, more
    c. more, less
    d. more, more

11. Adults with gender identity disorder are also known as _____.
    a. transsexuals
    b. transvestites
    c. bisexuals
    d. hermaphrodites

12. Researchers have found _____ of the brain.
    a. no gender differences in the functioning and organization
    b. gender differences in the functioning, but not the organization,
    c. gender differences in the organization, but not the functioning
    d. gender differences in the organization and the functioning

13. The process of adopting the behaviors and what we assume to be the thoughts and behaviors of others is called _____.
    a. differentiation
    b. identification
    c. assimilation
    d. socialization

14. Social cognitive theorists view identification as _____.
    a. the result of inappropriate rewards and punishments
    b. a one-time event occurring around the ages of 5 or 6
    c. an abnormal reaction to improper toilet training
    d. a broad, continuous process

15. A scientist claims that children learn to judge themselves according to the traits or constructs considered relevant to their genders through a process of observational learning and cognitive processing of their environment. This scientist is most likely a supporter of _____.
    a. social learning theory
    b. gender-schema theory
    c. social-cognitive theory
    d. humanistic theory

16. Girls have been fully integrated into the public school systems _____.
    a. since the times of ancient Greece and Rome
    b. since the Middle Ages and the Renaissance
    c. since the industrial revolution of the 1600s
    d. only in the 20th century

17. Which of the following is **NOT** true of boys, girls, and reading?
    a. Far more American boys than girls have reading problems.
    b. Cultural factors, stereotyping in particular, play a role in gender differences in reading.
    c. Reading is stereotyped as a feminine activity worldwide.
    d. Problems in reading generalize into nearly every area of academic life.

18. Which of the following is **NOT** a cost of gender-role stereotyping in the workplace?
    a. Women are less likely than men to be promoted into responsible managerial positions.
    b. Women are subjected to sexual harassment on the job.
    c. Women must act friendlier to coworkers and bosses to be respected on the job.
    d. Women who are flexible in their decision-making are more likely to be labeled "wishy-washy."

19. Which of the following is **NOT** a cost of gender-role stereotyping to the psychological well-being of men?
    a. Men who accept the traditional masculine gender role are more likely to be upset if their wives earn more money than they do.
    b. Men who accept the traditional masculine gender role are more likely to ask for help, including medical help, when they need it.
    c. Men who accept the traditional masculine gender role are less likely to be tolerant of their wives' or lovers' faults.
    d. Men who accept the traditional masculine gender role are less likely to be sympathetic and tender in their marital relationships.

20. The Hispanic ideal of femininity is one of _____.
    a. being strong-willed, vocal, and assertive
    b. being sexually aggressive and desirable
    c. being the provider of joy and suffering in silence
    d. being the logical, efficient planner who runs the household

True-False Questions

21. It is usually the Hispanic wife who has greater difficulty accepting a more flexible distribution of roles within the marriage and giving up a rigid set of expectations.   _____

22. Feminine traits in men contribute to marital happiness.   _____

23. Women talk more in social situations than men do.   _____

24. Gender identity is virtually the same as sexual orientation.   _____

25. Women earn less than men for comparable work.   _____

Essay Question

26. Compare and contrast the psychodynamic, social-cognitive, and gender-schema views of gender typing.

Student Activities

Name _____ **Date** _____

10.1 Riddles

These riddles have been around for quite a while, but they may still be useful for our purposes.

1. A man and his son are in a serious car accident. Both are rushed to the nearest hospital while unconscious. The boy needs emergency surgery, but the emergency room surgeon says, "I can't operate on him, he's my son." How is this possible?

2. If you enjoy sports, you might get this one. How can two softball teams play a complete softball game, and the score ends 1 to nothing, even though not one man for either team has crossed home plate?

3. I really doubt the riddles fooled you, given they are old and given the subject for this chapter. However, you may find they will work on a friend or acquaintance. Try them one at a time, separate them by a day or so, and see if your subject learns anything from the first to the second riddle, assuming you told him or her the answer to the first. What happens and what hypotheses might be generated from this information?

Activity continued on back

4. Do you think that people today would be more likely to answer the riddles correctly than people 40 years ago? Why or why not?

10.2 Reversal of Roles

It is not uncommon to read about or be entertained by people's real or imagined experience with role reversal. What kinds of answers do you come up with to the following questions?

1. Movies I can think of that have featured the theme of role reversal go back to such Hollywood classics as "Some Like It Hot," and include more recent films such as *Mr. Mom, Mrs. Doubtfire, Tootsie, Three Men and a Baby*, the *Alien* trilogy, and *Tomb Raider*. What movies can you add to this list?
    How have such films affected your views, if at all, of men's and women's roles in society?

2. Our nation's experiences in the Iraq War and the War in Afghanistan have brought home the reality of women in combat missions. Do you believe that women should be serving in combat roles in the military? Why or why not? What limits, if any, would you recommend for women serving in the armed services when it comes to combat missions, and/or the draft?

Activity continued on back

3. Ask someone else the same question found in 2 above. What is her or his opinion? Why do you think he or she is right or wrong?

4. In a related question, given the treatment of women in cultures such as that in Afghanistan (as imposed by the Taliban), do we have a right, as a culture to demand that this treatment be changed or to forcefully intervene to change it? Explain your reasons for your beliefs. Under what circumstances, if any, do we ever have that right?

10.3 Dear Old Sexist School Days

In the text, Nevid and Rathus detail how gender roles are reinforced in the education system. Researchers have found that sex bias continues beyond primary and secondary education right into the lecture halls and laboratories of American universities and colleges. For example, a University of Illinois study found that while high school valedictorians, salutatorians, and honor students were attending the University of Illinois, self-concepts remained steady for males, but dropped dramatically for females. Upon graduating from high school, 23 percent of the males and 21 percent of the females rated themselves as "far above average" in intelligence. By the time they were seniors in college, the numbers for the males and females were respectively, 25 percent and **zero**.

Are college instructors biased in the ways research suggests, such as calling on male students more, making better eye contact with males, supporting male students more, and coaching males more? To assess such possibilities at your school, select one class other than this adjustment class, and record for one week the following information.

1. Did the instructor favor one gender by disproportionately calling on, helping, encouraging, or agreeing with either the men or the women in that class? How can you accurately record this data? Can anyone else in the class you have chosen also record the same data, so you could check for agreement (which we call reliability)?

2. In addition to your effort to carefully look at one selected class, where else in your school have you run into gender bias? How did it affect you? I have been utterly astonished at the stories of blatant as well as less obvious sexism that are still reported on college campuses, where people are supposed to be "enlightened" enough to know better. If you cannot think of any examples from your own experience, ask your friends if they have had such experiences. What have you learned?

Activity continued on the Back

3. What hypotheses could you create to systematically test and document the effects of gender bias in higher education?

4. What other explanations might account for the University of Illinois findings?

5. What are at least four things people can do to effectively respond to biased and discriminatory behavior?

10.4 Thinking Makes It So

Shakespeare wrote: "Nothing is either good or bad, but thinking makes it so." What may be meat for one person may be poison for another. It's in the eye of the beholder. And so forth and so forth. By the same token, we can substitute an attractive synonym for something much less attractive, or we can turn things around the other way and make something wonderful or grand sound ugly or base. Word games like these can be used to create or maintain sexual bias. For each of the words below, think of two synonyms that can be substituted for the word—one positive and one negative. For example, we can substitute both "rational" and "unfeeling" for "stable," or "childish" and "creative" for "spontaneous."

	POSITIVE	NEGATIVE
consistent	_____	_____
warm	_____	_____
generous	_____	_____
stubborn	_____	_____
self-righteous	_____	_____
different	_____	_____
ambitious	_____	_____
serious	_____	_____
jaded	_____	_____
assertive	_____	_____
meticulous	_____	_____
sensitive	_____	_____
focused	_____	_____
intelligent	_____	_____
principled	_____	_____

Name _____ **Date** _____

10.5 Interviewing Others

Since we can learn so much from others, consider one or both of these possible interviews. One could be a child and the other an adult engaged in a career not typical for that person's gender, such as a male nurse, or a female firefighter.

1. With parental permission, question a child about issues raised in this chapter about early appearance of gender-role stereotyping. What questions can you think of and what are the child's answers?

2. Interview the adult with some questions prepared in advance, but also with flexibility to pursue some unanticipated but promising leads. What can you share from your conversations?

3. What did you learn from your questioning of these people? How did it change your thinking, if at all, on this matter?

11

Interpersonal Attraction: Of Friendship and Love

Chapter Outline

Chapter Overview

Factors that Contribute to Attraction.   Physical appeal appears to be the key factor. In our culture, slenderness is considered attractive in both men and women, whereas tallness is valued in men. Women tend to see themselves as heavier than the cultural ideal. Similarity in attitudes and sociocultural factors (ethnicity, education, and so on), proximity, and reciprocity in feelings of admiration also contribute to attraction.

Stereotypes About Attractive People.   There is an assumption that good things come in pretty packages. Physically attractive people are assumed to be more successful and well adjusted, but they are also perceived as more vain, self-centered, and likely to have sexual affairs.

Male and Female Preferences in Attractiveness. Both males and females emphasize the importance of physical appeal and personal qualities. However, males tend to place somewhat more emphasis on physical attractiveness, and females tend to place relatively more emphasis than males do on traits like vocational status, earning potential, consideration, dependability, and fondness for children. Some behavioral and social scientists believe that evolutionary forces favored the survival of ancestral men and women with these mating preferences because they conferred reproductive advantages.

The Matching Hypothesis. The matching hypothesis suggests that we are more likely to ask out and marry people who are similar to ourselves in attractiveness—largely because of fear of rejection.

Sexual Orientation. Sexual orientation refers to the direction of erotic interests. People with a heterosexual orientation are sexually attracted to members of the opposite sex. People with a gay male or lesbian sexual orientation are sexually attracted to people of their own gender. People with a bisexual orientation are attracted to both men and women.

Theories of Sexual Orientation. Psychodynamic theory connects sexual orientation with the resolution of the Oedipus and Electra complexes, Learning theorists focus on the role of reinforcement of early patterns of sexual behavior. Evidence of a genetic contribution to sexual orientation is accumulating. Sex hormones are known to have both organizing and activating effects. Sex hormones may have an effect on the developing brain during prenatal development that may affect later sexual orientation.

People's Reactions to Those Who Are Gay Males, Lesbians, or Bisexuals. Gay males and lesbians have generally met with strong—sometimes violent—social disapproval. Most people in the United States today favor granting gay males and lesbians equal access to jobs, but many would bar them from activities—such as teaching—in which they fear (mistakenly) that their sexual orientation might affect the sexual orientations of children.

Challenges Faced by Those With a Gay Male or Lesbian Orientation. Gay males and lesbians frequently struggle with coming out, both to themselves and others. They often have difficulty coming to terms with their sexual orientation—both recognizing and personally accepting their sexual orientation, and then deciding whether they will declare their orientation to other people. Gay males and lesbians are more likely than heterosexuals to be anxious, depressed, or suicidal. Their adjustment problems may be connected with society's negative treatment of them.

The Role of Friends. We share activities, interests, and confidences with friends. The key qualities we seek are ability to keep confidence, loyalty, social support, and general positive traits, such as frankness and intelligence.

Love. Love is a strong positive emotion characterized by feelings of attraction, attachment, and sexual arousal. Sternberg's theory postulates three components of love: intimacy, passion, and commitment. Romantic love is characterized by intimacy and passion; infatuation (fatuous love) by passion and commitment; companionate love by intimacy and commitment; and consummate love—which to many, is the ideal form of love—by all three components.

Learning Objectives

After studying this chapter you should be able to:

1. Define attraction, describe the various traits that contribute to physical attractiveness in our culture, and discuss the accuracy of the various stereotypes about attractive people.

2. Summarize research findings on gender and cultural differences in the perception of attractiveness

3. Explain what the matching hypothesis is and how it influences who we choose as potential partners.

4. Explain the roles of attitudinal similarity, proximity, and reciprocity in interpersonal attraction and discuss the specific areas where similar attitudes are most likely to affect a developing relationship.

5. Explain what sexual orientation is and how it is different from sexual preference, and summarize research findings in regard to the origins of sexual orientation, and the psychological adjustment of gay males and lesbians.

6. Compare and contrast the attitudes of various ethnic minorities toward gay males and lesbians.

7. Describe the role played by friends in our lives and identify the various qualities we seek in friends throughout childhood and into adulthood.

8. Identify and briefly describe each of the six styles of love discussed in the text.

9. Explain Sternberg's "love triangle" and identify at least five possible kinds of love that can emerge from this model.

10. Compare and contrast romantic love with companionate love.

11. Explain what loneliness is, describe the factors that contribute to it, and identify various measures that can be taken to cope with it.

Key Terms

attraction	organizing effects	storge
matching hypothesis	activating effects	pragma
proximity	cliques	mania
reciprocity	crowds	agape
sexual orientation	cliques	consummate love
heterosexual	love	empty love
homosexual	eros	fatuous love
bisexual	ludus	companionate love

Key Terms Review

Define each of the following terms:

1. Attraction: _____

_____

2. Matching Hypothesis: _____

_____

3. Proximity: _____

_____

4. Reciprocity: _____

_____

5. Sexual Orientation: _____

_____

6. Heterosexual: _____

_____

7. Homosexual: _____

_____

8. Bisexual: _____

_____

9. Organizing Effects: _____

_____

10. Activating Effects: _____

_____

11. Cliques: _____

_____

12. Crowds: _____

_____

13. Love: _____

_____

14. Eros: _____

_____

15. Ludus: _____

_____

16. Agape: _____

_____

17. Consummate Love: _____

_____

18. Empty Love: _____

_____

19. Fatuous Love: _____

_____

20. Companionate Love: _____

_____

Chapter Review

1. Two forms of interpersonal attraction are _____ and _____.

2. The key factor in determining romantic attraction is_____ _____.

3. A study of people in England and Japan found that men consider women with _____ eyes, _____ cheekbones, and _____ jaws to be most attractive.

4. In our society, tallness is a(n) _____ for men, and tall women tend to be viewed _____ attractively.

5. In the workplace, shortness is perceived to be a _____ for men and a _____ for women.

6. Men prefer women with _____ than average breasts, and perceive them as _____ intelligent, competent, moral, and modest than other women.

7. In Western culture, there is pressure on males to be _____ and females to be _____.

8. In Western culture today, both genders perceive obese people to be _____.

9. Men prefer women to be _____ than they expect, and women prefer men to be _____ than they expect.

10. In their choice of mates, males and females tend to value _____ traits..

11. Studies on attraction and choice of mates find that _____ place greater emphasis on vocational status, earning potential, expressiveness, and kindness, while _____ place greater emphasis on youth, physical attractiveness, and frugality.

12. In several studies of people in various cultures on choosing potential mates, men tend to emphasize _____ _____, while women tend to emphasize men's _____ status.

13. By and large, we rate beautiful people as _____ people.

14. Physically attractive people are judged and treated more _____ than their less attractive peers.

15. Physically attractive people have _____ self-esteem.

16. People from different cultures tend to rate physical beauty in _____ ways.

17. Men and women prefer female faces with _____ features and males faces with _____ features.

18. The major motive for asking out "matches" in physical attractiveness appears to be _____.

19. Marriages are made in the _____.

20. We tend to be attracted to people who have _____ attitudes, and men place _____ emphasis than women do on attitude similarity as a determinant of attraction.

21. In computer matched dates at the University of Nevada, men were more influenced by _____ attitudes, while women were influenced by _____ attitudes.

22. Proximity allows for repeated _____, which may kindle feelings of attraction.

23. Reciprocity is a _____ determinant of attraction.

24. People with a _____ orientation are sexually attracted to, and interested in forming romantic relationships with, members of their own gender.

25. People with a _____ orientation are sexually attracted to, and interested in forming romantic relationships with, members of the opposite gender.

26. Surveys in the United States and Europe find that about _____ percent of men identify themselves as gay and about _____ percent of American women surveyed say they have a lesbian sexual orientation.

27. Gay people have a gender identity that is _____ with their sexual orientation.

28. Researchers suspect that exposure of the fetus to _____ _____ during prenatal development may influence later sexual orientation.

29. Sex hormones have _____ effects and _____ effects on sexual behavior.

30. The origins of sexual orientation are _____ and _____.

31. Sexual orientation usually emerges during _____.

32. Gay males and lesbians are more likely than heterosexuals to experience feelings of _____ and _____, and they are more prone to _____ attempts.

33. Gay males and lesbians encounter stress from _____ oppression and _____.

34. For primary schoolers, friendship is based mostly on _____

_____,

whereas for middle schoolers it is based more on _____ _____.

35. By puberty, people want friends with whom they can share _____ _____.

36. Girls find _____ to be more important than boys do, and typically form

_____ friendships.

37. In high school and college, we tend to belong to _____ or _____.

38. The quality deemed most important in friends is _____

_____

39. Psychologists find that love is a _____ emotion involving _____,

_____, and _____ areas of experience.

40. **Matching:** Match the style of love on the left with its appropriate description on the right.

_____ a. Storge   1. characterized by intense, idealized passion and the belief that one is "in love"

_____ b. Agape

_____ c. Eros   2. similar to attachment and affection, also friendship love

_____ d. Ludus   3. similar to liking and respect

_____ e. Pragma   4. based on sharing, mutual respect, and willingness to sacrifice

_____ f. Mania   5. based on sexual attraction or lust

_____ g. Companionate love   6. selfless love, similar to generosity

_____ h. Romantic love   7. game-playing love

                                       8. practical, logical love

                                       9. possessive, excited love

41. According to Sternberg, love involves _____, _____, and _____.

42. **Matching:** Match the type of love (from Sternberg's model) on the left with its appropriate description on the right.

     _____ a. Romantic love   1. intimacy alone

     _____ b. Companionate love   2. intimacy and passion

     _____ c. Fatuous love   3. intimacy and commitment

     _____ d. Empty love   4. passion alone

     _____ e. Consummate love   5. passion and commitment

     _____ f. Infatuation   6. commitment alone

     _____ g. Liking   7. intimacy, passion, and commitment

43. _____ love is seen by the great majority of Americans as a prerequisite for marriage.

44. Romantic lovers _____ one another, _____ each other's positive features and _____ their flaws.

45. According to Sternberg's model, love at first sight is _____ love.

46. _____ love assails us in a flash and then dissipates when our involvement with the loved one grows. The relationship must develop _____ love if it is to last.

47. Companionate love is based on _____ _____ of the other person.

48. Loneliness tends to peak during _____, when most of us begin to replace close links to our parents with _____ relationships.

49. Loneliness is linked to feelings of _____. Also, lonely people are more likely to get _____.

50.   Five causes of loneliness are:

a.   _____

b.   _____

c.   _____

d.   _____

e.   _____

51.   Five steps to making friends and combating loneliness are:

a.   _____

b.   _____

c.   _____

d.   _____

e.   _____

Sample Test

Multiple-Choice Questions

1.   Undergraduate men prefer dates who are about _____ they are.
   a.   the same height as   c.   4.5 inches shorter than
   b.   2.5 inches shorter than   d.   8.5 inches shorter than

2.   American men prefer women to be _____.
   a.   thinner than most women can realistically become
   b.   thinner than most women expect
   c.   about the same size as most women expect
   d.   heavier than most women expect

3.   In initial attraction, men place greater emphasis than women on each of the following **EXCEPT**
   _____.
   a.   frugality   c.   cooking ability
   b.   physical allure   d.   dependability

4.   Which of the following is **NOT** true of our expectations of attractive people?
   a.   We expect them to be popular and successful.
   b.   We expect them to be persuasive.
   c.   We expect them to be good parents
   d.   We expect them to have less stable marriages.

278

5. According to the matching hypothesis, if you rated yourself as a "5" on a 1–10 scale, who would you most likely ask out?
   a. a "3"   c. a "7"
   b. a "5"   d. a "9"

6. The tendency to return feelings and attitudes that are expressed about us, or to seek what we perceive as a "balance" in a relationship between others' feelings towards us and our feelings towards them is called _____.
   a. propinquity   c. complementarity
   b. reciprocity   d. synergy

7. Research indicates that _____ choose their sexual orientation.
   a. neither gay males nor lesbians   c. lesbians, but not gay males
   b. gay males, but not lesbians   d. gay males and lesbians

8. According to psychodynamic theory, a boy is most likely to develop a homosexual orientation if he has a _____.
   a. close-binding mother and father
   b. close-binding mother and detached-hostile father
   c. a detached-hostile mother and a close-binding father
   d. a detached-hostile mother and father

9. Research on the causes of homosexuality indicate that _____.
   a. it appears to be the result of direct genetic transmission
   b. a variety of factors may influence prenatal sex hormones to create a predisposition toward homosexuality
   c. homosexuality is the result of faulty resolution of the Oedipus or Electra complex during the phallic stage of development
   d. homosexuality results from pleasurable sexual experiences during adolescence

10. Recent studies of gay males and lesbians have found that _____.
    a. they show lower levels of anxiety than heterosexuals
    b. they are more prone to suicide than heterosexuals
    c. they are more likely to have schizophrenia than heterosexuals
    d. they are as well-adjusted as heterosexuals

11. Jennifer is in puberty. Which of the following is **MOST** likely to characterize how she feels about friendship?
    a. Friends are people who keep confidences.
    b. Friends are people who are similar to you and share interests with you.
    c. Friends are those with whom you do things and have fun.
    d. Friends are those with whom you can share intimate feelings.

12. Your text mentions each of the following in regards to friends in adulthood **EXCEPT** _____.
    a. the quality of friendliness is associated with psychological well-being among older people
    b. adults with confidants are less depressed and lonely
    c. single people tend to have more confidants than married people
    d. having confidants can heighten morale even in the face of tragic events

13. Joshua is in love. He enjoys "game playing" on his beloved and says "I keep my lover up in the air about my commitment." His style of love is called _____.
    a. agape   c. pragma
    b. ludus   d. storge

14. According to your text, to experience romantic love, one _____.
   a. just needs to experience sexual arousal
   b. must be exposed to a culture that idealizes romantic love
   c. must be willing to be a martyr for the other person
   d. must only reach the age of puberty

15. According to Sternberg, _____ is the motivational force behind romantic love.
   a. intimacy
   b. trust
   c. passion
   d. commitment

16. Liking someone in a relationship is characterized by _____.
   a. commitment, without passion or intimacy
   b. intimacy, without passion or commitment
   c. commitment and intimacy without passion
   d. commitment and passion, without intimacy

17. According to Sternberg's model, couples are matched if they _____.
   a. are nearly opposite on all three components of his triangle
   b. are nearly identical on any one side of his triangle
   c. are nearly identical on any two sides of his triangle
   d. are nearly identical on all three sides of his triangle

18. A feeling of painful isolation involving a sense of being cut off from other people is called _____.
   a. stoicism
   b. separation anxiety
   c. loneliness
   d. shyness

19. Which of the following is **NOT** a characteristic typical of lonely people?
   a. lack of empathy towards others
   b. pessimism about life in general
   c. cynicism about human nature
   d. low self-criticism

20. Each of the following is true **EXCEPT** _____.
   a. some municipalities have instituted fines for inappropriate cell phone use in public places
   b. cell phones are causing people to retreat from face-to-face interactions
   c. cell phones are no longer simply a convenient form of voice communication
   d. learning the ropes of cell phone etiquette is becoming as important as learning good manners

True-False Questions

21. Tallness is generally found to be an attractive feature in men, but not in women. _____

22. "Opposites attract": We are more likely to be attracted to people who disagree _____
   with our attitudes than to people who share them.

23. Sexual activity with members of one's own gender defines one's sexual orientation. _____

24. Friends no longer play an important role in our happiness by late adulthood. _____

25. There is such a thing as love at first sight. _____

Essay Question:

26. Identify and briefly describe each of the six styles of love discussed in the text.

Student Activities

Name _____ **Date** _____

11.1 What Kind of Face Could Launch a Thousand Ships?

As the text says, it may not seem intelligent and sophisticated, but physical appearance is given a lot of importance in interpersonal attraction. Homer claimed that it was the face of Helen of Troy that precipitated the Trojan War. Certainly the Greeks knew how to appreciate physical appearance, and they left a classical, idealized legacy for Western civilization to admire, ponder, and replicate. They are often given credit for defining the ideal characteristics of faces still followed by plastic surgeons today. While most of us might not know much about art, or faces, we know what we like. However, before we examine this fascinating information, seriously try to draw an idealized face in the space below.

Many of you may not have a clue as to how to begin, so here are some rules for shaping the face at least basically.

1. Construct a rectangle so that the height is approximately 25 percent taller than the width (for example, four inches wide by five inches tall). Now divide the height by two horizontal lines so the rectangle is divided into equal thirds (for example, one line 1 and 2/3 inches from the top, and one line 1 and 2/3 inches from the bottom of the original rectangle).

2. Next, divide the length of the rectangle into equal fifths. In our example, this requires four vertical lines spaced 0.80 inches apart from each other and the sides of the original rectangle.

3. Now do what you do when you doodle, and doodle the ears between the middle horizontal lines.

4. Place the nose in the middle section, neatly fitting on the bottom line and between the two sides.

5. Place the eyebrows at the tops of the two sections to the sides of the nose section.

Activity continued on the back

6. Place the eyes under the eyebrows and fully between the side lines of this section.

7. In the section immediately below the nose place the lips, one third of the way down the section and fully extending to and slightly past the sides of the section.

8. Find a magazine photo of the most attractive face you can and report how well the face conforms to the specifications above.

9. Collect five photos of faces you find attractive, and identify any additional specifications for attractiveness that were omitted above. Believe me, there are many more.

11.2 Is Your Love Like a Red, Red Rose?

Clearly the word "love" gets overused when it can be applied to the most important person in our life and broccoli. Rathus and Nevid recognize this and make some suggestions about a more exact language of love, especially the different styles of love. The discussion suggests most people in love experience a combination of several different styles.

Think about the "ideal" you have of love, and see if you can assign some percentage from 0 to 100 percent to each of the styles. Beside each style enter your ideal percentage.

    1. _____ Eros or romantic love

    2. _____ Ludus or game-playing love

    3. _____ Storge or friendship love

    4. _____ Pragma or pragmatic, logical love

    5. _____ Mania or possessive, excited love

    6. _____ Agape or selfless love

Follow-Up Questions:

1. Would the relationship you describe above best be described as romantic love, companionate love, or some other love described in the text? How is it similar?

2. Looking back on a relationship in your past which ended, what percentages would you have assigned in that case?

Activity continued on the back

4. How is the relationship described in question 2 (above) similar to or different from the ideal relationship you described in question 1 (above)? Is there any lesson in that?

5. If you are involved in a relationship, have your partner write down the percentages for his or her vision of ideal love. How does this compare with your ideal? Is it similar to or different from what you expected?

6. Try comparing your ideal love with a relationship portrayed in a novel, on a television show, or in a movie. What percentages could you use to describe the couple's relationship?

7. Think about an influential couple you knew while growing up—perhaps your parents, grandparents, or close family friends. What percentages would you assign to their love? Would you want a relationship like theirs? If so, why? If not, how would you want it to be different?

11.3 Coffee Shop Observations

Next time you are in the student union, coffee shop, cafeteria, or any place where people sit at a table together, observe some of the nonverbal communication and answer these questions:

1. What body language do people use to convey they are "in love" with the other person?

2. What body mannerisms suggest to you that two people are not romantically interested in each other, even though they are talking?

Activity continued on the back

3. Looking at still another conversation, what can be deduced about the relationship being experienced by the two people at that table, and why?

11.4 Is Love Insane?

George Bernard Shaw is quoted as saying love is "the most violent, most insane, most delusive, and most transient of emotions."

1.   What arguments or examples from experience, could you use to **support** his characterization of love?

2.   What rebuttals could be used to refute his contentions?

Activity continued on the back

3. Based on your arguments (above), what reasons can you provide to argue that lifetime marriage should be based on love?

4. What reasons can you provide to argue that lifetime marriage should not be based on love?

12

Relationships and Communication: Getting From Here to There

Chapter Outline

Chapter Overview

Scientific Views of Stages in the Development of a Relationship. According to social-exchange theory, stages of development involve social exchanges, which balance the rewards and costs of maintaining the relationship.

Levinger's Stages in the Development of a Relationship. According to Levinger, relationships undergo a five-stage developmental sequence: attraction, building, continuation, deterioration, and ending. Relationships need not advance beyond any one of these stages.

Steps People Can Take to Build a Relationship. People can use opening lines, small talk, and self-disclosure to build relationships. Small talk is a broad exploration for common ground that permits us to decide whether we wish to advance the relationship beyond surface contact. Self-disclosure is the revelation of personal information. Self-disclosure invites reciprocity and can foster intimacy. However, premature self-disclosure suggests maladjustment and tends to repel people.

Factors that Contribute to the Continuation or Deterioration of a Relationship. Factors that contribute to the continuation of a relationship include enhancing variety (to fight boredom), trust, caring, commitment, evidence of continuing positive evaluation (e.g., Valentine's Day cards), absence of jealousy, perceived equity (e.g., a fair distribution of homemaking, child-rearing, and breadwinning chores), and mutual overall satisfaction.

The Role of Marriage Today. Today's marriages still provide a home life and an institution for rearing children and transmitting wealth. However, they are usually based on attraction and feelings of love, and they provide for emotional and psychological intimacy and security.

Factors that Contribute to Marital Satisfaction. These include good affective communication, problem-solving communication, sexual satisfaction, and agreement about finances and child-rearing. A marriage contract may help clarify a couple's values and goals. For example, it indicates whether the wife will take the husband's surname, who will be responsible for what chores, type of contraception to be used, methods of child-rearing, and how leisure activities will be decided on. By and large, married people seem to be happier with their lives than single people are.

Extramarital Affairs. Extramarital sex is viewed negatively by the great majority of people in the United States. Although people have become more permissive about premarital sex, they generally remain opposed to extramarital sex. The discovery of infidelity can evoke anger, jealousy, even shame. Affairs often, but not always, damage marriages.

Intimate Partner Violence. About one woman in eight is victimized by intimate partner violence each year. Women and men are equally likely to engage in intimate partner violence, but women are more likely to sustain serious injuries. Intimate partner violence is frequently connected with threats to men's dominance in relationships.

Divorce. About one-half of all marriages in the United States end in divorce. Reasons include relaxed restrictions on divorce, greater financial independence of women, and—ironically—continued positive expectations for marriage, particularly the belief that marriage should meet people's needs and be happy. Divorce typically lowers the standard of living for all parties involved. It is associated with an increased likelihood of suicide in men. Divorce can lead to family disorganization, making it more difficult to rear children.

Being Single. Many people are remaining single today by choice, and many are delaying marriage to pursue educational and vocational goals. Some people remain single because they have not found the right marital partner. Others prefer sexual variety and wish to avoid making a commitment.

Cohabitation. Cohabitation is living together without being married. The incidence of cohabitation has risen to the point where nearly half the population has cohabited at one time or another. For some, cohabitation is an alternative to marriage that confers many of the benefits of marriage without the depth of commitment. For others, cohabitation has, in effect, become a stage in courtship. People who cohabit before marriage may be more likely to get divorced. However, we shouldn't assume that cohabitation prior to marriage is a cause of later divorce.

Learning Objectives

After studying this chapter your students should be able to:

1. Explain what an intimate relationship is, and briefly describe Levinger's five stages in the development of a relationship.

2. Identify and discuss the positive and negative factors that affect each of Levinger's five stages in the development of a relationship.

3. Explain how cyber-dating is changing the dating scene, and identify at least five guidelines for safer cyberdating.

4. Discuss the importance of small-talk and self-disclosure in a developing relationship.

5. Discuss the roles of caring, trust mutuality, and commitment in a developing relationship.

6. Discuss jealousy, in terms of its causes, effects, and gender differences in reasons for jealousy.

7. Identify and briefly explain the steps people can take to improve their date-seeking skills at the easy practice level, medium practice level, and target behavior level.

8. Explain the factors involved in the deterioration and ending of relationships. Discuss whether this is inevitable, and what can be done to prevent it from happening.

9. Explain why people get married, describe who they marry, and discuss the factors that affect marital satisfaction.

10. Explain what emotional intelligence is, identifying its five main features, and discuss why it is important to relationships.

11. Discuss who has affairs, how many people have them, why they have them, how they affect the primary relationship, and how Americans feel about whether affairs are right or wrong.

12. Discuss how widespread intimate partner violence is, who engages in it, and what motivates it.

13. Discuss the reasons for changes in the divorce rate in recent years and explain the costs and effects of divorce on all of those involved.

14. Summarize research findings on adjustment in stepparent families. How common are stepparent families and why is it important to understand them?

15. Identify and briefly describe at least 5 guidelines for single parents who are about to begin dating again.

16. Describe the singles scene, explaining why more people have chosen to remain single in recent years, and the problems encountered by single people today.

17. Discuss cohabitation in terms of the reasons for and types of cohabitation, and why it has increased in recent years. Also discuss the risks for divorce among those who cohabit prior to marriage and those who do not.

18. Describe the various methods of coping with marital conflict described in your text.

19. Explain the various methods presented in your text for improving your communications and listening skills, as a means for resolving marital conflict.

20. Explain the methods presented in your text for learning about your partner's needs when trying to improve marital communication.

21. Describe the methods presented in your text for making requests when trying to improve marital communication.

22. Describe the methods presented in your text for delivering and receiving criticism when trying to improve marital communication.

23. Explain the methods presented in your text for coping with impasses when trying to improve marital communications.

Key Terms

intimate relationships	self-disclosure	marriage contract
social-exchange theory	mutual cyclical growth	emotional intelligence
ABCDE model	mutuality	divorce mediation
needs for affiliation	jealousy	cohabitation
surface contact	speed dating	part-time/limited cohabitation
small talk	equity	premarital cohabitation
confederates	homogamy	substitute marriage

Key Terms Review

Define each of the following terms:

1. Intimate Relationships: _____

_____

2. Social-Exchange Theory: _____

_____

3. ABCDE Model: _____

_____

4. Needs for Affiliation: _____

_____

5. Surface Contact: _____

_____

6. Small Talk: _____

_____

7. Confederates: _____

_____

8. Self-Disclosure: _____

_____

9. Mutual Cyclical Growth: _____

_____

10. Mutuality: _____

_____

11. Jealousy: _____

_____

12. Speed Dating: _____

_____

13. Equity: _____

_____

14. Homogamy: _____

_____

15. Marriage Contract: _____

_____

16. Emotional Intelligence: _____

_____

17. Divorce Mediation: _____

_____

18. Cohabitation: _____

_____

19. Premarital Cohabitation: _____

_____

20. Substitute Marriage: _____

_____

Chapter Review

1. Like individuals, relationships undergo different stages of _____.

2. According to the ABCDE model, the five stages through which relationships develop are:

   a. _____

   b. _____

   c. _____

   d. _____

   e. _____

3. The positive factors during the attraction stage of a relationship are _____, _____ emotions, and need for _____. The negative factors are physical _____, _____ emotions, and low need for _____.

4. Married people are most likely to have met their spouses through _____ _____, or by _____ _____.

5. The positive factors during the building stage of a relationship are matching _____ attractiveness, _____ similarity, and _____ _____ evaluations. The negative factors in this stage are nonequivalent _____ attractiveness, _____ dissimilarity, and mutual _____ evaluations.

6. _____ has become the hot new place for finding sweethearts.

7. Four steps in building a relationship are:

    a. _____

    b. _____

    c. _____

    d. _____

8. Men tend to be _____ willing than women to disclose their feelings, and gender differences in self-disclosure tend to be _____.

9. Psychologists have found that we can enhance social skills, such as date-seeking skills, through _____ _____.

10. Once a relationship is built, it enters the stage of _____.

11. When there is _____ in a relationship, partners feel secure that disclosing intimate feelings will not lead to ridicule, rejection, or other kinds of harm.

12. _____ is an emotional bond that allows intimacy to develop.

13. When two independent people come to see themselves as a "we" (as a couple), they have achieved _____.

14. Truly intimate relationships are marked by _____ or resolve to maintain the relationship through thick and thin.

15. Factors in the continuation stage that can throw the relationship into a downward spiral are lack of _____, _____, displaying evidence of negative _____, perceiving _____ in the relationship, and feelings of _____.

16. Feelings of _____ are often related to jealousy, as is low _____-_____ and a lack of self-_____.

17. Males get most upset about _____ infidelity, whereas females get most upset about _____ infidelity.

18. _____ involves feelings that one is getting as much from a relationship as one is giving to the relationship.

19. Deterioration is a stage in relationships that is neither _____ nor _____.

20. Two active responses to a deteriorating relationship are:

    a. _____

    b. _____

21. Passive responses to a deteriorating relationship are essentially characterized by _____ or _____ _____.

22. Relationships are likely to come to an end when:

    a. _____

    b. _____

    c. _____

23. Problems in _____ and _____ are among the most common reasons for ending a relationship.

24.   _____ is our most common lifestyle.

25.   In general, people want to get married because _____

_____.

26.   The concept of like marrying like is called _____.

27.   By and large, we tend to be attracted to and to get married to _____

_____

28.   Marriage contracts encourage couples to spell out their _____ and _____.

29.   Five items that should be included in a marriage contract are:

a. _____

b. _____

c. _____

d. _____

e. _____

30.   Studies show that _____ ability is a prime factor in satisfying relationships.

31.   Snyder found four factors that constantly predicted marital satisfaction. They are:

a. _____

b. _____

c. _____

d. _____

32.   Five main features of emotional intelligence are:

a. _____

b. _____

c. _____

d. _____

e. _____

33. Men are about _____ as likely as women to admit to affairs, and a _____ of married people admit to having affairs.

34. In explaining why they have affairs, _____ and desire for _____ _____ are cited as more common reasons than marital dissatisfaction.

35. Usually, men are seeking _____ in affairs, and women are seeking _____ _____.

36. Most married couples embrace the value of _____ as the cornerstone of their marital relationship.

37. Worldwide, one of _____ women have been beaten or sexually or emotionally abused by their partners.

38. Male domestic violence stems from factors that threaten their traditional _____ in relationships, such as _____ and _____ abuse. Women's violence often arises from the stress of coping with an _____ partner.

39. Domestic violence is reported most frequently among people of _____ socioeconomic status.

40. Male batterers often have low _____-_____ and a sense of personal _____.

41. Feminist theorists look upon domestic violence as a product of the _____ relationships that exist between men and women in our society.

42. In 1920, about one marriage in _____ ended in divorce. By 1960, this figure had risen to one in _____. Today about one in _____ marriages end in divorce.

43. Until the mid-1960s, _____ was the only legal grounds for divorce in New York State.

44. The most common reasons given for a divorce today are problems in _____ and

a lack of _____ .

45. Adjustment to divorce can be _____ difficult than adjustment to the death of a spouse.

46. People who are _____ and _____ have the highest rates of adjustment and psychological problems in the population.

47. The hardest aspect of divorce may be _____

_____

48. Children of divorced people are more likely to have _____ problems, engage in

_____ abuse, and earn _____ grades in school.

49. Researchers have found that living in stepfamilies as opposed to nuclear families may

have _____ psychological impact.

50. _____ divorced people remarry and remarriages are _____ than first marriages to end in divorce.

51. _____ is the most common lifestyle among people in their early to mid-twenties.

52. Three factors contributing to the rise in the number of single people are:

a. _____

b. _____

c. _____

53. _____ was once referred to as "living in sin" but today is more likely to be

termed _____ _____ .

54. More than half of all marriages today are preceded by a period of _____ .

55. Three styles of cohabitation are:

    a. _____

    b. _____

    c. _____

56. Cohabiting couples who eventually marry are _____ likely to get divorced than those who do not cohabit prior to marriage.

57. Cohabiters hold more _____ traditional views of marriage, are _____

    likely to say that religion is important to them, and are _____ committed to the

    values and interests traditionally associated with marriage.

58. Five methods of coping with marital conflict are:

    a. _____

    b. _____

    c. _____

    d. _____

    e. _____

59. Two ways to get started in improving communications are to:

    a. _____

    b. _____

60. Four methods of improving listening skills for more effective communication with your partner are:

    a. _____

    b. _____

    c. _____

    d. _____

61. Three methods for learning about your partner's needs are:

    a. _____

    b. _____

    c. _____

62. Three steps in making requests effectively are:

    a. _____

    b. _____

    c. _____

63. Six steps in delivering effective criticism are:

    a. _____

    b. _____

    c. _____

    d. _____

    e. _____

    f. _____

64. Five steps in receiving criticism effectively are:

    a. _____

    b. _____

    c. _____

    d. _____

    e. _____

65. Five techniques to help cope with communications impasses are:

a. _____

b. _____

c. _____

d. _____

e. _____

Sample Test

Multiple-Choice Questions

1. Most often, we meet potential romantic partners _____.
   a. by accident
   b. through computer match-ups
   c. on blind dates
   d. through dating services

2. An important prelude to a greeting or opening line is often _____.
   a. small talk
   b. eye contact
   c. physical intimacy
   d. a pheromone

3. Researchers have found that men are _____ than women to disclose their feelings.
   a. much less willing
   b. slightly less willing
   c. slightly more willing
   d. much more willing

4. John and Mary have reached the stage in their relationship where they think of themselves as a "couple" rather than as two separate individuals who happen to go out with each other. They are in the _____ stage of their relationship.
   a. self-disclosure
   b. surface contact
   c. mutuality
   d. romantic love

5. In Levinger's model, the final stage in the development of a relationship is _____.
   a. mutuality
   b. continuation
   c. ending
   d. deterioration

6. Which of the following is **NOT** true of marriage?
   a. It permits the orderly transmission of wealth from one generation to the other.
   b. It provides an institution for the financial support and socialization of children.
   c. It legitimizes women's equality and their rights.
   d. It regulates and legitimizes sexual relations.

7. Which of the following is **NOT** true of people we tend to marry?
   a. They seem to have opposite interests that complement ours.
   b. They seem likely to meet our psychological needs.
   c. They seem likely to meet our emotional and sexual needs.
   d. They are usually similar to us in physical attractiveness.

8. On average, husbands are about _____ years older than wives
    a. 0 to 1   c. 6-10
    b. 2 to 5   d. 11 to 15

9. The informal marriage contracts described in your text are _____.
    a. legally binding
    b. restrictive and often cause more problems than they solve
    c. likely to raise unrealistic expectations about the future marital relationship
    d. not legally binding

10. Patterns of _____ among couples planning a marriage predict marital satisfaction more than five years after the wedding vows are taken.
    a. sexual behavior   c. child-rearing
    b. career choice and development   d. communication

11. Research indicates that _____.
    a. both men and women tend to separate sex from love
    b. men tend to separate sex from love, but women tend to believe that sex and love go together
    c. women tend to separate sex from love, but men tend to believe that sex and love go together
    d. both men and women tend to believe that sex and love go together

12. In regards to a marital partner having an affair, _____ see the affair as an unforgivable blow to their ego.
    a. neither men nor women
    b. men are more likely than women to
    c. women are more likely than men to
    d. both men and women

13. Each of the following is true of domestic violence **EXCEPT** _____.
    a. women are far less likely than men to be violent
    b. it is found at all levels of society
    c. it often follows a triggering event such as criticism or rejection by one's partner
    d. male batterers are often overly dependent on their partners for emotional support

14. Each of the following is listed by your text as a factor contributing to today's high divorce rate **EXCEPT** _____.
    a. increased economic independence of women
    b. changes in people's expectations and attitudes
    c. the collapse of traditional morality
    d. relaxation of legal restrictions on divorce

15. The approach to divorce in which couples are guided through the proceedings in a cooperative spirit rather than as adversaries is called _____.
    a. the Reno divorce   c. divorce mediation
    b. dissolution   d. divorce resettlement

16. According to your text, the "singles scene" _____.
    a. does not exist, because singles are highly varied in intention and the style of daily life
    b. consists of singles bars and a string of short-term, sexually based relationships
    c. is limited to those people not yet mature enough to handle the responsibilities of marriage and family
    d. is basically for those people who cannot find a suitable partner for marriage

17. Each of the following is a style of cohabitation discussed by your text **EXCEPT** _____.
    a. part-time/limited cohabitation   c. premarital cohabitation
    b. alternative cohabitation   d. substitute marriage

18. John and Mary have been having conflicts in their relationship for some time. They each agree to change their behavior in return for the other making an equivalent change in behavior. This conflict-resolution technique is called _____.
    a. negotiating differences
    b. exchange contracting
    c. increasing pleasurable marital interactions
    d. complementarity

19. Which of the following is **NOT** one of the ways discussed in your text for learning about your partner's needs while improving marital communication?
    a. ask questions to draw your partner out
    b. use self-disclosure
    c. engage in passive listening techniques
    d. give your partner permission to say something that might be upsetting to you

20. Jim engages in small talk and exchanges "name, rank, and serial number." This is most likely to occur during the _____ level.
    a. initial attraction
    b. target behavior
    c. medium practice
    d. easy practice

True-False Questions

21. Rapid self-disclosure of intimate information is the best way to deepen a new relationship.

22. Jealousy is not always destructive to a relationship.

23. Women are more likely to be raped, injured, or killed by their current or former partners than by other types of assailants.

24. Adjustment to divorce can be more difficult than adjustment to the death of a spouse.

25. Disagreement is destructive to a marriage.

Essay Question

26. Describe the methods presented in your text for making requests when trying to improve marital communication.

Student Activities

Name _____ **Date** _____

12.1 Opening Lines

When we spy someone who is appealing and apparently available, most of us would like to know what to say, and we might rehearse a line or two to break the ice. What do you think is appropriate, and what do you think is shallow and a turn-off? Test your thoughts on this by writing examples of "good," "mediocre," and "shallow" opening lines in the space below. Then tell a friend what you are up to and ask him or her to evaluate the examples you have written.

Follow-Up Questions:

1. How well did you do? Was your friend able to tell correctly what your intentions were? If not, what went wrong? What could you do to fix the problem?

Activity continued on the back

2. Generally, what goals do you recommend people try to achieve with their opening remarks to someone they find attractive?

3. What do people of the opposite sex report are appropriate for opening lines? Ask your classmates or friends for ideas. If you cannot ask others, try to imagine what they would say. Write down what you can and ask your instructor to provide some feedback or class discussion.

12.2 It May Be in How We Say It

While the suave lines we invent to initiate relationships are important, the nonverbal cues we give may be even more significant. Try to imagine you are a screenwriter working on a movie. You are writing a line for the heroine or hero, whomever you identify with, who is approaching the other star for the first time, and simply says: "Good evening," or alternatively "Hi, my name is _____." Now write the stage direction, referring to vocal tone, eye contact, bodily postures, and movement.

1. First, write this for yourself.

2. Second, write this for someone who is very shy. How is this different from what you wrote for yourself? Is it better or worse? Why?

3. Finally, write this for your favorite actor or actress. Is this different from either or both of the first two you wrote? If so, how? Is it better or worse? Why?

Activity continued on the back

4. Describe how the president says this before a televised talk. How is it different from any of the others you wrote above? Is it better or worse? Why?

Follow-Up Questions:

1. What did you rely on most for creating different nonverbal communication in this exercise?

2. What would you most like to change about your own nonverbal communication and how can you change it?

12.3 It May Be When We Say It

After initial attraction, we are still "on approval," meaning we still want to keep Mr. or Ms. "Right" favorably impressed with us. In our first and early testing opportunities, we can, and likely must, disclose information to each other. Rathus and Nevid point out how we must consider what is safe to disclose and what could be self-damaging and prematurely revealing. Consider the research project discussed in Chapter 12 where researchers had their confederates reveal intimate information early in a ten-minute conversation, or late in the conversation, and as a consequence either come across as immature and phony if they revealed too early, or more attractive when revealing the same information toward the end of the ten minutes.

Write down three items of disclosure you think the researchers could have used in their study to create the effects they found.

1.

2.

3.

Activity continued on the back

You will need some feedback on how well you did, so share your three ideas with your confidant, your class, or your instructor. Be prepared for some criticism because these are judgment calls. Others may have a less than adequate idea of the context you have imagined. Let's hear them out because we are at least being sensitized to some of the relevant points the text is trying to make. How did you do? What could you do differently next time to do it better?

Name _____ **Date** _____

12.4 A Tall Job

A tall job is what Nevid and Rathus call the preparation of a marriage contract, even an informal one. But to avoid ending up like Donald Trump, let us do it anyway. Consider each of the eleven issues discussed in the questions below, and decide how each would be resolved for you.

1. What name will the wife use after marriage?

2. How will chores be allocated?

3. Will there be children, and if so, how many and when?

4. Will there be contraception, and if so, what kind?

5. How will child care be distributed?

Activity continued on the back

6. Whose career will determine where you live? Why?

7. Who will work and who will make financial decisions?

8. Which relatives will be visited and how often?

9. What leisure activities will be shared and unshared?

10. How will sexual issues be decided, and what will the decisions be?

11. How can changes in this contract be accommodated?

12. Do you agree with some experts who believe marriages should be free of such contractual specifications? Why?

13. What things might you add to this list? Why?

13

Sexual Behavior

Chapter Outline

Chapter Overview

Female Sexual Organs. The vulva, or external female sexual organs, include the mons veneris, clitoris, major and minor lips, and vaginal opening. The woman's internal sexual organs consist of the vagina, cervix, fallopian tubes, and ovaries. The cervix is the opening that connects the upper vagina to the uterus. Fallopian tubes connect the uterus with the abdominal cavity. Ovaries lie in the abdomen and produce ova and the sex hormones estrogen and progesterone. When an ovum is released, it travels through a fallopian tube, where fertilization in most likely to occur.

Male Sexual Organs. The major male sex organs include the penis, testes (or testicles), scrotum, and the series of ducts, canals, and glands that store and transport sperm and produce semen (the fluid that transports and nourishes sperm).

Hormones and the Menstrual Cycle. Levels of estrogen and progesterone vary and regulate the menstrual cycle. Following menstruation, estrogen levels increase, causing an ovum to ripen and the uterine lining to thicken. An ovum is released (ovulation occurs) when estrogens reach peak blood levels. In response to secretion of progesterone, the inner lining of the uterus thickens, gaining the capacity to support an embryo. If the ovum is not fertilized, estrogen and progesterone levels drop suddenly, triggering menstruation.

Hormones and Sexual Behavior. As a directional or organizing effect, sex hormones predispose animals toward masculine or feminine mating patterns. The activating effects of sex hormones influence the sex drive and facilitate sexual response. The sex drive and sexual response of both males and females is facilitated by testosterone.

Why Do Sexual Practices and Customs Vary so Widely Around the World? Sexual practices and customs vary largely because of differences in cultural attitudes and values toward sex.

Factors in Selecting a Method of Contraception. Considerations in the selection of a method of contraception include its convenience, its moral acceptability, its cost, the extent to which it enables partners to share the responsibility for contraception, its safety, its reversibility, whether it affords protection against sexually transmitted diseases (STDs), and its effectiveness.

The Sexual Response Cycle. The sexual response cycle describes the body's response to sexual stimulation and consists of four phases: excitement, plateau, orgasm, and resolution. The sexual response cycle is characterized by vasocongestion and myotonia. Excitement is characterized by erection in the male and lubrication in the female. Orgasm is characterized by muscle contractions and release of sexual tension. Following orgasm, males enter a refractory period during which they are temporarily unresponsive to sexual stimulation.

Rape. Rape apparently has more to do with power and aggressiveness than with sex per se. Social critics argue that men are socialized into sexual aggression by being generally reinforced for aggressiveness and competitiveness. Social and cognitive factors, such as viewing sex in adversarial terms and adopting rape myths that tend to blame the victim, also contribute to a climate that encourages rape. These include beliefs that women who dress provocatively deserve or are at least partially responsible for rape and that women who say "no" really mean "yes."

Preventing Rape. From a cultural perspective, prevention of rape involves publicly examining and challenging widely held cultural attitudes and ideals that contribute to rape. We can specifically encourage our colleges and universities to require students to attend lectures and seminars on rape. In terms of a woman's personal life, she can take precautionary measures to reduce the risk of rape, such as avoiding deserted areas, dating in groups, and being assertive in expressing her sexual limits. but let us not forget that the act of rape is a crime of violence and is always the fault of the rapist.

Sexual Dysfunctions. Sexual dysfunctions are persistent or recurrent problems in becoming sexually aroused or reaching orgasm. They include hypoactive sexual desire disorder (lack of interest in sex), female sexual arousal disorder and male erectile disorder (characterized by inadequate vasocongestion), orgasmic disorder, and premature ejaculation. Sexual dysfunctions may be caused by physical health problems, negative attitudes toward sex, lack of sexual knowledge and skills, problems in the relationship, and performance anxiety. Sexual dysfunctions are treated by sex therapy, which focuses on reducing performance anxiety, changing self-defeating attitudes and expectations, teaching sexual skills, enhancing sexual knowledge, and improving sexual communication. There are also some biological treatments, such as drugs that enhance vasocongestion.

Learning Objectives

After studying this chapter you should be able to:

1. Discuss the reasons why sexual practices vary so much from culture to culture and describe some of the differences that exist in these cultures.

2. Describe the male and female sex organs and explain the functions of the various components of these organs.

3. Explain what a clitoridectomy is, why it is performed, the dangers associated with it, and where it is most commonly performed.

4. Identify the hormones involved in human sexual response and explain what role they play in human sexual arousal and behavior.

5. Summarize current research on the varieties of sexual expression and the importance of values in sexual expression.

6. Compare and contrast at least five major methods of contraception in terms of their effectiveness, how they prevent pregnancy, their reliability, and reversibility.

7. Summarize the research on cybersex addiction, and discuss the warning signs of cybersex addiction.

8. Identify the four stages of the sexual response cycle and briefly explain what happens during each stage of the cycle.

9. Explain what pheromones are and discuss their role in sexual arousal in animals and in humans.

10. Describe the prevalence of rape in the United States, discuss the reasons for this prevalence, and identify at least three myths about rape.

11. Explain the possible strategies for reducing the risk of being raped by a stranger.

12. Explain the possible strategies for reducing the risk of date rape.

13. Identify the various sexual dysfunctions and briefly explain the causes for each of them as well as for sexual dysfunctions in general.

14. Briefly explain what sex therapy is and what its goals are.

15. Explain what STDs are and identify the various causes of five of the most prevalent STDs. Also, briefly discuss which STDs can and cannot be treated or cured.

16. Identify and briefly explain various measures you can take to protect yourself from AIDS and other STDs.

Key Terms

vulva
pudendum
urethral
mons veneris
clitoris
glans
major lips
minor lips
vagina
cervix
uterus
fallopian tubes
ovaries
ovum
clitoridectomy
circumcision
infibulation
penis

testes
scrotum
sperm
semen
testosterone
prostate
estrogen
progesterone
menstruation
endometrium
ovulation
organizing effects
activating effects
estrus
menopause
contraception
sexual response cycle
vasocongestion

myotonia
excitement phase
cybersex addiction
plateau phase
orgasmic phase
resolution phase
refractory period
pheromones
rape
sexual dysfunctions
hypoactive sexual desire disorder
female sexual arousal disorder
male erectile disorder
orgasmic disorder
premature ejaculation
performance anxiety
sex therapy

Key Terms Review (Due to the number and complexity of the terms in this chapter, there are two review sections. The first deals with sexual anatomy. The second deals with the sexual response cycle and sexual disorders.)

Key Terms Review #1

Define each of the following terms:

1. Vulva: _____

_____

2. Pudendum: _____

_____

3. Urethra: _____

_____

4. Mons Veneris: _____

_____

5. Clitoris: _____

   _____

6. Glans: _____

   _____

7. Major Lips: _____

   _____

8. Minor Lips: _____

   _____

9. Cervix: _____

   _____

10. Fallopian Tubes: _____

    _____

11. Clitoridectomy: _____

    _____

12. Testes: _____

    _____

13. Scrotum: _____

    _____

14. Prostate: _____

    _____

15. Estrogen: _____

    _____

16. Progesterone: _____

_____

17. Menstruation: _____

_____

18. Endometrium: _____

_____

19. Ovulation: _____

_____

20. Estrus: _____

_____

Key Terms Review # 2

Define each of the following terms:

1. Sexual Response Cycle: _____

_____

2. Vasocongestion: _____

_____

3. Myotonia: _____

_____

4. Excitement Phase: _____

_____

5. Plateau Phase: _____

_____

6. Orgasmic Phase: _____

_____

7. Resolution Phase: _____

_____

8. Refractory Period: _____

_____

9. Pheromones: _____

_____

10. Rape: _____

_____

11. Sexual Dysfunctions: _____

_____

12. Hypoactive Sexual Desire Disorder: _____

_____

13. Female Sexual Arousal Disorder: _____

_____

14. Male Erectile Disorder: _____

_____

15. Orgasmic Disorder: _____

_____

16. Premature Ejaculation: _____

_____

17. Performance Anxiety: _____

_____

18. Sex Therapy: _____

_____

Chapter Review

1. The residents of Inis Beag don't believe that women experience _____, and

    men believe that sex saps their _____.

2. From an early age, Mangaian children are encouraged to get in touch with their

    sexuality through _____.

3. Nearly every society has an _____ taboo.

4. Kissing is nearly universal in the United States but is unpopular in _____ and

    is _____ in some cultures.

5. Among the Aleut people of Alaska, it is considered good manners for a man to offer

    his _____ to a houseguest.

6. While the United States has romanticized Valentine's Day, Japan has eroticized

    _____ eve.

7. Perhaps no other natural function has been influenced so strongly by religious and

    moral beliefs, cultural tradition, folklore, and superstition, as _____ has been.

8. **Matching:** Match the term on the left with its appropriate description on the right.

_____ a. Vulva

_____ b. Mons veneris

_____ c. Clitoris

_____ d. Glans

_____ e. Major lips

_____ f. Minor lips

_____ g. Cervix

_____ h. Urethra

_____ i. Vagina

_____ j. Ovaries

_____ k. Fallopian tube

1. the tubelike organ that contains the penis during sexual intercourse

2. a tube that conducts urine from the body

3. the female external genital organs

4. the folds of the skin that enclose the urethral and vaginal openings

5. the lower part of the uterus that opens into the vagina

6. the tip or head

7. the female sex organ whose only known function is the transmission and reception of sensations of sexual pleasure

8. the large folds of skin that run along the sides of the vulva

9. the pad of fatty tissue that covers the joint of the pubic bones and cushions the female during intercourse

10. the female sexual organs that produce ova and the hormones estrogen and progesterone

11. the tubelike organ that connects the ovaries to the uterus

9. Conception normally takes place in the _____ _____, but the embryo becomes implanted and grows in the _____.

10. Cultures in some parts of Africa and the Middle East mutilate or remove a woman's _____, to ensure female _____..

11. The Greeks held their _____ when offering testimony.

12. The _____ produce sperm and the male sex hormone _____.

13. The _____ allows the testes to hang away from the body.

14. The male urethra transports _____ as well as _____.

15. _____ transports, activates, and nourishes sperm.

16. The penis consists mainly of _____ _____ tissue.

17. In the penis, engorgement with _____ produces an erection.

18. The ovaries produce _____ and _____.

19. _____ occurs each month in women when estrogen reaches peak blood levels,

20. _____ is triggered by sudden drops in estrogen and progesterone levels,

   whereas _____ occurs when estrogen levels peak.

21. Sex hormones have _____ and _____ effects on sexual behavior.

22. The hormones _____ and _____ regulate the menstrual cycle in females,

   while the hormone _____ affects sexual desire and drive in males and females.

23. While sex hormones affect sexual behavior, _____ factors also play a role.

24. Survey evidence indicates that oral sex has now become the _____, and

   anal intercourse has become _____ common.

25. Five issues one should consider when choosing a method of contraception are:

   a. _____

   b. _____

   c. _____

   d. _____

   e. _____

26. **Matching:** Match the birth control technique on the left with its appropriate description on the right.

_____ a. Birth control pills

_____ b. Rhythm methods

_____ c. IUDs

_____ d. Diaphragms

_____ e. Depo-Provera

_____ f. Male condom

_____ g. Vasectomy

_____ h. Coitus interruptus

_____ i. Tubal litigation

_____ j. Norplant

_____ k. Cervical cap

1. a barrier method that covers the cervix to prevent passage of sperm

2. tracking the ovulation cycle and avoiding intercourse for 3 days prior to ovulation and 2 days afterward

3. Long-acting, synthetic for of the female sex hormone progesterone that inhibits ovulation

4. surgical procedure in which the fallopian tubes that carry egg cells (ova) from the ovary to the uterus are severed and tied back

5. a device that is inserted and left in place in the uterus by a physician to prevent conception or implantation of a fertilized egg

6. female sex hormones delivered through match-stick-sized implants in the upper arm

7. removal of the penis from the vagina prior to ejaculation

8. female sex hormones that inhibit ovulation or interfere with implantation of a fertilized egg

9. surgical procedure in which the tube through which sperm is transported from the testes to the penis is severed, so that no sperm can be ejaculated

10. device made of rubber or plastic that is fitted over the cervix; works in a similar way as a diaphragm

11. a barrier device worn on the penis to prevent passage of sperm

27. About one-_____ of visits to the internet are directed toward sexually oriented sites.

28. As with other addictions, people can develop a tolerance to _____ stimulation.

29. The sexual response cycle is characterized by _____ and _____.

30. The four phases of the sexual response cycle are the _____ phase, the

_____ phase, the _____ phase, and the _____ phase.

323

31. Erection, vaginal lubrication, and orgasm are all _____.

32. Unlike women, men enter a _____ period after orgasm in which they cannot experience another _____ or _____.

33. Scientists believe that natural "love potions" exist in the form of chemical secretions known as _____, which are detected by humans through the _____ organ.

34. The great majority of rapes are committed by _____

_____.

35. Many rapists appear to be using rape as a means of expressing social _____ over, or _____ toward, women, rather than for sexual satisfaction.

36. Social scientists contend that our society socializes men into becoming _____ by reinforcing males for _____ and _____ behavior.

37. Four myths about rape are:

    a. _____

    b. _____

    c. _____

    d. _____

38. Rape myths contribute to a sexual climate that is _____ toward rapists and _____ toward rape victims.

39. The aftermath of rape can include physical _____, _____, _____, sexual _____, sexually transmitted _____, and/or _____.

40. Five things a woman can do to prevent rape by a stranger are:

    a. _____

    b. _____

c. _____

d. _____

e. _____

41. Five things a woman can do to avoid date rape are:

a. _____

b. _____

c. _____

d. _____

e. _____

42. **Matching:** Match the term on the left with its appropriate description on the right.

_____ a. Hypoactive sexual desire	1. lack of interest in sexual activity
_____ b. Female sexual arousal disorder	2. difficulty achieving orgasm despite adequate sexual arousal
_____ c. Male erectile disorder	3. difficulty becoming sexually aroused as defined by vaginal lubrication
_____ d. Orgasmic disorder	
_____ e. Premature ejaculation	4. ejaculation that occurs prior to the couple's desires
	5. difficulty in becoming aroused as defined by achieving erection

43. Obesity increases the risk of _____ disease, _____, and _____ dysfunction.

44. Sexual competencies are based largely on _____ and _____.

45. Sexual dysfunctions are usually treated with sex _____, that generally incorporates _____ and _____ components.

46. Sex therapy is largely indebted to the pioneering work of _____ and _____.

47. Sex therapy generally focuses on:

    a. _____

    b. _____

    c. _____

    d. _____

    e. _____

48. _____ cases of sexual dysfunctions can be treated successfully.

49. Sexually transmitted diseases (STDs) are _____ in our society, especially among _____ people.

50. Perhaps a total of _____ million Americans are infected with HIV, whereas _____ million cases of STDs among preteens and teens are reported in the United States each year.

51. AIDS is a fatal condition in which the person's _____ system is so weakened that he or she falls prey to _____ that would otherwise be eradicated.

52. HIV kills _____ cells.

53. HIV is transmitted by infected _____, _____, _____, and _____ secretions, and _____ _____.

54. The most effective way to deal with AIDS is _____.

55. **Matching:** Match the sexually transmitted disease on the left with its appropriate symptoms and cause on the right

_____ a. Gonorrhea

_____ b. Genital Herpes

_____ c. AIDS

_____ d. Candidiasis

_____ e. Chlamydia

_____ f. Genital Warts

_____ g. Bacterial Vaginosis

1. caused by a bacterium; symptoms in men include a yellowish thick penile discharge, burning urination. In women, increased vaginal discharge, burning urination, irregular menstrual bleeding

2. In women, thin foul-smelling vaginal discharge. Irritation of genitals and mild pain during urination. In men, inflammation of penile foreskin and glans, urethritis, and cystitis. May be assymptomatic in both genders

3. caused by a virus; reddish painful bumps around the genitals, thigh, or buttocks; in women, may also be in the vagina or on the cervix. Bumps become blisters or sores that fill with pus and break.

4. caused by a fungus; vaginal irritation and white cheesy foul-smelling discharge; vulval itching and soreness

5. caused by a bacterium; in men—itching and burning on urination, or a reddening of the penis. In women, frequent and painful urination, lower abdominal pain and inflammation, and vaginal discharge, but most women are symptom free

6. Appearance of painless warts, often resembling cauliflowers, on the penis, foreskin, scrotum, or internal urethra in men, and on the vulva, labia, vagina or cervix in women. May occur around the anus and in the rectum.

7. caused by a virus; destroys immune system by killing white blood cells; fatal; no cure

Sample Test

Multiple-Choice Questions

1. The men on Inis Beag believe that sex _____.
   a. saps your strength
   b. increases your virility
   c. should be an equally pleasurable experience for both men and women
   d. is primarily for recreation, not procreation

2. The woman's most sensitive sexual organ is the _____.
   a. vagina   c. scrotum
   b. mons veneris   d. clitoris

3. High in the vagina is a small opening called the _____, which links the vagina to the uterus.
   a. cervix   c. mons veneris
   b. clitoris   d. "G" spot

4. Most clitoridectomy victims are _____.
   a. Muslims   c. Ethiopian Jews
   b. Christians   d. animists

5. The male reproductive organ(s) that produce(s) sperm cells and male sex hormones _____.
   a. is the penis   c. is the scrotum
   b. are the testes   d. is the glans

6. The directional effects of sex hormones, which point development along masculine or feminine direction, are called _____ effects.
   a. organizing   c. peripheral
   b. subliminal   d. activating

7. Female mice, rats, cats, and dogs are receptive to the sexual advances of males only during _____.
   a. menstruation   c. estrus
   b. menarche   d. early summer

8. Of the following, the **LEAST** reliable method of birth control is _____.
   a. the pill   c. Norplant
   b. the IUD   d. coitus interruptus

9. Myotonia refers to _____.
   a. near-sightedness   c. muscle tension
   b. rapid, shallow breathing   d. flushing of the skin

10. About one rape in _____ is carried out by a complete stranger.
    a. two   c. four
    b. three   d. five

11. Which of the following is **NOT** true of rape?
    a. Our culture may socialize some men into becoming rapists.
    b. Our culture may socialize women into unjustly accusing men of rape as a means of getting revenge against those men.
    c. Social attitudes such as "some women want to get raped" tend to encourage leniency toward rapists.
    d. Many social attitudes blame the rape victim for a rape as much or more than they blame the rapist.

12. On the National Health and Social Life Survey, women were more likely than men to report each of the following sexual dysfunctions **EXCEPT** _____.
    a. painful sex   c. performance anxiety
    b. lack of interest in sex   d. lack of pleasure

13. Which of the following has **NOT** been shown to cause sexual dysfunction?
    a. physical factors, such as disease   c. too much sexual activity
    b. traditional sex-negative attitudes   d. lack of sexual skills

14.	_____ college students appear to be reasonably well-informed about AIDS.
	a.	Almost no
	c.	Most
	b.	A large minority of
	d.	Virtually all

15.	HPV is linked to the development of _____.
	a.	AIDS
	c.	breast cancer
	b.	SIDS
	d.	cervical cancer

16.	A few days after having sexual intercourse, Amy develops lower abdominal pain, a need to urinate frequently and urinating becomes quite painful. Her menstrual cycle becomes irregular, she develops a vaginal discharge and eventually, pelvic inflammatory disease. She appears to have contracted _____.
	a.	chlamydia
	c.	syphilis
	b.	AIDS
	d.	herpes

17.	Which of the following is **NOT** a way that the AIDS virus appears to be transmitted?
	a.	vaginal intercourse
	c.	breastfeeding
	b.	anal intercourse
	d.	close-mouthed kissing

18.	The part of the world hardest hit by the AIDS epidemic is _____.
	a.	North America
	c.	Southeast Asia
	b.	South and Central America
	d.	Sub-Saharan Africa

19.	Worldwide, the clear majority of people who are infected with HIV/AIDS, contracted it through _____.
	a.	homosexual activity
	c.	intravenous drug use
	b.	infected blood transfusions
	d.	heterosexual activity

20.	Pheromones are chemicals that are detected by the _____.
	a.	vomeronasal organ
	c.	basal ganglia
	b.	organ of Corti
	d.	caudate nucleus

True-False Questions

21.	Kissing is considered highly erotic by nearly every culture on Earth.	_____

22.	Testosterone stokes sexual desire in men but not women.	_____

23.	Women say no to sex when they really mean yes.	_____

24.	Everyone experiences sexual dysfunctions at one point or another.	_____

25.	There is no cure, nor vaccine, for AIDS.	_____

Essay Question

26.	Describe the prevalence of rape in the United States, discuss the reasons for this prevalence, and identify at least three myths about rape..

Student Activities

Name _____ **Date** _____

13.1 The Perfect Sex Questionnaire

In this chapter we learn how reliant we are on information from surveys and questionnaires to understand sexual behavior. We also learn that many questionnaires are open to some methodological flaws, or are dated, or just didn't ask the "right" people. There is only one way to find the "perfect sex questionnaire." You will have to write it. Try writing five relevant questions about sexual behavior that would answer questions that are important to you. They may reflect a concern, or an issue related to your interests.

1.

2.

3.

4.

5.

Your instructor may wish to follow up this exercise with class discussion.

13.2 Sex and Entertainment

The last movie or television show you saw that included sexual intimacy will serve as our target for this exercise. The answers may tell us much about the attitudes and behaviors being encouraged today.

1. Did the script suggest that safe sex was being practiced? If so, how?

2. What kind of relationship was the couple involved in? Was it a long-term relationship, such as a marriage or cohabitation, or a brief fling, or what?

3. What was the state of the relationship at the end of the movie? Was there an implication of any type of long-term commitment that would extend after the end of the movie? If so, what was it?

Activity continued on the back

4. Do you think there are different standards of sexual behavior for yourself, for others, or for entertainment? If so, what are those standards and how are they different from yours?

13.3 What Are Your State's Laws?

The laws governing sexual behavior differ from state to state. Occasionally we read about obviously outdated laws that are still on the books, but not enforced. Missouri once had a law forbidding a woman from refusing her husband's sexual advances.

What does your state say about the following sexual issues? Answer a) what you believe the law says, and then b) find a good source for the law to check yourself.

1. What is your state's age for statutory rape?

    a)

    b)

2. What constitutes being labeled a "sexual predator" in your state?

    a)

    b)

3. What is your state's age for legally being allowed to get married?

    a)

    b)

4. Does your state allow cohabitation or recognize common law marriage? If so, under what conditions?

    a)

    b)

Activity continued on the back

5. Does your state require a blood test for a marriage license, and if it does, is AIDS included in the screening? What other diseases are screened for, if any?

   a)

   b)

6. Does your state limit where sexual predators can live or work, if so where are they excluded from living or working, and how does your state track them?

   a)

   b)

6. Which of the laws are not enforceable? Why not?

7. Would you like to see any of these laws changed? Why?

13.4 Critical Thinking

Researchers have found evidence that rape victims tend to be less dominant and less self-assertive than nonvictims. The results suggested that women who appear to be vulnerable are more likely to be attacked. If we look critically at this research, we will see that it is a bit premature to conclude that women have been socialized into the role of victims who are "asking for it."

1.   What other explanations could account for research findings such as this?

2.   What kind of study could more successfully test the hypothesis that being less dominant and self-assertive could increase the risk of being a rape victim? Explain how you would design such a study.

13.5 Sexual Expectations

Historically, adolescents in this country have faced numerous stereotypic expectations regarding their sexual behavior. At one extreme, males were supposed to be ready, willing, and eager at every sexual opportunity no matter who the partner or what kind of commitment they have to someone else. Females were divided into "nice girls" who saved themselves until marriage, and "bad girls" who were sexually promiscuous. Males encouraged each other to have sex with the "bad girls," but them labeled them "sluts," and gave them "reputations" that were unappealing at best. The males on the other hand were labeled "studs" and looked up to by other males. Males would then marry the "nice girls," while the "bad girls" were left to mend their own reputations and fend for themselves.

1. How are these stereotypic expectations different today, if at all, from years past?

2. Who have they changed more for, men or women? Why do you believe this is so?

3. Do you see the changes as for the better or the worse? Why?

Activity continued on the back

4. Have you ever found yourself under pressure to behave sexually in a way you did not want to? What happened, how did you handle it, and how did it affect you afterwards?

5. What do you think can be done to lower the amount of sexual pressure on adolescents today?

14

Adolescent and Adult Development: Going Through Changes

Chapter Outline

Module 14.1: Adolescence

Module 14.2: Young and Middle Adulthood

Module 14.3: Late Adulthood

Module 14.4: Psychology in Daily Life: Live Longer and Healthier Lives

Chapter Overview

Physical Development in Adolescence. Adolescence is a period of life that begins at puberty and ends with assumption of adult responsibilities. Changes that lead to reproductive capacity and secondary sex characteristics are stimulated by increased levels of testosterone in the male and of estrogen and androgens in the female.

Cognitive Development in Adolescence. Formal operational thinking appears in adolescence, but not everyone reaches this stage. Two consequences of adolescent egocentrism are the imaginary audience and the personal fable. the imaginary audience refers to the adolescent beliefs that they are the center of attention and that other people are as concerned with their appearance and behavior as they are. The personal fable refers to the adolescent belief that one's feelings and ideas are special, even unique, and that one is invulnerable. Feelings of invulnerability can be connected with risky behavior.

Social and Personality Development in Adolescence. Adolescents and parents are often in conflict because adolescents desire more independence and may experiment with things that can jeopardize their health. Despite bickering, most adolescents continue to love and respect their parents. According to Erikson, adolescents strive to forge an ego identity—a sense of who they are and what they stand for. The changes of puberty prepare the body for sexual activity and reproduction, but many adolescents lack the maturity to make responsible decisions regarding their sexual activities.

Adulthood and Emerging Adulthood. Historically speaking, marriage has been a marker of adulthood. In American society today, making independent decisions, accepting responsibility for oneself, and financial independence are key markers. Emerging adulthood is a hypothesized period that exists in wealthy societies. It roughly spans the ages of 18-25 and affords young people extended periods of role exploration.

Physical Development in Young and Middle Adulthood. People are usually at the height of their physical powers during young adulthood. Menopause, the cessation of menstruation, is associated with a great many myths, including the belief that hormonal changes naturally lead women to become depressed and anxious during this period of life. Men undergo a more gradual decline of reproductive functioning.

Cognitive Development in Young and Middle Adulthood. People are usually at the height of their cognitive powers during early adulthood, but people can be creative for a lifetime. Memory functioning declines with age, but the decline is not usually as large as people assume. People tend to retain verbal ability, as shown by vocabulary and general knowledge, into advanced old age. Crystallized intelligence—one's vocabulary and accumulated knowledge—generally remains intact. Fluid intelligence—the ability to process information rapidly—declines more rapidly, but workers' familiarity with solving specific kinds of problems is often more important than declines in fluid intelligence.

Social and Personality Development in Young and Middle Adulthood. Young adulthood is generally characterized by efforts to become established and advance in the business world, and by the development of intimate ties. Many young adults reassess the directions of their lives during the "age-30 transition." Many theorists view middle adulthood as a time of crisis (the "midlife crisis") and further reassessment. Many adults try to come to terms with the discrepancies between their achievements and the dreams of youth during middle adulthood. Some middle-aged adults become depressed when their youngest child leaves home (the "empty-nest syndrome"), but many report increased satisfaction, stability, and self-confidence. Many people in middle adulthood experience "middlescence"—a phase during which they redefine themselves and their goals for the 30 to 40 healthy years they expect lie ahead.

Physical Development in Late Adulthood. Older people show less sensory acuity, and their reaction time lengthens. Changes in the elasticity of the skin lead to wrinkling and production of melanin declines, producing a graying of the hair, Our lung capacity , muscle mass, metabolic rate, and bone density decline. Our immune system weakens and our cardiovascular system becomes less efficient. Though we also encounter age-related changes in sexual functioning, people who maintain their general health can adjust to these changes and continue to enjoy sexual experience throughout their lifetimes.

Cognitive Development in Late Adulthood. Cognitive changes beginning in middle adulthood continue, which mostly affect memory and tasks requiring fluid intelligence. Crystallized intelligence remains relatively intact and people can continue to be creative throughout their lifetimes.

Alzheimer's Disease. Alzheimer's disease is a brain disease of unknown origin. It is not a consequence of normal aging. It is characterized by cognitive deterioration in memory, language, and problem-solving.

Gender and Ethnic Differences in Life Expectancy. Women outlive men by nearly seven years, and European and Asian Americans tend to outlive other ethnic groups in the United States. By and large, the groups who live longer are more likely to seek and make use of health care.

Personality and Social Development in Late Adulthood. Erikson characterizes late adulthood as the stage of ego integrity versus despair. He saw the basic challenge as a maintaining the belief that life is worthwhile in the face of physical deterioration. Despite common stereotypes, most older people life independently and are not living in poverty. Older adults rate their life satisfaction and health as generally good. Retirement can be a positive step, so long as it is voluntary. Having social support is a major contributor to emotional well-being among older people.

Death and Dying. Kubler-Ross has identified five stages of dying among people who are terminally ill: denial, anger, bargaining, depression, and final acceptance. However, other investigators find that psychological reactions to approaching death are more varied than Kubler-Ross suggests. Hospices support terminally ill patients and their families. Euthanasia is a controversial topic with varied legal status. Scholars have identified certain stages of bereavement that many people experience when they lose a loved one.

Learning Objectives

After studying this chapter your students should be able to:

1. Discuss the physical changes that take places during adolescence and the issues those changes present for adolescents and their parents.

2. Describe cognitive development in adolescence, and the effects on behavior that result from the cognitive style typical of adolescents.

3. Describe the characteristics of adolescent social, personality, and sexual development.

4. Explain what emerging adulthood is and why it is only found in industrialized societies.

5. Compare and contrast the physical changes that occur in young, middle, and late adulthood.

6. Describe what menopause and the climacteric are and discuss how they affect women in middle adulthood.

7. Explain whether or not there is a male equivalent of menopause and describe the physiological changes men experience during middle age.

8. Compare and contrast cognitive development in young, middle, and late adulthood.

9. Compare and contrast social and personality development in young, middle, and late adulthood.

10. Compare and contrast authoritarian, authoritative, and permissive styles of parenting in terms of how they differ from each other and how they affect children.

11. Identify the various causes of child abuse and discuss the effects of abuse and neglect on children who are abused or neglected.

12. Explain what the "midlife transition," "midlife crisis," "middlescence," and "empty nest syndrome" are and how they affect male and female behavior in middle adulthood.

13. Explain what empty-nest syndrome is and discuss what evidence there is to support or refute this concept.

343

14. Describe the physical and sexual functioning changes that occur in late adulthood.

15. Describe cognitive development in late adulthood and identify the factors that contribute to intellectual functioning across the lifespan.

16. Summarize the research on the prevalence, causes, and effects of Alzheimer's disease. What can be done to treat and cope with Alzheimer's disease?

17. Describe the effects of gender, ethnicity, and social class on aging, and explain why those differences exist.

18. Describe personality and social development in late adulthood, and explain how the living arrangements of most elderly people differ from the stereotypes about them.

19. Discuss the impact of retirement on older persons and present the reasons for the differences between happily retired persons and retired persons who deteriorate and are unhappy in their retirement.

20. Identify Elisabeth Kübler-Ross's stages of death and dying and discuss what evidence there is in support or rebuke to her theory.

21. Explain what hospices are and what their goals are. Also compare and contrast positive and negative euthanasia, and discuss if their is ever a situation where either type is justified.

22. Explain what successful aging is, and identify and briefly explain the three components of successful aging.

Key Terms

adolescence
growth spurt
puberty
secondary sex characteristics
menarche
formal-operations stage
egocentrism
imaginary audience
personal fable
sturm and drang
ego identity versus role diffusion
ego identity
role diffusion
emerging adulthood

young adulthood
menopause
climacteric
osteoporosis
andropause
crystallized intelligence
fluid intelligence
trying twenties
the dream
intimacy versus isolation
individuation
age 30 transition
catch 30s
instrumental competence

authoritative
authoritarian
permissive
generativity versus stagnation
midlife crisis
middlescence
empty nest syndrome
late adulthood
reaction time
Alzheimer's disease
ego integrity versus despair
euthanasia
hospice
bereavement

Key Terms Review

Define each of the following terms:

1. Puberty: _____

_____

2. Secondary Sex Characteristics: _____

_____

3. Menarche: _____

_____

4. Egocentrism: _____

_____

5. Personal Fable: _____

_____

6. Role Diffusion: _____

_____

7. Emerging Adulthood: _____

_____

8. Menopause: _____

_____

9. Climacteric: _____

_____

10. Osteoporosis: _____

_____

11. Crystallized Intelligence: _____

_____

12. Fluid Intelligence: _____

_____

13. Individuation: _____

_____

14. Authoritative: _____

_____

15. Mid-Life Crisis: _____

_____

16. Middlescence: _____

_____

17. Empty-Nest Syndrome: _____

_____

18. Alzheimer's Disease: _____

_____

19. Euthanasia: _____

_____

20. Bereavement: _____

_____

Chapter Review

1. _____ is a time of transition from childhood to adulthood.

2. One of the most noticeable physical developments of adolescence is a _____ spurt.

3. _____ is the period during which the body becomes sexually mature, and

   begins with the appearance of _____ _____ characteristics.

4. In girls, a critical body weight of about _____ pounds is thought to trigger hormonal secretions that stimulate the growth of breast tissue and supportive tissue in the hips and buttocks.

5. In girls, the beginning of menstruation, or _____, usually begins between the

   ages of _____.

6. According to psychologist Jean Piaget, children typically develop _____-

   _____ thinking during adolescence.

7. Formal operational thought involves the ability to _____, _____, and

   carry arguments to their _____ conclusions.

8. Adolescent egocentrism gives rise to two cognitive developments: the _____

   audience, and the personal _____.

9. Adolescents typically experience "storm and stress" in three areas:

   a. _____

   b. _____

   c. _____

10. Adolescents strive to become more _____ from their parents.

11. _____ is the period of life when people are most likely to engage in risky behaviors.

12. According to Erikson, the major "crisis" in adjustment faced by adolescents is that of

   _____

13. Western culture often sends adolescents _____ messages about sex.

14. Rates of sexual intercourse among American teens have been _____ in recent years.

15. James Marcia has identified four identity statuses. They are:

    a. _____

    b. _____

    c. _____

    d. _____

16. Most teenage girls who become pregnant do so because _____

    _____, or _____

17. Many young gay people do not come to fully accept their sexual orientation until

    _____.

18. The period of development spanning the ages of 18–25 that bridges adolescence and

    independence is known as _____ _____.

19. For many young adults today, the threshold of full-fledged adulthood has been moved

    up to age _____.

20. Most of us reach our physical and cognitive peaks during _____ _____.

21. The years between 40 and 60 are reasonably _____. There is _____

    physical decline, but it is _____.

22. _____ is the final stage of a broader female experience called the _____,

    in which _____ and reproductive capacity draw to an end.

23. Five myths about menopause are:

    a. _____

    b. _____

    c. _____

    d. _____

    e. _____

24. In men, testosterone production begins to decline at around age _____, resulting in reduced muscle _____, reduced _____ drive, and lack of _____.

25. People are at their height of cognitive development during _____ _____.

26. _____ intelligence represents one's lifetime intellectual achievements, and generally _____ as one ages, whereas _____ intelligence represents mental flexibility and tends to _____ as one ages.

27. People tend to grow psychologically _____ as they advance from adolescence through middle age.

28. Many young adults adopt what Levinson calls the _____—the drive to "become" someone, to leave their mark on history.

29. According to Erikson, young adulthood is the stage of _____ versus _____ and we are not capable of committing ourselves to others in a meaningful way until we have achieved _____ _____.

30. In young adulthood, men's development seems to be guided mainly by needs for _____ and _____, while for women the establishment and maintenance of _____ _____ is of primary importance.

31. For men and women, the late 20s and early 30s are commonly characterized by _____.

32. The later thirties are often characterized by _____ _____, or planting _____.

33. Havighurst's seven developmental tasks for young adulthood are:

a. _____

b. _____

c. _____

d. _____

e. _____

f. _____

g. _____

34. Five reasons **FOR** having children are:

a. _____

b. _____

c. _____

d. _____

e. _____

35. Five reasons for **NOT** having children are:

a. _____

b. _____

c. _____

d. _____

e. _____

36. According to Baumrind, parents can foster _____ _____, in children, so that they can manipulate their environments to achieve desired results.

37. **Matching:** Match the parenting style on the left with its appropriate description on the right.

     _____ a. Authoritative

     _____ b. Authoritarian

     _____ c. Permissive

1. high restrictiveness (use of force), moderate demands for mature behavior, low communications ability and low warmth and support

2. high restrictiveness (use of reasoning), high demands for mature behavior, high communications ability, and high warmth and support

3. Low (easygoing) restrictiveness, low demands for mature behavior, low communications ability, and low warmth and support

38. Children of _____ parents have greater self-esteem, self-reliance, social competence, and achievement motivation than other children do.

39. Children of _____ parents are often withdrawn or aggressive.

40. Children of _____ parents are less mature than other children.

41. Five methods of promoting competence in children are:

    a. _____

    b. _____

    c. _____

    d. _____

    e. _____

42. Child abuse arises in families in which parents turn to increasingly _____ means of controlling their children's behavior.

43. Seven factors contributing to child abuse include:

    a. _____

    b. _____

    c. _____

    d. _____

    e. _____

f. _____

g. _____

44. Abused children are at increased risk of developing _____ problems,

_____ problems, _____ behaviors, and failure to venture out and

_____ the world.

45. Being abused creates feelings of _____ that are then expressed against others, including one's children.

46. The typical sexual abuser of children is a _____, and ninety percent of

molesters are _____.

47. Five guidelines for dealing with suspected child sexual abuse are:

a. _____

b. _____

c. _____

d. _____

e. _____

48. Erikson labels the life crisis of the middle years as that of _____ versus

_____.

49. According to Levinson, there is a _____ _____ at about age 40 to 45, characterized by a shift in psychological perspective.

50. The midlife transition may trigger a crisis called the _____ _____.

51. According to Sheehy, women enter midlife at about age _____, whereas men

enter it at about age _____.

52. Sheehy has labeled the years from age 45 to 65 as the "age of _____."

53. Despite years of emphasis on the so-called _____ _____ syndrome, studies indicate that most middle-aged women show increased _____, self-_____, and _____ after the children have left home.

54. Hair becomes gray as people age because the body produces less _____.

55. Age-related changes in vision usually begin in the mid-_____, as the lenses of the eyes become more _____.

56. Between the ages of 20 and 70, lung capacity may decline by _____ percent.

57. As we age, reaction time _____ and metabolic rate _____.

58. Bones begin to lose density in early middle age, frequently leading to _____.

59. Older men and women may both experience less interest in sex, which is related to lower levels of _____.

60. In late adulthood, _____ and willingness of partners to _____ are crucial factors in sexual fulfillment.

61. _____, a cognitive skill, is not negatively impacted by age.

62. Five factors that contribute to intellectual functioning across the lifespan are:

    a. _____

    b. _____

    c. _____

    d. _____

    e. _____

63. By the middle of the twenty-first century, the prevalence of Alzheimer's disease is expected to _____.

64. At its most severe stage, people with Alzheimer's disease become essentially _____.

65. Women in the United States outlive men by _____ years, and their prospects for a happy and healthy old age are _____.

66. Members of ethnic minority groups are _____ likely to be poor, and tend to eat _____ nutritious diets, encounter _____ stress, and have _____ access to good quality health care.

67. According to Erikson, late adulthood is the stage of _____ _____ versus _____.

68. Peck's six psychological shifts that aid us in adjusting to aging are:

   a. _____

   b. _____

   c. _____

   d. _____

   e. _____

   f. _____

69. Havighurst's seven developmental tasks for late adulthood are:

   a. _____

   b. _____

   c. _____

   d. _____

   e. _____

   f. _____

   g. _____

70. Most old people who deteriorate rapidly after retirement were _____ prior to retirement.

71. Atchley's six phases of retirement are:

    a. _____

    b. _____

    c. _____

    d. _____

    e. _____

    f. _____

72. The majority of people in their 70s are _____ with their lives.

73. _____ is the last great taboo.

74. Kübler-Ross's five stages of death and dying are _____, _____,

    _____, _____, and _____.

75. _____ is also referred to as "mercy killing."

76. A _____ is a homelike environment in which the terminally ill can face death

    with dignity.

77. After the death of a loved one, usually the most intense grief is encountered

    _____ the funeral.

78. Three components of successful aging are:

    a. _____

    b. _____

    c. _____

79.	Four benefits of physical exercise are:

a. _____

b. _____

c. _____

d. _____

80.	Regular exercise helps boost _____ well-being, mental _____, and may

combat _____ later in life.

Sample Test

Multiple-Choice Questions

1.	The adolescent growth spurt typically lasts about _____.
	a.	3 to 6 months			c.	1 to 2 years
	b.	6 months to a year		d.	2 to 3 years

2.	During adolescence, people typically become capable of _____ thought.
	a.	concrete operational		c.	formal operational
	b.	preoperational			d.	postconventional

3.	Adolescents who appear to suffer the least amount of storm and stress are those who _____.
	a.	experience cultural disconnectedness
	b.	closely follow and imitate media trends and imagery
	c.	identify closely with risk-taking peers
	d.	have strong traditional roots

4.	Emerging adulthood refers to a period of development spanning the ages from _____.
	a.	12-18				c.	25-31
	b.	18-25				d.	31-38

5.	The multiyear process triggered by a falloff in production of sex hormones in which menstrual periods become irregular and finally cease is called _____.
	a.	menarche			c.	ovulation
	b.	the climacteric			d.	midlife crisis

6.	Which of the following is **NOT** a myth about menopause?
	a.	menopause is abnormal
	b.	menopause signals an end to a woman's sexual interests
	c.	menopause is accompanied by depression and anxiety
	d.	menopause is a major life change for women

7.	Research indicates that we reach the peak of our cognitive powers during _____.
	a.	childhood			c.	young adulthood
	b.	adolescence			d.	middle adulthood

8. At work, George shows great ability to solve the routine day-to-day problems that arise as part of his job duties. He is demonstrating a high level of _____.
   a. primary intelligence
   b. secondary intelligence
   c. crystallized intelligence
   d. fluid intelligence

9. At which age did Erikson feel the major conflict was one of intimacy versus isolation?
   a. adolescence
   b. young adulthood
   c. middle adulthood
   d. late adulthood

10. Levinson labeled the period in which we tend to reassess the choices made in the early 20s is called the _____.
    a. midlife transition
    b. midlife crisis
    c. age 30 transition
    d. climacteric

11. Today, _____ percent of households were made up of married couples with children.
    a. 25
    b. 45
    c. 65
    d. 85

12. Little Joey is conflicted and irritable. He is less friendly and spontaneous in social interactions and more withdrawn than other children, is cautious in relating to others and is less competent than other children both socially and academically. His parents were most likely _____ in their parenting style.
    a. authoritarian
    b. authoritative
    c. permissive
    d. nonconformist

13. Which of the following is **NOT** a factor that contributes to the probability that parents will abuse their children?
    a. parental overattachment to the child
    b. situational stress
    c. a history of child abuse in at least one of the parent's families of origin
    d. rigid attitudes about child-rearing

14. The point in people's lives where they shift from viewing themselves in of years already lived to viewing themselves in terms of years left to live is called _____.
    a. the age 30 transition
    b. midlife transition
    c. midlife crisis
    d. the age 50 transition

15. According to Sheehy, women enter midlife about _____ men.
    a. 5 years earlier than
    b. about the same time as
    c. 5 years later than
    d. 10 years later than

16. Which of the following is **NOT** one of the psychological shifts Peck believes aids people in adjusting to late adulthood?
    a. disengaging from the complex and fast-paced world around us
    b. shifting interest from the world of work to retirement activities
    c. retaining mental flexibility
    d. coming to value wisdom more than physical strength and power

17. _____ elderly heads of households own their own homes.
    a. Almost no
    b. A large minority of
    c. A majority of
    d. Virtually all

18. Alvin has recently retired. He now has a more realistic view of his possibilities than in the first few weeks after his retirement. He is planning to join a volunteer group and increase his civic involvement to increase the meaningfulness of his activities. He is in the _____ stage of retirement.
    a. disenchantment
    b. reorientation
    c. stability
    d. termination

19. A doctor gives a terminally ill patient high doses of morphine that will induce death painlessly (after the patient has requested death). This is called _____.
   a. positive euthanasia
   b. primary euthanasia
   c. negative euthanasia
   d. secondary euthanasia

20. Which of the following is **NOT** one of the characteristics of "successful aging" presented in your text?
   a. focusing on what is important and meaningful
   b. a positive outlook
   c. challenging oneself
   d. withdrawing from social obligations and commitments

True-False Questions

21. Puberty begins with the appearance of primary sex characteristics.   _____

22. Women tend to lose their sexual desire at menopause.   _____

23. Children with strict parents are more likely to become competent.   _____

24. Alzheimer's disease is a normal part of aging.   _____

25. Most elderly people are generally dissatisfied with their lives.   _____

Essay Question

26. Explain what empty-nest syndrome is and discuss what evidence there is to support or refute this concept.

Student Activities

Name _____ **Date** _____

14.1 Where Are You?

From the discussion in this chapter, where would you place your current development? In what ways is your experience consistent with the discussion and in what ways is your experience inconsistent with the discussion?

1. Current development:

2. Consistent experiences:

3. Inconsistent experiences:

14.2 Our Parents as Subjects

Consider one or both of your parents for a while. Where are they in terms of their adult development? Would they tend to nod agreeably if they were reading this chapter, or would they look puzzled or even openly disagree?

1. Try to create their reaction in your mind and describe it.

2. This might be a good time to call home and check out your attempt to empathize with either or both parents. What can it accomplish? What will they say to these questions?

    a. When in their lives did they experience the greatest amount of freedom?

    b. When did they experience the greatest physical change? How did it affect them?

    c. When did they feel most in control of their lives? If not now, how is it different now?

Activity continued on the back

d. What changes do they look forward to?

e. What could you add to this set of questions?

14.3 Getting Ready for the Rest of Life

Support groups help us through so many of life's experiences. There are support groups in our locale for victims of diseases, former patients of various disorders, survivors of suicide, and parents who experience the loss of a child. There are also informal social supports we enjoy when lunching with colleagues, bowling with friends, or talking over the fence with a neighbor.

Where will we get support for growing older and dealing with the challenges of aging? Will we just have to laugh at ourselves as our eyes lose their focus, our waistlines fight for space, and our children's tuition bills come due? It may be that the most reliable support will come from within ourselves.

Taking Shakespeare's dictum that "nothing is either good or bad, but thinking makes it so," reword the following changes that can come with aging so that the glass is half full instead of half empty, so to speak.

> The first half of life consists of the capacity to enjoy without the chance; the last half consists of the chance without the capacity.
>
> Mark Twain

1. Imagine you discovered you have just passed the halfway point of your predicted lifespan. Will this be the half of life described by Mark Twain as the "half that consists of chance without the capacity?" How could the last half be described in positive language?

2. Suppose you are holding the newspaper at arm's length and still squinting to read the print which you feel "isn't as good as it used to be." If you give in to nature and start wearing glasses, you would be showing your age. How could this turn of events be described positively?

Activity continued on the back

363

3. Soon there will be no child living in your home. Growing up and moving out is creating the "empty nest." What can be positive about this?

4. Of all the challenges or changes outlined in this chapter, what one would you add to this exercise? How could you reconstruct it in a more positive light?

5. What is the next major life change you anticipate? Consider the chapter discussion relevant to your age and use it to compare or contrast this next major life change, again, viewing it in a positive light.

6. Identify one change or challenge in this chapter that you will **not** be experiencing because of your abilities, beliefs, strengths, or choices. How will it be possible to avoid this one?

Name _____ **Date** _____

14.4 Aging and Stereotypes

Television and movie scriptwriters often take advantage of negative stereotypes about aging, and thereby contribute to some of the myths surrounding it. Please identify an example of ageism that is perpetuated by the entertainment media, and bring your example to class to contribute to a discussion.

1.   Describe your example here.

2.   How is this portrayal of aging inaccurate or different from your real-life experience of older people?

3.   In contrast to question 1, illustrate a case where the writer has helped provide some accurate insight.

14.5 A Fountain of Youth

As your text describes, there are many scientific efforts underway to slow down the deterioration associated with aging. Drugs such as DHEA, HGH, and melatonin are just the first wave of what may someday be true anti-aging drugs. Some experts in aging believe that within just a few generations (at most) science will be able to "stretch" the human lifespan out to around 150 years, with the person feeling young and healthy virtually the entire time. A few researchers believe that within 100 years science will be able to expand human life expectancy to around 300 to 400 years, with people being youthful and vigorous most during most of their extended lives. Some extremely optimistic researchers believe that at some point we will be able to stop the aging process entirely, and while people will still die from war, accidents, crime, and some diseases, no one will die from old age. This raises some interesting questions about the impact such changes will have on society.

1. How do you think extended or unlimited aging would affect or change society?

2. What potential problems do you see this creating for society itself, and the world in general?

Activity continued on the back

3. If a pill were available that would stop aging completely, would you take it? Why or why not? If you would take it, can you imagine reasons why someone else might not? What would those reasons be?

Name _____ **Date** _____

14.6 Personal Experience: Part I

Having children can be among the most exciting experiences in your life, while at the same time being among the scariest experiences once the awesome responsibility you have taken on by having a child really sinks in. Once you get the child home you also realize how unprepared you are for many of the things with which you will now have to cope. While there are hundreds of child-rearing manuals, some much more helpful than others, each child is different and no child comes with a set of "operating instructions" custom-tailored to that particular child.

1.   Visit your favorite library and/or bookstore. How many child-rearing books can you find on the shelves or in the indexes?

2.   Please identify and characterize the one that appeals to you most and explain why.

Name _____ **Date** _____

14.7 What Are the Odds?

1. What odds do you give yourself for becoming a parent? Write it as a percentage, and write down what you think the odds are for college students. Are your odds higher or lower than the odds you gave to college students in general? Why?

2. Ask several friends the same thing and write down their responses here.

Activity continues on the back

3. Compare the odds given by you and your friends with the likelihood given for parenting in the United States and Canada (approximately 80 percent). Do you and others have very different ideas about the odds in general or your odds in particular? If so, why do believe your odds are different?

4. What classes on parenting, if any, are offered on your campus? Where else could you go in your community or region to enroll in such classes?

14.8 To Have or Have Not

First read the reasons presented in Chapter 14 to have or not to have children and check the items that seem to apply to you. Now take a position to have or to have not, even if only for this exercise. If you cannot decide, flip a coin.

1.   Identify the strongest reason that is inconsistent with your chosen or coin-determined position. Explain why you are not influenced by that reason.

2.   Write a rebuttal that challenges that reason. Explain why you are so strongly influenced by that rebuttal.

Activity continued on the back

3. Now do the same for the strongest reason in support of your position. Explain why you believe so strongly in this reason.

Name _____ **Date** _____

14.9 Are You Feeling the Pressure?

Have others ever tried to influence your choice about having children? Was it strong persuasion or subtle hints? If this has not happened to you, has it happened to one of your siblings or friends?

1. Record here any influences you detect from friends, family or other sources (for you or your sibling/friend).

2. What position gets the heaviest support—not just in terms of sheer numbers, but also in terms of strengths and influence? For example, an argument from a friend may be more manipulative than an ad for Huggies, and a casual comment from a relative may be more weighty than a lecture from a confirmed bachelor professor.

Name _____ **Date** _____

14.10 In Your Judgment

Since how our parents raised us can influence how we will or would raise children and because you now have some sound basis for judging, please characterize your parents' child rearing with regard to the emphasis they placed on authoritarian, authoritative, or permissive styles.

Also, please describe the strengths or weaknesses you think you will bring to the tasks of parenting, and explain what you can do to help correct or compensate for your weaknesses.

What do you look forward to the most about having children, if you choose to have them?

Activity continued on the next page

What is your biggest fear about having children or your ability to raise children, should you choose to have them?

What are some steps you can take ahead of time to alleviate your fears or minimize the problems you anticipate?

If you choose to have children, about how old do you want to be when you have your first child? Why this age and not an older or younger age?

15

The Challenge of the Workplace

Chapter Outline

Module 15.1: Career Development

Module 15.2: Adjustment in the Workplace

Module 15.3: Women in the Workplace

Module 15.4: Psychology in Daily Life: Finding a Career That Fits

Chapter Overview

Reasons for Working. Workers are motivated by both extrinsic rewards (money, status, security) and intrinsic rewards (the work ethic, self-identity, self-fulfillment, self-worth, and the social values of work). The work ethic holds that we are morally obligated to engage in labor, to avoid idleness.

Stages of Career Development. Stage theorists identify various stages of career development, including the fantasy, tentative, realistic-choice, maintenance, career change, and retirement stages.

Writing a Resume. Your resume is a summary of your background and qualifications. Your resume is you—until the interview. It should summarize your background in education and work experience, most recent experiences first. General rule to break (sometimes): Any color ink is fine as long as it's black. Include e-mail address and cell phone number. don't lie—you may lie your way into a job for which you are not qualified; then what do you do?

The Cover Letter. The cover letter can explain how you learned about the opening, briefly show how you are qualified, can state salary and geographical needs, request an interview, offer to send references upon request, and thank the prospective employer for her or his consideration.

The Job Interview. Make a good first impression by being well-groomed, well-dressed, and as well-spoken as you can be. Maintain eye contact, but look engaged, not challenging. Answer questions briefly and have some questions of your own to ask. Emphasize how your qualifications fit this job. Never be sarcastic or impatient. Ask for a reasonably high salary. Don't volunteer weaknesses.

Getting Ahead on the Job. Your adjustment may begin with recognizing that you're going from the "top" of your educational experience to a relatively low rung in the world outside. Learn how to do your specific job tasks and take responsibility for them. Show that you can get along with co-workers and supervisors. Seek a mentor to "show you the ropes."

Factors Associated with Job Satisfaction. Actually the great majority of workers in the United States report being completely or somewhat satisfied with their jobs. Older workers and workers with higher incomes are more likely to say they are satisfied. Workers do not like being left out of decision-making processes and profit from constructive rather than destructive criticism. Many workers complain of stress, low pay, lack of recognition, and unsatisfactory job benefits in areas like health insurance and retirement.

Enhancing Job Satisfaction. Measures that contribute to job satisfaction include careful recruitment and selection of workers, training and instruction, unbiased appraisal and feedback, goal setting, linking financial compensation to productivity, allowing workers to make appropriate decisions, and flexible schedules such as flextime and job sharing.

Sources of Workplace Stress. There are physical, individual, group, and organizational stressors. For example, the workplace can be polluted. The workers' personality may not fit the job. Co-workers may be criticizers or "back-stabbers." Organizations may have strict hierarchies that do not permit input from lower-level workers.

Decreasing Stress in the Workplace. The organization can study the workplace environment to reduce stressors such as pollution and abrasive supervisor-employee relationships. Many organizations provide health or fitness facilities and activities. Workers also need to evaluate whether their jobs truly fit their personalities and skills.

Burnout. Burnout is characterized by emotional exhaustion, feelings of depersonalization, and reduced achievement. The typical "setup" for burnout is frustration on the job when encountered by highly conscientious workers. Workers can prevent burnout by measures such as creating clear priorities, setting reasonable goals, and limits, sharing their feelings (with people they can trust!), building supportive relationships, and setting aside time to pursue personally rewarding activities outside the workplace.

Women in the Workplace. Women work mainly for the same reasons that men do—financial independence, self-esteem, social interaction, self-identity. However, women often encounter greater stress in the workplace, such as pressure of balancing childbearing and career needs, role overload, sexism and sexual harassment, and dealing with the gender-related earnings gap.

"Men's Work" and "Women's Work." The very question is sexist because it assumes that there are such things as "men's work" and "women's work." Areas that have been traditional male preserves—especially medicine and law—are now seeing equal or nearly equal numbers of women entering them. However, because these areas were shut off to women, older men usually remain in positions of power. Other areas are still dominated by men—for example, the military, science, and engineering, truck driving, and the construction industry.

The Gender-Related Earnings Gap. The earnings gap narrowed at the end of the twentieth century such that women earned about 65% of the income of men. There is no simple explanation for the remaining earnings gap. Reasons include discrimination, women's "choices" (based on a lifetime of exposure to gender role stereotypes) to enter traditionally lower-paying fields, and the fact that the fields formerly restricted to women tend to remain dominated by older men.

Reducing the Earnings Gap. Women profit from realistic career planning, maintaining employment continuity, child-care facilities, and training programs. (Lack of discrimination wouldn't hurt either.)

Sexual Harassment. One commonly accepted definition of sexual harassment consists of deliberate or repeated unsolicited verbal comments, gestures, or physical contact of a sexual nature that is unwelcome. People who are sexually harassed can adopt a cool (not necessarily nasty) "professional" attitude in relating to harassers, directly inform the harasser to stop, avoid being alone with the harasser, keep a record of incidents, complain to the organization, and seek legal remedies. Harassment usually will not go away by itself.

Learning Objectives

After studying this chapter your students should be able to:

1. Compare and contrast the various intrinsic and extrinsic motives for working.

2. Identify and briefly explain Super's stages of vocational development.

3. Explain what a resume and a cover letter are, and provide a detailed description of what each should, or should not, contain.

4. Summarize, in detail, the things you should do to make a good impression at a job interview.

5. Identify and discuss the various developmental tasks in taking a new job.

6. Describe the various measures that can be taken to enhance job satisfaction

7. Identify the various sources of stress in the workplace. Describe their effects, including burnout, and explain what steps can be taken to cope with job stress.

8. Describe discrepancies in pay and promotion for women in the workplace. Identify and explain the steps that can be taken to improve the workplace for women.

9. Discuss the types of behavior that represent sexual harassment. Explain what steps a person can take to protect himself or herself against sexual harassment.

10. Explain what a balance sheet is and describe how it can be used to enhance the process of making career decisions.

11. Identify at least two psychological tests that could be useful in the career decision-making process and explain how psychological tests can help us make better career decisions.

12. Describe the six coping styles proposed in Holland's theory and explain how certain coping styles "fit" better in certain occupations than in others.

Key Terms

extrinsic motives	résumé	sexual harassment
intrinsic motives	cover letter	balance sheet
fantasy stage	job satisfaction	realistic type
tentative choice stage	quality circle	investigative type
realistic stage	hoteling	artistic type
maintenance stage	flextime	social type
career change stage	burnout	enterprising type
retirement stage	the earnings gap	conventional type

Key Terms Review

Define each of the following terms:

1. Extrinsic Motives:_____

    _____

2. Intrinsic Motives: _____

    _____

3. Fantasy Stage: _____

    _____

4. Maintenance Stage: _____

    _____

5. Résumé: _____

    _____

6. Cover Letter: _____

    _____

7. Job Satisfaction: _____

    _____

8. Quality Circle:_____

    _____

9.   Flextime: _____

_____

10. Hoteling: _____

_____

11. Burnout: _____

_____

12. The Earnings Gap: _____

_____

13. Sexual Harassment: _____

_____

14. Balance Sheet: _____

_____

15. Realistic Type: _____

_____

16. Investigative Type: _____

_____

17. Artistic Type: _____

_____

18. Social Type: _____

_____

19. Enterprising Type: _____

_____

20. Conventional Type: _____

_____

Chapter Review

1. In a society free of traditional castes or hereditary aristocracies, _____ prestige is a major determinant of social status and respect.

2. Three factors that help explain how adolescents and young adults choose particular careers are:

    a. _____

    b. _____

    c. _____

3. Many of us _____ _____ our careers because of _____

    _____.

4. The major reason for working is _____.

5. The *Dictionary of Occupational Titles* currently lists more than _____ occupations.

6. Three extrinsic reasons for working are:

    a. _____

    b. _____

    c. _____

7. Five intrinsic reasons for working are:

    a. _____

    b. _____

    c. _____

    d. _____

    e. _____

8.   The six stages of Super's theory of vocational development are:

a.   _____

b.   _____

c.   _____

d.   _____

e.   _____

f.   _____

9.   When you apply for a job, you usually send a _____ with a _____

_____.

10.   A résumé is a _____ of your job qualifications and should be kept to

_____ page(s) if at all possible.

11.   The five parts of a résumé are:

a.   _____

b.   _____

c.   _____

d.   _____

e.   _____

12.   A cover letter should include each of the following:

a.   _____

b.   _____

c.   _____

d.   _____

e.   _____

f.   _____

g.   _____

13. A job interview is a _____ occasion and a _____.

14. Women interviewers rate applicants who wear perfume or cologne more _____.

   Male interviewers rate fragrant applicants more _____.

15. Five developmental tasks in taking a job are:

   a. _____

   b. _____

   c. _____

   d. _____

   e. _____

16. American workers see themselves as hardworking, but _____, _____,

   and _____.

17. A sense of control is important for job _____, and employees _____ and

   _____-_____.

18. Personality traits such as self-_____, self-_____, and _____
   stability are associated with greater job satisfaction.

19. Increasing job satisfaction also is associated with lower employee _____,

   and _____ and enhanced _____.

20. Five methods for enhancing job satisfaction and productivity are:

   a. _____

   b. _____

   c. _____

   d. _____

   e. _____

21. When appraising employees' work efforts, supervisors tend to focus on the

_____ rather than the worker's _____.

22. Quality circles give workers a greater sense of _____ over their jobs and

increase _____ to the company.

23. Four sources of stress in the workplace are:

a. _____

b. _____

c. _____

d. _____

24. Burnout is characterized by feeling emotionally _____, a lack of _____

at work, and a sense of _____ or _____.

25. Burnout is common among people who have high levels of role _____, role

_____, and role _____.

26. Five signs of job burnout are:

a. _____

b. _____

c. _____

d. _____

e. _____

27. Five suggestions for preventing burnout are:

a. _____

b. _____

c. _____

d. _____

e. _____

28. Working mothers are primarily concerned about their _____.

29. All things considered, working women are putting in about _____ of work a day.

30. Working women usually work two shifts. One in the _____ and one in the

_____.

31. The average female worker earns about _____ as much as the average male.

32. About one in _____ working wives now outearns her husband.

33. Six measures for reducing the earnings gap are:

a. _____

b. _____

c. _____

d. _____

e. _____

f. _____

34. Five types of sexual harassment are:

a. _____

b. _____

c. _____

d. _____

e. _____

35. Women are much _____ likely than men to suffer sexual harassment, and

women of color are _____ likely than are white women.

36.   Sexual harassment may have more to do with _____ and the abuse of

        _____ than with sexual desire.

37.   Most women who are sexually harassed do not file complaints because of:

        a. _____

        b. _____

38.   It may be that as many as one in _____ women encounters some form of sexual
        harassment on the job or in college.

39.   Five ways to resist sexual harassment are:

        a. _____

        b. _____

        c. _____

        d. _____

        e. _____

40.   Two methods for gathering information for making career decisions are a

        _____ _____ and _____ _____.

41.   Three types of information necessary to make satisfying career decisions are:

        a. _____

        b. _____

        c. _____

42.   The most widely used intelligence tests are the _____ and the _____-

        _____.

43. **Matching:** Match the coping style from Holland's theory on the left with its appropriate description on the right.

_____ a. Realistic

_____ b. Investigative

_____ c. Artistic

_____ d. Social

_____ e. Enterprising

_____ f. Conventional

1. abstract in thinking, creative, and introverted; well-adjusted in research or college and university teaching

2. adventurous, impulsive, domineering, and extraverted; gravitates toward leadership and planning roles in industry and government

3. high self-control, needs for order, desire for social approval, enjoys routine, not very creative; well-adjusted in banking, accounting, and clerical work

4. concrete thinkers, mechanically oriented, enjoy using their hands; well-adjusted in farming, unskilled labor, skilled trades

5. creative, emotional, intuitive, interested in feelings; gravitate toward visual and performing arts

6. extraverted, socially concerned, high verbal ability, strong needs for affiliation; gravitate toward social work, teaching, or counseling

Sample Test

Multiple-Choice Questions

1. Samantha works because she likes the intellectual challenge of her job and the sense of accomplishment she feels after successfully completing a work assignment. Her reasons for working are primarily _____.
   a. pragmatic
   b. extrinsic
   c. active
   d. intrinsic

2. The belief that we are morally obligated to engage in productive labor and to avoid idleness and laziness is called _____.
   a. philanthropy
   b. the work ethic
   c. the blue-collar mentality
   d. the Golden Rule

3. People who choose a job or career because it offers them opportunities to express personal needs, interests, and values through their work have focused on which of the following motivations for working?
   a. self-worth
   b. self-identity
   c. self-fulfillment
   d. the work ethic

4. Chad is 20 years old and in his sophomore year in college. He has really narrowed down his career choices to a couple of specialty areas in which there are lucrative positions that will allow him to do things in which he is interested. He has changed his major so that it fits the career direction he is heading toward. According to Super, he is in the _____ stage of vocational development.
   a. fantasy
   b. tentative choice
   c. realistic choice
   d. maintenance

390

5. Each of the following is true of a résumé **EXCEPT** _____.
   a. it should have a photograph of you attached to it
   b. it is intended to convince a hiring manager that you are well qualified for the position for which you are applying
   c. it should be kept to one page, if at all possible
   d. it should be neat, complete, legible, and compatible with the job's requirements

6. Each of the following should be included in your cover letter **EXCEPT** _____.
   a. an explanation of the purpose of the letter
   b. a summary of your educational background
   c. a request for an interview or other response to the letter
   d. a statement of desired salary and geographic limitations

7. According to your text, you should do each of the following in an interview **EXCEPT** _____.
   a. maintain alert, but friendly eye contact with the interviewer
   b. try to anticipate the interviewer's questions
   c. try to do most of the talking in the interview
   d. look your best

8. According to a 1999 Gallup survey, of the following, workers are **MOST** satisfied with _____.
   a. the amount of stress on the job
   b. the flexibility of their work schedules
   c. the recognition they receive for their work
   d. the physical safety of the workplace

9. Each of the following is true **EXCEPT** _____.
   a. job satisfaction depends more on the job duties than the worker's personality
   b. genetic factors may influence whether people are satisfied with their jobs
   c. a person's attributional style affects job satisfaction
   d. a sense of personal control is important to job satisfaction

10. According to your text, which of the following workers is most likely to receive the best evaluation from a supervisor?
    a. a well-liked worker who works hard but makes mistakes
    b. an unliked worker who works hard and does the job well
    c. a well-liked worker who doesn't work very hard but does the job well
    d. an unliked worker who doesn't work hard and makes mistakes

11. A "mother's shift," four 10-hour day work weeks, and scheduling someone's hours around other outside commitments are all examples of _____.
    a. work redesign   c. stimulus control
    b. peripheral timing   d. flextime

12. Edgar faces too many competing demands for his time. He feels pulled in about nine different directions at once, and doesn't have the time or energy to meet any of the competing demands he is facing. He is experiencing _____.
    a. role conflict   c. role overload
    b. role ambiguity   d. role diffusion

13. About _____ percent of working women, including married and single mothers, continue to bear the major responsibility for child-care.
    a. 60   c. 80
    b. 70   d. 90

14. Which of the following is **NOT** listed in your text as a measure to help reduce the earnings gap?
    a. more realistic career planning
    b. increasing job flexibility and providing child-care facilities
    c. providing employers with accurate information about women in the work force
    d. increasing the number of lawsuits against employers who discriminate against women

15. Which of the following is **NOT** a type of information needed to make satisfying career decisions?
    a. intellectual and educational appropriateness
    b. intrinsic factors
    c. extrinsic factors
    d. response factors

16. One of the two most widely used intelligence tests is the _____.
    a. WAIS   c. WPPSI
    b. MMPI   d. SCII

17. As part of her career exploration, Janet goes to a counselor who gives her a test. This test pairs numbers of statements and asks her to choose which statement is more descriptive of herself. Her answers are then used to calculate scores on 15 different scales of psychological needs. The test Janet took is the _____.
    a. TAT   c. EPPS
    b. WAIS   d. MMPI

18. Over the next several years, opening in occupations that require a bachelor's degree will grow at about _____ the rate projected for jobs that require less education and training.
    a. half   c. twice
    b. equal   d. six times

19. Irwin is a concrete thinker. He is mechanically oriented and interested in jobs that involve motor activity such as farming, carpentry, and auto mechanics. According to Holland's theory, Irwin is a(n) _____ type.
    a. realistic   c. enterprising
    b. investigative   d. conventional

20. Rita is adventurous, impulsive, extroverted, and domineering. She is a natural leader and has a thriving career as a real-estate developer. She likes working with other people, but only in situations where she is in control. According to Holland's theory, she is a(n) _____ type.
    a. social   c. enterprising
    b. realistic   d. artistic

True-False Questions

21. Many million-dollar lottery winners feel aimless and dissatisfied if they quit their jobs after striking it rich. _____

22. You should develop a résumé that you can use to apply for all positions. _____

23. Criticism is necessary if workers are to improve. _____

24. Women miss twice as much work as men when the children are sick. _____

25. Sexual harassment is one of the most common and vicious obstacles people face in the workplace. _____

Essay Question

26. Describe the various measures that can be taken to enhance job satisfaction.

Student Activities

Name _____ **Date** _____

15.1 Resources for Career Information

There are some fantastic resources waiting at your library that can provide important information about the career you have chosen or are considering. You will find the reference librarian **very** helpful and able to direct you to titles such as *The Dictionary of Occupational Titles* and *The Occupational Outlook Handbook*. The latter is updated yearly and is quite complete in coverage of the nature of occupations. Both titles are widely held at libraries designated as Federal Depository Libraries and generally are available at local, regional, and campus libraries. Ask the person behind the reference desk for directions, and answer these questions about your chosen career, or what you might consider for a career:

1. What is the nature of the work? Does it seem to fit your preconceptions?

2. What work conditions are associated with the occupation?

3. How many people are currently employed in this occupation?

4. What education, training and other qualifications are required?

5. What is the outlook for this career choice? How many more people are expected to be needed in the future?

Activity continued on the back

6. What earnings and advancement opportunities are associated with this career choice?

7. What health benefits are associated with this job?

8. Is your interest in this career enhanced or reduced by this exercise? What exactly was influential?

9. Which stage of vocational development is associated with this exercise?

10. If you won the lottery, would you still choose this career? Why or why not? If not, what else would you do?

Name _____ **Date** _____

15.2 Our Work and Our Identity

The text points out the tendency for us to say "I am a _____" rather than "I work as a _____," and thus, we intertwine career with self-identity. We will be or already are sensitive at those times people ask us what our major is, what our career plans are, and what work we do.

Ask three people who are unfamiliar with your career interests to grade the "prestige" they associate with five jobs that you identify, including your first choice. Use a scale of 1 to 10, with 10 being the most prestigious job. Also ask all participants to give an example of a job they would rate a 1 and one they would rate a 10.

Follow-Up Questions:

1. Is it alarming or comforting to learn what others think of your choice? Why?

2. How much did the three judgments vary? In what ways did they vary?

Activity continued on the back

3. Do the opinions of others regarding your career choice have any value to you? Why or why not?

Name _____ **Date** _____

15.3 Supercharging Your Formal Education

It is hard to find it in writing, but students generally know that there are courses outside their major, called electives, that are extremely useful, exciting, and valuable.

1. What courses outside your major could you describe to your class that you would highly recommend? Why are these courses valuable? What benefits do they provide?

2. Ask a friend for his or her recommendation for an elective course and the reason for the recommendation. What did the friend recommend and why does he or she recommend it?

Activity continued on the back

3. Ask a faculty member for his or her recommendation for an elective course and the reason for the recommendation. What did the faculty member recommend and why did she or he recommend it?

4. Please bring these to class for sharing, and indicate which class or classes intrigue you.

Name _____ **Date** _____

15.4 What Matters on the Job?

Since most of us have work experience, we can judge the relative contribution of several of the components that influence job satisfaction or dissatisfaction. Rank each item from 1 to 10, with 1 representing the most important and 10 representing the least important. Briefly explain your rating.

1. _____ The boss

2. _____ Geographic location

3. _____ Fellow workers

4. _____ Work environment

5. _____ Hours

6. _____ Salary/Money

7. _____ Advancement potential

8. _____ Benefits (health insurance, etc.)

9. _____ Status/Prestige

10. _____ Daily tasks on the job

Follow-Up Questions:

1. This is an exercise that is also good to share with other members of your class. It probably would be useful to discover what your classmates' experiences are, especially if they are quite different from your own. For example, working nights or weekends might not be part of your experience, so the insights of others might be valuable if you are thinking of a career in a medical field.

2. Given the possible effects of criticism, goal setting, linkage of pay to productivity, work redesign, flextime, and stress at the workplace, how would you change the workplace you rated in this exercise?

Activity continued on the back

3. How would you monitor, measure, and document improvements that your recommendations could create?

Answer Key

Chapter 1

Chapter Review

1. behavior, mental (6)
2. Multitasking (6)
3. Adjustment (7)
4. the same (8)
5. Adjustment, personal growth (8)
6. genetic, environmental (8)
7. Genes, chromosomes (8)
8. environmental, choice (8-9)
9. predisposition (9)
10. clinical (9)
11. healthy personality (9)
12. Positive (9)
13. Ethnic groups (11)
14a. experiences of ethnic groups highlight the impact of social, political, and economic factors on human behavior and development (11)
  b. the dramatically changing ethnic make-up of the United States (11)
  c. to enable students to appreciate the cultural heritage and historical problems of various ethnic groups (11)
  d. to help psychologists understand how ethnic diversity concerns psychological intervention and consultation (11)
15. Asian, Hispanic (12)
16. Gender (13)
17. critical (14)
18a. be skeptical (15)
  b. examine the definition of terms (15)
  c. examine the assumptions or premises of arguments (15)
  d. be cautious in drawing conclusions from "evidence" (15)
  e. consider alternative interpretations of research evidence, especially evidence that seems to show cause and effect (15)
  f. do not oversimplify (15)
  g. do not overgeneralize (15)
  h. apply critical thinking to all areas of life (16)
19. pseudoscience (16)
20. Barnum (16)
21. science (17)
22. evidence (17)
23. any five of the following ten (18)
  a. don't judge a book by its cover or title (18)
  b. avoid books that make extravagant claims (18)
  c. check authors' credentials (18)
  d. check authors' affiliations (18)
  e. consider authors' complaints about the conservatism of professional groups to be a warning (18)
  f. check the evidence reported in the book (18)
  g. check the reference citations for evidence (18)

23h.   ask your instructors for advice (18)

   i.   read textbooks and professional books, like this book, rather than self-help books (18)

   j.   stop by and chat with your psychology instructor (18)

24.   skeptical (19)

25.   scientific method (20)

26a.   formulate a research question (20)

   b.   develop a hypothesis (20)

   c.   test the hypothesis (20)

   d.   draw conclusions about the hypothesis (20)

27.   Correlation (20)

28.   selection factor (21)

29.   replicate (21)

30.   men (22)

31.   case studies (22)

32.   sample, population (23)

33.   random (23)

34.   volunteer (23)

35.   descriptive, causes (26)

36.   +1.00 and −1.00 (26)

37.   positive (26)

38.   negative (26)

39.   experimental (28)

40a.   4 (25)   d. 2 (22)

   b.   1 (22)   e. 5 (28)

   c.   3 (26)

41.   independent (28)

42.   experimental, control (28)

43.   placebo (28)

44.   double-blind (29)

45a.   plan ahead (33)

   b.   study different subjects each day (33)

   c.   become an active note taker (33)

   d.   expand your attention span (33)

   e.   eliminate distractions (34)

   f.   practice self-reward (34)

   g.   stick with it (34)

46a.   survey (34)

   b.   question (34)

   c.   read (35)

   d.   recite (35)

   e.   review (35)

47a.   identify irrational catastrophizing thoughts (35)

   b.   construct incompatible rational alternatives (35)

   c.   substitute rational alternative thoughts (35)

   d.   reward yourself for making changes (35)

Sample Test

1. D, 5	6. C, 13	11. C, 22	16. A, 28	21. F, 9
2. D, 6	7. B, 14	12. C, 22	17. B, 28	22. F, 13
3. A, 7	8. D, 20	13. A, 25-26	18. D, 28-29	23. F, 21
4. C, 8	9. A, 21	14. D, 26	19. C, 29	24. T, 25
5. D, 9	10. B, 22	15. D, 27	20. A, 28	25. F, 26

26. This essay is a short-answer essay which requires you to identify the key differences between the two major approaches to healthy personality: a clinical or a healthy-personality approach. In your answer you

must identify the key elements of each approach as discussed in your text. The clinical approach focuses mainly on the ways in which psychology can help people correct problems and cope with stress. Books written from this approach are frequently written from a psychodynamic or behaviorist perspective. The healthy-personality approach primarily focuses on healthful patterns of personal growth and development, including social and vocational development. Books written from this approach are likely to be written from a phenomenological perspective.

Chapter 2

Chapter Review

1.	Sigmund Freud (40)		
2.	struggle (40)		
3.	physician (40)		
4.	iceberg (40)		
5.	conscious, preconscious, unconscious (40)		
6.	unconscious (40)		
7.	repression (40)		
8.	psychoanalysis (41)		
9.	id, ego, superego (41-42)		
10.	id, pleasure (41)		
11.	reality (41)		
12.	defense mechanism (42)		
13.	superego, identification (42)		
14a.	4 (43)	e.	3 (43)
b.	6 (43)	f.	7 (43)
c.	1 (43)	g.	5 (43)
d.	8 (43)	h.	2 (43)
15.	eros, libido (42)		
16.	oral, anal, phallic, latency, genital (42-44)		
17.	fixation (42)		
18.	anal (43)		
19.	Jung, Adler, Horney, Erikson (45-46)		
20.	self (45)		
21.	personal, collective (45)		
22.	superiority, inferiority complex (45)		
23.	awareness (45)		
24.	penis, power, authority (46)		
25.	interpersonal relationships (46)		
26.	psychosocial (46)		
27a.	6 (47)	e.	1 (47)
b.	8 (47)	f.	7 (47)
c.	2 (47)	g.	5 (47)
d.	4 (47)	h.	3 (47)
28a.	the abilities to love and work (48)		
b.	ego strength (48)		
c.	a creative self (48)		
d.	compensation for feelings of inferiority (48)		
e.	positive outcomes (48)		
29.	behaviorist (50)		
30.	Classical (50)		
31a.	2 (51)		
b.	4 (51)		
c.	1 (51)		
d.	3 (51)		

32a.	4 (52)	e.	13 (52)	i.	12 (53)
b.	10 (52)	f.	3 (53)	j.	6 (53)
c.	11 (50)	g.	8 (53)	k.	2 (53)
d.	7 (52)	h.	1 (53)		

33. observation, or modeling (55)
34. competencies, encoding, expectancies, regulatory (55-57)
35a. learning by observing others (57)
b. learning competencies (57)
c. accurate encoding of events (57)
d. accurate expectations and positive self-efficacy expectations (59)
e. efficient self-regulatory systems (59)
36. the meaning of life (60)
37. humanism (60)
38. biological, safety, love and belongingness, esteem, self-actualization (61)
39. self (62)
40. conditional, conditions of worth, unconditional, self-esteem (62-63)
41. client-centered (63)
42a. experiencing life in the here and now (63)
b. being open to new experience (63)
c. expressing true feelings and beliefs (63)
d. seeking meaningful activities (63)
e. being capable of making major changes in their life (63)
f. becoming their own persons (63)
43. trait (64)
44. introversion-extraversion, emotional stability-instability (neuroticism) (64-65)
45. extraversion, neuroticism, conscientiousness, agreeableness, openness (66)
46. label, explain (68)
47. sociocultural (69)
48. individualists, collectivists (70)
49. bicultural (71)
50a. balancing competing cultural demands (73)
b. coping effectively with discrimination (73)
c. becoming acculturated without losing your cultural identity (73)
51. Objective (74)
52. projective (75)
53. Rorschach, TAT (76)

Sample Test

1. A, 40	6. D, 42-44	11. B, 47	16. D, 55	21. T, 42
2. A, 41	7. C, 44	12. A, 50	17. D, 60	22. F, 53
3. D, 42	8. C, 45-46	13. B, 51	18. A, 62	23. F, 57
4. D, 43	9. A, 46	14. D, 52	19. B, 66	24. T, 63
5. B, 42	10. A, 46	15. D, 53-54	20. D, 70	25. T, 76

26. In this question, you must first identify the two major humanistic theorists discussed in the text—Abraham Maslow and Carl Rogers. You should then explain that phenomenological theory generally focuses on subjective experience rather than empirical evidence in its approach to understanding the human condition. Then identify the common points expressed by Maslow and Rogers who both propose that the personal, subjective experiencing of events is the most important aspect of human nature and that, as unique individuals, we are our own best experts on ourselves. Furthermore, in discussing the elements of a healthy personality, the phenomenologists all agree that healthy people experience life in the here and now, are open to new experiences, express their feelings and ideas, trust their intuitive feelings, engage in meaningful activities, are capable of making major changes in their lives, and are their own persons. You might wish to offer brief explanations for each of the above qualities (similar to those presented in the text). Then you must briefly contrast this approach with psychodynamic, behavioral, and social-cognitive theories.

Chapter 3

Chapter Review

1.	stress (83)
2.	adapt, cope, adjust (83)
3a.	daily hassles (84)
b.	life changes (84)
c.	pain and discomfort (84)
d.	conflict (84)
e.	irrational beliefs (84)
f.	Type A behavior (84)
g.	environmental factors (84)
4.	stress (84)
5a.	household hassles (85)
b.	health hassles (85)
c.	time-pressure hassles (85)
d.	inner-concern hassles (85)
e.	environmental hassles (85)
f.	financial responsibility hassles (85)
g.	work hassles (85)
h.	future-security hassles (85)
6a.	Many life changes are positive. Hassles are, by definition, negative (86)
b.	Hassles occur regularly. Life changes occur at irregular intervals (86)
7.	least (89)
8.	tension, stress, older (89)
9.	Prostaglandins (90)
10.	Analgesic, prostaglandins (90)
11.	endorphins (91)
12.	chemical (90)
13a.	obtaining accurate information (91)
b.	distraction and fantasy (91)
c.	hypnosis (91)
d.	relaxation training and biofeedback (91)
e.	taking control of your thoughts (92)
f.	gate theory (92)
g.	acupuncture (92)
14.	gate (92)
15.	placebo (92)
16.	frustration (92)
17.	emotional (93)
18.	lowers (93)
19.	Conflict (93)
20a.	approach-approach (93)
b.	avoidance-avoidance (93)
c.	approach-avoidance (94)
d.	multiple approach-avoidance (94)
21.	opposite (94)
22.	beliefs (94)
23.	activating, beliefs, consequence (95)
24.	irrational beliefs (95)
25.	anxiety, depression (95)
26.	Type A, Type B (96-97)
27a.	disasters (98)
b.	terrorism (98)
c.	noise (100)

27d. temperature (101)
 e. air pollution (102)
 f. crowding (102)
28. life changes (98)
29. noise (101)
30. aggressive (101)
31. lead (102)
32. mortality (102)
33. All (102)
34. Personal space (102)
35. protective, communicative (102)
36. Self-efficacy (104)
37. commitment, challenge, perceived control (104)
38. internal (104)
39. inconclusive (104)
40. control, moderates (105)
41. control (105)
42. optimistic (106)
43a. emotional concern (107)
 b. instrumental aid (107)
 c. information (108)
 d. appraisal (108)
 e. socializing (108)
44. Defensive (109)
45a. withdrawal (109)
 b. denial (109)
 c. substance use (109)
 d. aggression (109)
46. Active (109)
47a. Don't bite off more than you can chew. (109)
 b. Reduce daily hassles (110)
 c. Develop time management skills (110)
48. Meditation (112)
49. relaxation (112)
50. progressive muscle relaxation (112)

Sample Test

1. A, 84	6. C, 90	11. D, 94	16. D, 102	21. F, 85
2. A, 85	7. D, 91	12. D, 96-97	17. D, 102	22. T, 90
3. A, 86	8. C, 92	13. C, 101	18. D, 104	23. T, 92
4. B, 89	9. B, 93	14. A, 100-101	19. A, 108	24. T, 102
5. B, 90	10. B, 94	15. C, 101-102	20. B, 109	25. F, 103

26. This question requires you to define frustration and conflict in a way that highlights how they are similar and/or different from each other. Whereas frustration is a feeling resulting from anything which blocks or thwarts a motive, either intentionally or unintentionally, conflict results when two opposing motives exist and the gratification of one motive necessarily prevents the gratification of the other.
Then you must identify the four types of conflict discussed in the text. Even though the question only asks you to identify each conflict (which could be interpreted to mean list them), it is a good idea to write down a one-sentence explanation of each conflict you list such as:

approach-approach conflict: a conflict in which a person must choose between two desirable options and in choosing one option must forfeit the other option.

The other three types of conflicts are: an approach-avoidance conflict, an avoidance-avoidance conflict, and a multiple approach-avoidance conflict.

Chapter 4

Chapter Review

1. Health (120)
2. Stress (120)
3. general adaptation syndrome, alarm, resistance, exhaustion (120)
4. fight or flight (120)
5. endocrine, hormones (120)
6. autonomic, sympathetic, parasympathetic (120-120)
7. corticosteroids, adrenaline, noradrenaline (121-122)
8. lower (123)
9. adaptation (124)
10. tend, befriend, oxytocin (123)
11a. anxiety (124)
  b. anger (124)
  c. depression (124)
12. trait, state (124)
13. enduring (124)
14. parasympathetic (125)
15. disease, cells (125)
16. leukocytes, pathogens, antigens, antibodies (125)
17. immune (125)
18. contract, dilate (125)
19. psychoneuroimmunology (125)
20. corticosteroids, immune (126)
21a. correlational evidence (126)
  b. positive versus negative life changes (127)
  c. personality differences (127)
  d. cognitive appraisal (127)
22. multifactorial (128)
23. healthier (128)
24. seven (130)
25. one-half, three-quarters (131)
26. African (131)
27. African (131)
28. less, earlier, more (132)
29. estrogen (132)
30. five (133)
31. better, longer, education (133)
32. Headaches (134)
33. muscle tension, migraine (134)
34. Tension, migraine (134)
35. serotonin (134)
36. 50 to 75 (135)
37. biological (135)
38. estrogen, progesterone, serotonin, GABA (136)
39. any five of the following eleven items:
  a. don't blame yourself (136)
  b. keep track of your menstrual symptoms to help identify patterns (136)
  c. develop strategies for dealing with days that you experience the greatest distress (136)
  d. ask yourself if you harbor any self-defeating attitudes toward menstruation (136)
  e. see a doctor about your concerns (136)
  f. develop nutritious eating habits (136)
  g. eat smaller meals throughout the day (136)
  h. make exercise a part of your lifestyle (136)

39i. check with your doctor about vitamin and mineral supplements (136)
  j. ask your doctor for a recommendation regarding pain-relieving drugs (136)
  k. remind yourself that menstrual problems are time-limited (136)
40. Coronary heart (137)
41a. family history (137)
  b. physiological conditions (137)
  c. lifestyle factors (137)
  d. Type A behavior (137)
  e. negative emotions (138)
  f. job strain (139)
42a. stopping smoking, controlling weight, and following a healthful diet (140)
  b. reducing hypertension (140)
  c. lowering LDL serum cholesterol (140)
  d. modifying Type A behavior (140)
  e. exercising (140)
43. Any 5 of the 14 suggestions from pages 140-141
44. Any 5 of the 8 suggestions from page 141
45. cancer (142)
46. smoking, diet (143)
47a. avoid smoking and heavy use of alcohol (146)
  b. modify our diet (146)
  c. exercise regularly (146)
  d. have regular screenings for cancer (146)
  e. regulate exposure to stress (146)
  f. if struck by cancer, maintain hope and a fighting spirit (146)
48a. describe your symptoms and complaints as clearly and fully as possible (146)
  b. don't accept a treatment recommendation that you don't want (146)
  c. insist on explanations in plain language (146)
  d. don't be swayed by a doctor who says your problems are "in your head" (147)
49a. Look under the hood before joining an HMO (147)
  a. discuss coverage for hospital stays (147)
  b. insist on your right to see a specialist (147)
  c. learn what to do in case of emergencies (147)
  d. if you are refused coverage, file an appeal (147)

Sample Test

1. D, 120	6. C, 123	11. C, 125	16. A, 134	21. F, 124
2. D, 120	7. D, 124	12. B, 126	17. A, 136	22. F, 125
3. A, 120	8. C, 125	13. B, 130	18. C, 138	23. T, 132
4. A, 120	9. A, 125	14. A, 131-132	19. D, 140	24. F, 135
5. B, 121	10. C, 125	15. C, 133	20. B, 146	25. T, 142

26. In the first section of this question, even though it is not explicitly requested, you should identify the three clusters of symptoms related to menstrual problems: menstrual pain, physiological discomfort during menstruation, and premenstrual syndrome. Then you should note that the causes of most menstrual problems are biological but that beliefs and attitudes toward menstruation can heighten physiologically caused problems.

Having done this, you should identify the suspected causes of specific menstrual problems such as: Primary dysmenorrhea: caused by organic problems such as endometriosis, pelvic inflammatory disease, ovarian cysts, etc. Secondary dysmenorrhea: linked to hormonal changes. PMS: may reflect unusually high levels of estradiol and progesterone or an imbalance between the two, as well as secretions of prostaglandins that can cause cramping and painful discomfort. Psychological factors reflecting cultural beliefs about menstruation being a period of "pollution" and "raging hormones" may increase subjective discomfort and result in greater mood changes and more missed time from work.

In discussing the effects, you should note that the physical effects are usually pain and discomfort and that the mood changes, as discussed above, are often tied to psychological rather than purely physiological factors.

Finally, in discussing ways to cope with menstrual distress, you need to list the methods discussed on page 137 of the text. Since the question doesn't specify how many of the methods you should list, you should ask your instructor (in a real test situation). It is possible that an instructor might want you to list all ten methods presented in the text. Most instructors would probably be satisfied with four or five. But you can never assume this. You should always ask, or write them all down if you are not sure.

Chapter 5

Chapter Review

1. nutrients (154)
2. proteins, carbohydrates, fats, vitamins, minerals (154)
3. amino, hormones, enzymes, antibodies (154)
4. meat, poultry, eggs, fish, dairy (154)
5. Carbohydrates (154)
6. Sugars, starches (154)
7. stamina, skin, vitamins (155)
8. organic (156)
9. anti-oxidants, free radicals (156)
10. fruits, vegetables (156)
11. heredity, adipose, metabolism (158)
12. fat (159)
13. Biological, psychosocial, inactivity (158-159)
14. Dieting (161)
15. anorexia nervosa, bulimia nervosa (161)
16. adolescence, young (161)
17. depression (161)
18. control, perfectionism (165)
19. anaerobic, aerobic (168)
20. fitness (168)
21. metabolic, calories (172)
22. raises, lowers (172)
23. depression, sustain (172)
24. 30 minutes (172)
25. seven, nine (174)
26. attention, learning, memory (176)
27. taking sleeping pills (177)
28a. relax (177)
  b. challenging irrational beliefs (177)
  c. don't ruminate in bed (177)
  d. establish a regular routine (178)
  e. use fantasy (178)
29a. 3 (179)   d. 6 (179)
  b. 1 (179)   e. 2 (179)
  c. 5 (179)   f. 4 (179)
30. predisposition (180)
31. Alcohol (181)

32. binge drinking (181)
33. stomach, liver (183)
34. as likely as (183)
35. Alcoholics anonymous (183)
36. serotonin (184)
37. narcotic, morphine, heroin (184)
38. morphine (184)
39. heroin (185)
40. pain, epilepsy (185)
41. depressants (185)
42. nicotine (187)
43. highly, quickly (186)
44. curbs, raises (186)
45. 450,000 (186)
46. seven (186)
47. hydrocarbons (186)
48. Passive (186)
49. benzadrine, dexadrine, methamphetamine, ritalin (187-188)
50. methamphetamine (188)
51. cognitive, emotional, neurological (188)
52. Ecstasy (188)
53. euphoria, hunger, pain, self-confidence (188)
54. highly, withdrawal (189)
55. dangerous, collapse (189)
56. constricts, thickens, quickens (189)
57. Sigmund Freud (190)
58a. 5 (184)   f. 10 (188)
  b. 8 (185)   g. 3 (189)
  c. 9 (185)   h. 7 (189)
  d. 1 (185)   i. 4 (189)
  e. 6 (188)   j 2 (187)
59. marijuana, LSD, PCP, mescaline (189)
60. tolerance, psychological, physiological (189)
61. elevate, hallucinations (189)
62. headaches, pain (189)
63. Marijuana (189)
64. learning, memory, cancer (190)

Sample Test

1. A, 154	6. C, 162-164	11. C, 179	16. D, 184	21. T, 164
2. C, 154	7. A, 168	12. B, 179	17. C, 187	22. F, 167
3. D, 157	8. C, 174	13. A, 180	18. B, 189	23. T, 177
4. A, 159	9. C, 176	14. D, 180	19. C, 189	24. F, 181
5. A, 162	10. A, 176	15. A, 180	20. C, 189	25. F, 189

26. To answer this question you must first properly identify the two psychological views regarding the causes of substance abuse, the psychodynamic view and the social-cognitive view. Then you must briefly explain the theoretical perspective of each view. Then you must present a synopsis of the biological view of the causes of substance abuse.

In your explanation of the psychodynamic view, you must mention that psychodynamic theorists see drug use and abuse as an attempt by people to control unconscious needs and impulses that they do not feel they can control without drugs. Social-cognitive theorists, however, feel that people often begin drug use on the basis of modeling the behavior of others (such as peers or parents), following the recommendations of others (usually peers), and because of positive expectancies about the effects of the drug.

The biological view emphasizes that some people may inherit genetic predispositions or sensitivities toward physiological dependence on certain substances such as alcohol, nicotine, or cocaine. These inherited tendencies do not guarantee someone will become a substance abuser, but they do increase the chances of it happening.

Chapter 6

Chapter Review

1. role, person, self (197-198)
2. schemas (198)
3. physical, social, personal (198-200)
4. happier, higher (199)
5. personal (200)
6. attitudes (201)
7. values, ethics (201-202)
8. adolescence (203)
9. self-concept (204)
10. esteem, ideal (204)
11. self-esteem (207)
12. more, highly (207)
13. ideal self (207)
14. ideal, concept (207)
15. positively (208)
16. identity (208)
17. normal, growth (208)
18a. 2 (208)
    b. 3 (210)
    c. 4 (210)
    d. 1 (210)
19. sexual morality (211)
20. complicated (212)
21. primacy, recency (214)
22. Any five of the following seven choices are correct:
    a. Be aware of the first impressions you make on others. (214)
    b. Make your visa or resume neat and list your important accomplishments at the beginning. (214)
    c. Plan or rehearse your first few remarks for a date or job interview. (214)
    d. Smile. (214)
    e. Be aware of your style of dress and your physical mannerisms (214)
    f. Attend to your penmanship. (214)
    g. Seek eye contact with your instructors or others with whom you communicate. (214)
23. face, toward (215)
24. assertive, open, deception, depression (215-216)
25. provocations, anger (216)
26a. Be aware of what other people are telling you with their body language (216)
    b. Pay attention to your own body language as a way of helping you to make the desired impressions on other people (216)
    c. Pay attention to your own body language as a way of learning about yourself (216)
27. prejudice, discrimination (217)
28. stereotypes (217)

29a.   dissimilarity (218)
   b.   social conflict (218)
   c.   social learning (218)
   d.   information processing (218)
   e.   social categorization (219)
30a.   role reversal (219)
   b.   intergroup contact (219)
   c.   seeking compliance with the law (220)
   d.   self-examination (220)
   e.   raising tolerant children (220)
31.   attribution (221)
32.   attribution (221)
33.   dispositional, situational (221)
34a.   5 (222)
   b.   3 (221)
   c.   4 (222)
   d.   1 (221)
   e.   2 (221)
35.   Western (223)
36a.   expand your competencies (224)
   b.   challenge the tryanny of the "oughts" and "shoulds" (224)
   c.   have a crisis (226)
   d.   substitute realistic, attainable goals for unattainable goals (226)
   e.   build self-efficacy expectations (226)

Sample Test

1. D, 200	6. C, 207	11. A, 215	16. B, 221	21. T, 197
2. A, 200	7. B, 207	12. D, 215	17. C, 221	22. F, 199
3. D, 201	8. B, 208-210	13. B, 216	18. B, 222	23. F, 200
4. D, 207	9. B, 210	14. D, 217	19. D, 223	24. T, 215
5. C, 207	10. A, 214	15. A, 218	20. C, 226	25. F, 217

26. To answer this question you must first specifically identify each of the three parts of the self—the physical self, the social self, and the personal self—and briefly describe what each part is or does. For example, the physical self is your body and affects you through your physical appearance and your health. It can affect the hobbies, activities, and job choices you make and may affect how others interact with you because of your outward appearance. Your social self reflects the social masks you wear in your interactions with others and the social roles you play throughout your life. Finally, the personal self is the part of you that only you know about. It is hidden from others and reflects the day-to-day experience of being you.

The second part of the question demands that you take these three parts and describe how they meld together to form the "self." In answering this, it is usually helpful to focus on the idea that you need all three parts to be effectively self-aware and effective in your interactions with others. A couple of situations in which you need more than one part to function effectively can be helpful here.

Chapter 7

Chapter Review

1.   influence (231)
2.   elaboration likelihood (232)
3.   central, peripheral (233)
4.   central, peripheral (233)
5.   enhance (234)
6a.   repeated exposure (234)
  b.   two-sided arguments (234)
  c.   emotional appeal (234)
  d.   arguments that run counter to the interests of the communicator (234)
7.   credibility, likeability, trustworthiness, attractiveness, similarity (234)
8.   environment (234-235)
9.   good (235)
10.   low, high (235)
11.   foot-in-the-door, lowballing, bait and switch (235-236)
12.   social, groups (237)
13.   compliance, approval, morality (238)
14.   the effects of punishment on learning (239)
15.   65 (239)
16a.   propaganda (240)
  b.   socialization (240)
  c.   lack of social comparison (240)
  d.   perception of legitimate authority (240)
  e.   the foot-in-the-door technique (240)
  f.   inaccessibility of values (240)
  g.   buffers (240)
17.   conform (242)
18.   Asch (242)
19.   collectivist, liked, low, shyness, familiarity, size, support (243)
20.   four or five (243)
21.   deindividuation (244)
22a.   anonymity (244)
  b.   diffusion of responsibility (244)
  c.   arousal due to noise and crowding (244)
  d.   conforming with the social norms of the group rather than one's own core values (244)
23.   prosocial (245)
24.   bystander effect (245)
25a.   bystanders must recognize that a need for help exists (246)
  b.   bystanders must decide an emergency exists (246)
  c.   bystanders must assume the responsibility to act (246)
  d.   bystanders must choose a way to help (246)
  e.   bystanders must implement the plan (246)
26.   similar, similarly (247)
27.   attractive, unaccompanied (247)
28.   assertive, unassertive, aggressive (248)
29a.   self-monitoring (249)
  b.   confronting irrational beliefs (250)
  c.   modeling (250)
  d.   behavioral rehearsal (250)
30.   broken-record (251)

Sample Test

1. B, 233	6. A, 238	11. B, 243	16. B, 247	21. T, 236
2. C, 234	7. D, 238	12. D, 244	17. C, 248	22. F, 239
3. D, 234-235	8. D, 239	13. C, 245	18. D, 248	23. F, 244
4. A, 235	9. B, 241	14. A, 246	19. A, 251	24. F, 247
5. C, 235	10. A, 242	15. C, 246-247	20. D, 252	25. T, 248

26. To answer this question, you must first define assertive behavior, passive behavior, and aggressive behavior, perhaps giving an example of each, and the differences in the consequences of each type of behavior. Then you must identify the techniques of self-monitoring, confronting irrational beliefs, modeling, and behavioral rehearsal, and briefly explain or give an example of each one.

Chapter 8

Chapter Review

1.   Most (257)
2.   behaviors, mental (258)
3a.   unusualness (258)
   b.   socially unacceptability in a given culture (259)
   c.   faulty perception or interpretation of reality (258)
   d.   significant personal distress (258)
   e.   self-defeating behavior (259)
   f.   dangerousness (259)
4.   Diagnostic and Statistical Manual (259)
5a.   4 (259)
   b.   5 (259)
   c.   3 (259)
   d.   1 (259)
   e.   2 (259)
6.   half (260)
7.   Adjustment, mildest (261)
8.   subjective, behavioral, physical (262)
9a.   phobias (262)
   b.   panic disorder (264)
   c.   generalized anxiety disorder (265)
   d.   obsessive-compulsive disorder (265)
   e.   posttraumatic stress disorder (265)
   f.   acute stress disorder (265)
10.   specific, social, agoraphobia (262-263)
11.   extreme, free floating (264-265)
12.   obsession, compulsion (265)
13.   long, persist (266)
14.   complex, simple (267)
15.   serotonin, norepinephrine, GABA (268)
16.   whole (269)
17.   dissociative identity (269)
18.   somatoform (270)
19a. dissociative amnesia (270)
   b.   dissociative fugue (270)
   c.   dissociative identity disorder (270)
   d.   depersonalization disorder (271)

20a.	6 (270)	f.	4 (264)
b.	3 (270)	g.	9 (265)
c.	7 (270)	h.	2 (265)
d.	1 (271)	i.	5 (265)
e.	8 (262)	j.	10 (265)

21. repression (272)
22. conversion, hypochondriasis (272-273)
23. la belle indifférence (272)
24. uterus (273)
25. major depression, bipolar disorder (274-275)
26. depression (274)
27. twice, adolescence (276)
28. distract, ruminate (276)
29. bipolar (275)
30. depression, bipolar (277)
31. anger (277)
32. learned helplessness (277)
33. internal, stable, global (281)
34. serotonin (281)
35. severe, persistent (282)
36. hallucinations, delusions (282)
37. memory, attention, communication (282)
38. grandeur, reference, persecution (283)
39. disorganized, catatonic, paranoid (283)
40. 1, 40-50 (282-284)
41. more, earlier, more (282)
42. brain, dopamine (284)
43 Personality (285)
44a. 5 (286)
 b. 2 (286)
 c. 3 (286)
 d. 1 (286)
 e. 4 (286)
45a. 1 (286)
 b. 5 (286)
 c. 2 (286)
 d. 3 (286)
 e. 4 (286)
46. prefrontal (287)
47. depression, bipolar (287)
48. stressful, social support (288)
49a. people who threaten suicide are only seeking attention (289)
 b. discussing suicide with a person who is depressed will prompt the person to attempt suicide (289)
 c. only "insane" people would attempt to take their own lives (289)
50. any five of the following seven:
 a. keep talking/draw the person out (289)
 b. be a good listener (289)
 c. suggest that measures other than suicide may solve the problem (289)
 d. emphasize how the person's suicide would be devastating to you and to others who care (289)
 e. ask how the person intends to commit suicide (289)
 f. suggest that the person go with you to obtain professional help now (289)
 g. do not tell the person threatening suicide that he or she is silly or crazy (289)

Sample Test

26. In this question you must provide a description of anxiety disorders in general as well as a brief explanation of each of the specific types of anxiety disorders such as follows:

Anxiety disorders are characterized by nervousness, fears, feelings of dread and foreboding and sympathetic overarousal. The anxiety is either out of proportion to the threat or exists where there is no apparent threat at all. The specific types of anxiety disorders include:

1. Phobias—irrational fears of objects, situations, public scrutiny, or open spaces and crowds.
2. Panic Disorder—a recurrent experience of extreme anxiety (panic attacks) in the absence of any external anxiety-eliciting source.
3. Generalized Anxiety Disorder—persistent feelings of dread and foreboding which is "free floating," combined with sympathetic arousal which lasts for at least six months.
4. Obsessive-Compulsive Disorder—A disorder in which a person experiences either recurring thoughts or images which seem beyond control, irresistible urges to repeat an act or engage in ritualistic behaviors that serve no functional purpose, other than to relieve anxiety, or both.
5. Posttraumatic Stress Syndrome—A delayed reaction to a psychologically stressful event which is characterized by intense fear, reliving of the event, and avoidance of stimuli associated with the event.
6. Acute Stress Disorder—A reaction to a psychologically stressful event which is similar to PTSD except that it appear within two to four weeks of the experiencing of the event and the symptoms do not persist as long as those of PTSD.

Chapter 9

Chapter Review

1a. it is a systematic interaction between a client and a therapist (294)
 b. it brings psychological principles to bear on the client's problems or goals (294)
 c. it influences a client's thoughts, feelings, and behaviors (294)
 d. it helps the client overcome psychological disorders, adjust to problems in living, or develop as an individual (294)
2. Psychoanalysis, insight (294)
3. hypnosis, free association (295)
4. transference (296)
5. wish fulfillment (297)
6. manifest, latent (297)
7. briefer, less (297)
8. ego, id (297)
9. internal, unconscious, here-and-now (298)
10. client-centered, frames of reference (298)
11. self-actualization (299)

12a.   unconditional positive regard (299)

  b.   empathic understanding (299)

  c.   genuineness (299)

13.   integrate conflicting parts of their personality and become whole (300)

14a.   the dialogue (300)

  b.   I take responsibility (300)

  c.   playing the projection (300)

15.   dialogue (300)

16.   think, feel, do (301)

17.   classical, operant, observational (302)

18.   flooding, gradual exposure, systematic desensitization, modeling (303-304)

19.   learned, counterconditioning (304)

20.   observational (304)

21.   aversive (304)

22a.   token economy (305)

  b.   social skills training (305)

  c.   biofeedback training (305)

23.   Cognitive (306)

24.   cognitive (307)

25.   themselves, world, future (307)

26.   active, directive (308)

27.   behavioral, cognitive (308)

28a.   5 (294)

  b.   3 (298)

  c.   2 (300)

  d.   1 (307)

  e.   4 (308)

29.   Eclectic (309)

30a.   it is economical (311)

  b.   it provides more information and life experiences to draw on than one-to-one therapy (311)

  c.   appropriate behavior receives group support (311)

  d.   it reassures patients that others suffer from similar doubts, problems, and failures (311)

  e.   group members who show improvement provide hope for other patients (311)

  f.   it provides a place for group members to practice needed social skills (311)

31.   communication, conflict (311)

32.   systems (312)

33.   scapegoat (312)

34.   meta-analysis (314)

35.   effective, more (314)

36.   twice (315)

37.   Empirically supported (315)

38.   multicultural (317)

39.   prejudice, discrimination (317)

40a.   interacting with clients in the language requested by them, or referring them to someone who can (318)

  b.   using methods consistent with the client's values and levels of acculturation (318)

  c.   developing therapy methods that incorporate clients' cultural values (318)

41.   identity, pride, cohesion (318)

42.   gender-role, male (318)

43.   content, pressure, prejudice (319)

44.   sociocultural, individual (319)

45.   chemotherapy (drug therapy), electroconvulsive, psychosurgery (320)

46.   Psychotropic (320)

47.   minor, major (321)

48.   Sedation, rebound (321)

49a. antianxiety drugs (321)
  b. antipsychotic drugs (321)
  c. antidepressants (321)
  d. lithium (322)
50. antipsychotic (321)
51a. monoamine oxidase (MAO) inhibitors (321)
  b. tricyclic antidepressants (321)
  c. serotonin-uptake inhibitors (321)
52. Lithium (322)
53. depression (322)
54. prefrontal lobotomy (322)
55. tardive dyskinesia (323)
56. temporary, skills, coping (323)
57. any five of the following twelve
  a. monitor your reactions in angering situations (325)
  b. stop and think (325)
  c. practice competing responses and competing thoughts (325)
  d. practice coping thoughts in place of angering self-statements (326)
  e. practice self-relaxation (326)
  f. don't impose unrealistic expectations upon others (326)
  g. replace anger with empathy (326)
  h. depersonalize the situation (326)
  i. keep your voice down (326)
  j. act assertively, not aggressively (326)
  k. express positive feelings (326)
  l. give yourself a pat on the back for keeping your cool (326)
58a. pleasant events (326)
  b. rational thinking (326)
  c. exercise (326)

Sample Test

1. B, 295	6. A, 302	11. D, 308	16. A, 320	21. F, 301
2. D, 295	7. C, 304	12. D, 312	17. B, 321	22. T, 303
3. D, 297	8. A, 305	13. D, 312	18. A, 321	23. F, 304
4. A, 297	9. B, 305	14. D, 314	19. D, 322	24. F, 314
5. C, 300	10. C, 307	15. C, 318	20. D, 313	25. T, 319

26. In this question you must first identify the three major biological approaches to therapy: drug therapy, electroconvulsive therapy, and psychosurgery. Within the category of drug therapy there are antianxiety drugs, antidepressant drugs, antipsychotic drugs, and lithium. Antianxiety drugs work by lowering activity of the central nervous system. This, in turn, reduces heart and respiration rates and feelings of nervousness and tension. Problems include tolerance, sedation effects, physical dependence, and rebound anxiety.

Antipsychotic drugs appear to work by blocking dopamine receptors in the brain. Not all patients are responsive to them, however.

Antidepressants work by increasing the amounts of noradrenaline and serotonin available to the brain. They tend to work better when combined with psychotherapy.

Lithium appears to work by moderating the effects of neurotransmitters such as glutamate. Its major drawbacks include memory loss and depressed motor speed.

No one knows why ECT works, but it does help patients with major depression who do not respond to antidepressant drugs. The major problems associated with it are tied to the reluctance many have of passing an electric current through someone's brain, the fact that no one knows why it works, and loss of memory.

Finally, psychosurgery has been used mainly in the form of the prefrontal lobotomy. It calms down agitated patients by severing neural pathways between the frontal lobes and the thalamus. It has many side effects, ranging from hyperactivity and distractibility to impaired learning, seizures, and even death.

Chapter 10

Chapter Review

1.   gender roles (334)
2.   gender stereotypes (334)
3.   women, men (335)
4.   widespread (335)
5.   Machismo, marianismo (336)
6.   opposite, independent (337)
7.   masculine (337), feminine (337), androgynous (337), undifferentiated (337)
8.   androgynous (337)
9.   femininity, femininity (338)
10. independence, assertiveness (339)
11. the systematic exclusion of women from science, industry, and world affairs (340)
12. similar (341)
13. verbal, visual-spatial (341)
14a. in most cases, the differences are small (342)
  b. they are group differences (342)
  c. some differences may largely reflect sociocultural influences (342)
15. shallower, less (343)
16. just as talkative as women (343)
17. closer, more (343)
18. men, women (343)
19. Boys, girls (343)
20. aggression (343)
21. gender identity (344)
22. transsexuals, transgendered (344)
23. functioning, organization (346)
24. specialized (346)
25. landmark, geometric (346)
26. Prenatal (346)
27. social-cognitive, gender-schema (347)
28. identification (347)
29. Oedipus and Electra complexes (347)
30. observational, identification, socialization (347-348)
31. anxious, strike (348)
32. Gender-schema (348-349)
33. 3 (349)
34. testosterone, testosterone (349)
35. biological, social (349-350)
36. more, feminine (351)

37a.	fathers are more likely than mothers to help children with math homework (352)
  b.	advanced math courses are more likely to be taught by men (352)
  c.	teachers often show higher expectations for boys in math courses (352)
  d.	math teachers spend more time working with boys than with girls (352)
38.	less, less (351)
39a.	appear to have lower self-esteem (353)
  b.	find stressful events more aversive (353)
  c.	are less capable of bouncing back from failure experiences (353)
  d.	are more likely to believe that women should be seen and not heard (353)
  e.	are more likely to conform to group pressure (353)
40a.	are more likely to be upset if their wives earn more money than they do (353)
  b.	are less likely to feel comfortable performing activities involved in caring for children (353)
  c.	are less likely to ask for help – including medical help – when they need it (353)
  d.	are less likely to be sympathetic and tender and to express feelings of love in their marital relationships (353)
  e.	are less likely to be tolerant of their wives' or lovers' faults (353)

Sample Test

1. A, 337	6. C, 339	11. A, 344	16. D, 351	21. F, 336
2. A, 337	7. C, 341	12. D, 346	17. C, 351	22. T, 338
3. A, 337	8. C, 342	13. B, 347	18. C, 352	23. F, 342
4. D, 337	9. C, 343	14. D, 348	19. B, 353	24. F, 344
5. D, 338	10. C, 343	15. B, 348-349	20. C, 336	25. T, 352

26.	In this question you must explain each of the perspectives individually with an emphasis on their common points and their areas of disagreement. The three perspectives are as follows:

Freud: believed that gender identity results from children identifying with the same-sex parent during the resolution of the Oedipus and Electra complexes. In his model, gender identity remains flexible until the age of 5 or 6, when the Oedipus and Electra complexes are typically resolved.

Social-cognitive theory: states that observational learning, identification, and socialization are all involved in the formation of gender identity and gender roles. Children identify through a broad, continuous process affected by rewards, punishments, and observations of the frequencies with which men and women engage in certain behaviors.

Gender-schema theory: states that children use gender as a way to organize their perceptions of the world. They learn that some behaviors more than others affect how they are perceived by others and they learn to judge themselves according to the traits perceived as important for their gender.

All three approaches involve some level of identification; however, for Freud, that identification is limited to same-sex parents whereas with the other theories it is a much broader, more fluid process. Freud's theory does not take into account rewards and punishments or observational learning. Gender-schema theory does not emphasize direct rewards and punishments but focuses more on the indirect rewards and punishments that are tied to how people are perceived. Both social-cognitive and gender-schema theories take into account a broader social context for the development of gender identity, although they focus on somewhat different aspects of that broader context.

Chapter 11

Chapter Review

1. friendship, love (357)
2. physical appearance (358)
3. large, high, narrow (358)
4. asset, less (359)
5. liability, liability (358-359
6. larger, less (360)
7. slender, slender (360)
8. unattractive (360)
9. heavier, thinner (361)
10. similar (361)
11. women, men (361)
12. physical attractiveness, financial (361)
13. good (362)
14. positively (362)
15. higher (362)
16. similar (362)
17. feminine, feminine (363)
18. fear of rejection by more attractive people (363)
19. neighborhood (363)
20. similar, less (364)
21. sexual, religious (364)
22. contact (364)
23. powerful (365)
24. homosexual (365)
25. heterosexual (365)
26. three, two (365)
27. consistent (366)
28. sex hormones (366)
29. organizing, activating, (366)
30. obscure, complex (367)
31. adolescence (368)
32. anxiety, depression, suicide (368)
33. societal, rejection (368)
34. who lives next door and who sits next to whom, similar interests (370)
35. intimate feelings (371)
36. intimacy, closer (372)
37. cliques, crowds (372)
38. the ability to keep confidences/loyalty (373)
39. complex, emotional, cognitive, motivational (373)
40a. 2 (373)　　　　　　　　　　e. 8 (374)
  b. 6 (374)　　　　　　　　　　f. 9 (374)
  c. 5 (373)　　　　　　　　　　g. 4 (378)
  d. 7 (373)　　　　　　　　　　h. 1 (374)
41. intimacy, passion, commitment (374)
42a. 2 (376)　　　　　　　　　　e. 7 (376)
  b. 3 (376)　　　　　　　　　　f. 4 (376)
  c. 5 (376)　　　　　　　　　　g. 1 (376)
  d. 6 (376)
43. Romantic (375)
44. idealize, magnify, overlook (375)
45. fatuous (375)
46. Romantic, companionate (376-378)

47.   genuine knowledge (378)
48.   adolescence, peer (379)
49.   depression, sick (379)
50.   any five of the following eleven:
   a.   lack of social skills (379)
   b.   lack of interest in other people (379)
   c.   lack of empathy (379)
   d.   high self-criticism concerning social behavior (379)
   e.   fear of rejection (379)
   f.   failure to disclose information about themselves to potential friends (379)
   g.   cynicism about human nature (379)
   h.   demanding too much too soon (379)
   i.   general pessimism (379)
   j.   external locus of control (379)
   k.   lack of sense of community (379)
51.   any five of the following nine:
   a.   make frequent social contacts (379)
   b.   combat shyness (379)
   c.   be assertive (379)
   d.   become a good listener (379)
   e.   let people get to know you (380)
   f.   fight fair (380)
   g.   tell yourself that you're worthy of friends (380)
   h.   find an on-campus job (380)
   i.   go to the counseling center (380)

Sample Test

1. D, 359	6. B, 365	11. D, 371	16. B, 376	21. T, 359
2. D, 361	7. A, 366	12. C, 371	17. D, 376	22. F, 364
3. D, 361	8. B, 366	13. B, 373	18. C, 378	23. F, 365
4. D, 362	9. B, 366	14. B, 374	19. D, 379	24. F, 371
5. B, 363	10. B, 368	15. C, 375	20. B, 372	25. T, 375

26.   This is a straightforward question in which you simply list the six styles of love discussed in the text with a brief one- or two-sentence explanation of each style. They are as follows:

Eros: romantic love; mostly sexual attraction or lust combined with an idealized view of one's partner and the feeling of being "in love"
Ludus: game-playing love
Storge: friendship love similar to affection and attachment
Pragma: pragmatic, practical, or logical love
Mania: possessive, excited love
Agape: selfless, generous love

Chapter 12

Chapter Review

1.   development (383)
2a.   attraction (383)
  b.   building (383)
  c.   continuation (383)
  d.   deterioration (383)
  e.   ending (383)
3.   propinquity, positive, affiliation, distance, negative, affiliation (384)
4.   mutual friends, introducing themselves (384)
5.   physical, attitudinal, mutual positive, physical, attitudinal, negative (386)
6.   Online (385)
7a.   the opening line (386)
  b.   (surface contact) exchanging name, rank, and serial number (386)
  c.   not-so-small talk (386)
  d.   self-disclosure (387)
8.   less, small (387)
9.   successive approximations (389)
10.   continuation (387)
11.   trust (389)
12.   caring (387)
13.   mutuality (388)
14.   commitment (388)
15.   commitment, boredom, evaluation, unfairness, jealousy (388)
16.   possessiveness, self-esteem, confidence (390)
17.   sexual, emotional (390)
18.   Equity (391)
19.   desirable, inevitable (392)
20a.   taking action that might improve the relationship (392)
  b.   end the relationship (392)
21.   waiting, doing nothing (392)
22a.   alternative partners are available (392)
  b.   barriers to leaving the relationship are low (392)
  c.   there is little satisfaction in the relationship (392)
23.   communication, jealousy (392)
24.   Marriage (393)
25.   believe they will be happier (394)
26.   homogamy (394)
27.   the boy or girl next door (395)
28.   values, goals (395)
29.   any five of the following eleven items:
  a.   whether the wife will take her husband's surname, or retain her maiden name, or whether both will use a hyphenated last name (395)
  b.   how household tasks will be allocated and who will be responsible for what everyday activities—such as cleaning, washing, etc. (395)
  c.   whether or not the couple will have children, and if so, how many and at what time in the marital life cycle (395)
  d.   what type(s) of contraception to use and who will take responsibility for birth control measures (395)
  e.   how child-care responsibilities will be divided between the husband and wife (395)
  f.   whether they will rent or buy a place to live and whether residential decisions will accommodate the husband's or wife's career plans (395)
  g.   how the breadwinning functions will be divided, who will control the family finances, and how economic decisions will be made (395)
  h.   how in-law relations will be handled, and whether vacations will be spent visiting relatives (395)

i. what proportion of leisure activities will be spent apart from the spouse and what leisure activities will be spent together (395)

j. how sexual relations will be arranged and whether fidelity will be preserved (395)

h. how they will go about changing specific parts of their marital contract as the marriage progresses (395)

30. communication (396)

31a. affective communication (396)

b. problem-solving communication (396)

c. sexual satisfaction (396)

d. agreement about finances (396)

32a. recognizing your emotions (397)

b. managing your emotions (397)

c. using your emotions effectively (397)

d. identifying emotions in others (397)

e. handling emotions in relationships (397)

33. twice, minority (398)

34. curiosity, personal growth (398)

35. sex (playmates), soul mates (400)

36. fidelity (400)

37. three (401)

38. dominance, unemployment, substance, abusive (401)

39. lower (401)

40. self-esteem, inadequacy (401)

41. power (401)

42. seven, four, two (402)

43. adultery (402)

44. communication, understanding (402)

45. more (403)

46. separated, divorced (403)

47. separating psychologically from one's "ex" (403)

48. behavioral, substance, lower (403)

49. little (404)

50. Most, more (404)

51. Singlehood (406)

52a. people are getting married at later ages (408)

b. people are delaying marriage to pursue educational goals (408)

c. more people are deciding to live together rather than marry (408)

53. Cohabitation, living together (408)

54. cohabitation (408)

55a. part-time/limited cohabitation (409)

b. premarital cohabitation (410)

c. substitute marriage (410)

56. more (410)

57. less, less, less (410)

58a. challenge irrational expectations (411)

b. negotiate differences (412)

c. make a contract for exchanging new behaviors (412)

d. increase pleasurable marital interactions (412)

e. enhance communication skills (412)

59a. talk about talking (413)

b. request permission to raise a topic (413)

60a. engage in active listening (413)

b. use paraphrasing (413)

c. reinforce your partner for communicating (413)

d. use unconditional positive regard (413)

61a. ask questions designed to encourage your partner to communicate (413)
  b. use self-disclosure (413)
  c. give your partner permission to say something that might be upsetting to you (413)
62a. take responsibility for what happens to you (413)
  b. be specific (413)
  c. Use "I" talk (413)
63a. evaluate your motives (414)
  b. pick a good time and place (414)
  c. be specific (414)
  d. express dissatisfaction in terms of your own feelings (414)
  e. keep complaints to the present (414)
  f. try to phrase criticism positively (414)
64a. ask clarifying questions (414)
  b. paraphrase the criticism (414)
  c. acknowledge the criticism (414)
  d. acknowledge your mistake, if you have made a mistake (414)
  e. negotiate differences (414)
65a. try to see the situation from your partner's perspective (414)
  b. seek validating information (415)
  c. take a break (415)
  d. tolerate differentness (415)
  e. agree to disagree (415)

Sample Test

1. A, 384	6. C, 394	11. B, 400	16. A, 408	21. F, 387
2. B, 386	7. A, 394-395	12. B, 400	17. B, 409-410	22. T, 390
3. B, 387	8. B, 394	13. A, 401	18. B, 412	23. T, 401
4. C, 388	9. D, 395	14. C, 402	19. C, 413	24. T, 403
5. C, 392	10. D, 396	15. C, 403	20. C, 389	25. F, 411

26. Your book lists three suggestions (page 414) on how to make requests when trying to improve marital communication. You need to list each of these and provide a one- or two-sentence explanation for each one. For example:

> Be specific: Don't make general statements like "Be nicer to me," because your partner may not understand what that involves or that he or she is currently behaving in a way that is not "nice." It is much more effective to make specific statements focused on specific behaviors such as "Please don't cut me off in the middle of a sentence."

Chapter 13

Chapter Review

1. orgasm, strength (419)
2. masturbation (419)
3. incest (420)
4. Japan, unknown (420)
5. wife (420)
6. Christmas (420)
7. sex (420)

8a.	3 (421)		g.	5 (422)
b.	9 (421)		h.	2 (421)
c.	7 (421)		i.	1 (422)
d.	6 (421)		j.	10 (422)
e.	8 (422)		k.	11 (422)
f.	4 (422)			

9. fallopian tube, uterus (422)
10. clitoris, chastity (422)
11. testes (423)
12. testes, testosterone (423)
13. scrotum (423)
14. urine, sperm (423)
15. Semen (423)
16. loose erectile (423-424)
17. blood (424)
18. estrogen, progesterone (424)
19. Ovulation (425)
20. Menstruation, ovulation (424)
21. organizing, activating (424)
22. estrogen, progesterone, testosterone (425)
23. psychological (425)
24. norm, more (426)
25. choose any 5 of the following 8:
   a. convenience (427)
   b. moral acceptability (428)
   c. cost (429)
   d. sharing responsibility (429)
   e. safety (429)
   f. reversibility (429)
   g. protection against sexually transmitted infections (429)
   h. effectiveness (429)

26a.	8 (428)		g.	9 (428)
b.	2 (428)		h.	7 (428)
c.	5 (428)		i.	4 (428)
d.	1 (428)		j.	6 (428)
e.	3 (428)		k.	10 (428)
f.	11 (428)			

27. third (431)
28. cybersex (431)
29. vasocongestion, myotonia (430)
30. excitement, plateau, orgasmic, resolution (430)
31. reflexes (432)
32. refractory, orgasm, ejaculate (432)
33. pheromones, vomeronasal (433)
34. people the victims know (434)
35. dominance, anger (436)
36. rapists, aggressive, competitive (436)
37a. women are responsible for rape if they dress provocatively (437)
   b. women say no when they mean yes (437)
   c. rapists are crazed by sexual desire (437)
   d. deep down inside, women want to be raped (437)
38. lenient, unsympathetic (437)
39. harm, anxiety, depression, dysfunction, disease, pregnancy (438)

40.   any five of the following fifteen suggestions:
- a. establish signals and arrangements with other women in an apartment neighborhood (438)
- b. list only first initials in the telephone directory or mailbox (438)
- c. use deadbolt locks (438)
- d. keep windows locked and obtain iron grids for first-floor windows (438)
- e. keep entrances and doorways brightly lit (438)
- f. have keys ready for the front door or car (438)
- g. do not walk alone in the dark (438)
- h. avoid deserted areas (438)
- i   never allow a strange man into your apartment or home without checking his credentials (438)
- j. drive with the car windows up and the doors locked (438)
- k. check the rear seat of the car before entering (438)
- l. avoid living in an unsafe building (438)
- m. do not pick up hitchhikers, including women (438)
- n. do not talk to strange men on the street (438)
- o. shout "Fire!" not "Rape!" (438)

41.   any five of the following eight suggestions:
- a. communicate your sexual limits to your date (438)
- b. meet new dates in public places, and don't drive with strangers (439)
- c. state your refusal in definitive terms (439)
- d. become aware of your fears (439)
- e. trust your gut-level feelings (439)
- f. be especially cautious if you are in a new environment (439)
- g. don't let an ex-boyfriend or lover who you do not like or feel good about into your place (439)
- h. stay sober and see that your date does too (439)

42a. 1 (440)   d. 4 (441)
  b. 3 (441)   e. 2 (441)
  c. 5 (441)

43.   heart, diabetes, erectile (442)
44.   knowledge, skill (443)
45.   therapy, cognitive behavioral (444)
46.   Masters, Johnson (444)
47a. reducing performance anxiety (444)
  b. changing self-defeating attitudes and expectations (444)
  c. teaching sexual skills (444)
  d. enhancing sexual knowledge (444)
  e. improving sexual communication (444)
48.   Most (444)
49.   widespread, young (445)
50.   1, 3 (445)
51.   immune, diseases (445-446)
52.   white blood (or CD4 lymphocytes) (447)
53.   blood, semen, vaginal, cervical, breast milk (448)
54.   prevention (450)
55a. 1 (447)   e. 5 (446)
  b. 3 (447)   f. 2 (446)
  c. 7 (446)   g. 6 (447)
  d. 4 (446)

Sample Test

1. A, 419	6. A, 424	11. B, 436-438	16. A, 446	21. F, 420
2. D. 421	7. C, 425	12. C, 440	17. D, 448	22. F, 425
3. A, 422	8. D, 428	13. C, 442-443	18. D, 447	23. F, 437
4. A, 422	9. C, 430	14. C, 445	19. D, 447	24. F, 440
5. B, 423	10. D, 434	15. D, 445	20. A, 433	25. T, 449

26. This question requires you to provide an overview (which should include some statistics) on the frequency of rape in the United States, who commits rape, and who gets raped. For example, 70,000 rapes were reported in 1990, but since only about one in five rapes is believed to be reported, about 350,000 may have actually occurred. Only one in five is perpetrated by a stranger; most rapes are committed by acquaintances. Many more cases of forced rape occur within marriages and some people consider those to be rape. Date rape is also a problem. Surveys indicate 9% of college women may be victims, although there is still much controversy in these cases as to exactly what constitutes rape.

While sex may be one reason men rape women, most experts see it as an expression of anger at women or an attempt to physically dominate women. Many rapists have long histories of violent offenses and appear to use violence as a source of sexual arousal. Many rapists may also be encouraged by cultural myths that imply that when a woman says no, she is really playing "hard to get" and "wants to be dominated," so she really means yes. Or they may be responding to cultural pressures to be a "real man" which means using physical force to dominate others, including women. Other myths, such as the myth that "only bad girls get raped" create an atmosphere where the victim is often either not believed or is perceived as having "asked for it" and therefore her charges are not taken seriously or are almost impossible to prosecute effectively, particularly in cases of date rape. This may result in the offender "getting away with it" which discourages women from prosecuting and may encourage men to continue sexually aggressive behavior by confirming that what they have done is acceptable.

Chapter 14

Chapter Review

1. Adolescence (456)
2. growth (456)
3. Puberty, secondary sex (456)
4. 100 (457)
5. menarche, 11 and 14 (457)
6. formal-operational (458)
7. classify, hypothesize, logical (458)
8. imaginary, fable (458)
9a. family conflict (459)
  b. coping with physical and emotional changes (459)
  c. carving out a personal identity for themselves (459)
10. independent (459)
11. Adolescence (460)
12. ego identity versus role diffusion (461)
13. mixed (462)
14. declining (462)
15a. identity achievement (462)
  b. foreclosure (462)
  c. moratorium (462)
  d. identity diffusion (462)
16. they misunderstand reproduction and contraception, they miscalculate the odds of conception (463)
17. young and middle adulthood (463)
18. emerging adulthood (464)
19. 30 (464)
20. young adulthood (465)
21. stable, gradual, minor (465)
22. Menopause, climacteric, menstruation (or ovulation) (466)

23.   any five of the following six myths:
- a.   a woman's body no longer produces estrogen after menopause (467)
- b.   women normally become depressed or anxious during menopause (467)
- c.   menopause is a physical event, not a psychological one (467)
- d.   women can expect to experience severe hot flashes during menopause(467)
- e.   menopause signals an end to women's sexual interests (467)
- f.   menopause brings an end to a woman's child-bearing years (467)

24.   40, strength, sex, energy (467)

25.   early adulthood (468)

26.   Crystallized, increases, fluid, decreases (468)

27.   healthier (468)

28.   dream (469)

29.   intimacy, isolation, ego integrity (469)

30.   separation, individuation, social relationships (469)

31.   reassessment (469)

32.   settling down, roots (469)

33a.   getting started in an occupation (470)
- b.   selecting and courting a mate (470)
- c.   learning to live contentedly with one's partner (470)
- d.   starting a family and becoming a parent (470)
- e.   assuming the responsibilities of managing a home (470)
- f.   assuming some civic responsibilities (470)
- g   finding a congenial social group (470)

34.   any five of the following nine:
- a.   personal experience (470)
- b.   personal pleasure (470)
- c.   personal extension (470)
- d.   relationship (471)
- e.   personal status (471)
- f.   personal competence (471)
- g.   personal responsibility (471)
- h.   personal power (471)
- i.   moral worth (471)

35.   use any five of the following thirteen reasons:
- a.   strain on resources (471)
- b.   increase in overpopulation (471)
- c.   choice, not mandate (471)
- d.   time together (471)
- e.   freedom (471)
- f.   other children (471)
- g.   dual careers (471)
- h.   financial security (471)
- i.   community welfare (471)
- j.   difficulty (471)
- k.   irrevocable decision (471)
- l.   failure (471)
- m.   danger (471)

36.   instrumental competence (471)

37a.   2 (472)
- b.   1 (473)
- c.   3 (473)

38.   authoritative (473)

39.   authoritarian (473)

40.   permissive (473)

41a. be flexible, but not without limits (473)
b. set high but reasonable expectations (474)
c. explain to your children why you make certain demands (474)
d. listen to your children's opinions (474)
e. show warmth (474)
42. coercive (474)
43a. stress (474)
b. a history of child abuse in at least one of the parents' families of origin (474)
c. parents with poor anger management skills (474)
d. alcohol or substance abuse (474)
e. acceptance of violence as a way of coping with stress (474)
f. failure to become attached to the children (474)
g. rigid attitudes toward child-rearing (474)
44. behavioral, emotional, immature, explore (474)
45. hostility (475)
46. relative, men (475)
47a. give the child a safe environment in which to talk to you or another trusted adult (475)
b. reassure the child that he or she did nothing wrong (475)
c. seek mental health assistance for the child (475)
d. arrange for a medical examination for the child (475)
e. be aware of state laws that may require you to report suspected abuse to authorities (475)
48. generativity, stagnation (476)
49. midlife transition (476)
50. midlife crisis (477)
51. 35, 40 (476)
52. mastery (477)
53. empty-nest, mellowness, confidence, stability (477)
54. melanin (479)
55. 30s, brittle (480)
56. 40 (480)
57. increases, declines (479-480)
58. osteoporosis (480)
59. testosterone (481)
60. expectations, adjust (481)
61. Creativity (482)
62a. general health (482)
b. socioeconomic status (482)
c. stimulating activities (482)
d. marriage to a spouse with a high level of intellectual functioning (482)
e. openness to new experience (482)
63. quadruple (482)
64. helpless (483)
65. six or seven, dimmer (483)
66. more, less, more, less (483)
67. ego integrity, despair (484)
68a. coming to value wisdom more than strength and power (484)
b. coming to value friendship and social relationships more than sexual prowess (484)
c. retaining emotional flexibility so that we can adjust to changing family relationships and the ending of a career (484)
d. retaining mental flexibility so that we can form new social relationships and undertake new leisure activities (484)
e. keeping involved and active and concerned about others so that we do not become preoccupied with physical changes or the approach of death (484)
f. shifting interest from the world of work to retirement activities (484)

69a. adjusting to physical changes (484)
   b. adjusting to retirement and to change in financial status (484)
   c. establishing satisfying living arrangements (484)
   d. learning to live with one's spouse in retirement (484)
   e. adjusting to the death of one's spouse (484)
   f. forming new relationships with aging peers (484)
   g. adopting flexible social roles (484)
70. unhealthy (485)
71a. the preretirement phase (485)
   b. the honeymoon phase (485)
   c. the disenchantment phase (485)
   d. the reorientation phase (485)
   e. the stability phase (485)
   f. the termination phase (485)
72. satisfied (485)
73. Death (486)
74. denial, anger, bargaining, depression, acceptance (486)
75. Euthanasia (486)
76. hospice (487)
77. after (487)
78a. reshaping one's life to concentrate on what people find to be important and meaningful (488)
   b. a positive outlook (488)
   c. self-challenge (489)
79a. slowing down the physical effects of aging (489)
   b. reducing the risk of certain cancers (489)
   c. reducing the risk of other major killers such as heart disease, strokes, and diabetes (489)
   d. reducing the risk of osteoporosis (489)
80. mental, sharpness, depression (489)

Sample Test

1. D, 456	6. D, 467	11. A, 470	16. A, 484	21. F, 456
2. C, 458	7. C, 468	12. A, 473	17. C, 484	22. F, 466
3. D, 459	8. C, 468	13. A, 474	18. B, 485	23. T, 473
4. B, 464	9. B, 469	14. B, 476	19. A, 486	24. F, 482
5. B, 466	10. C, 469	15. A, 476	20. D, 488-489	25. F, 485

26. This question requires you to define the concept of "empty-nest syndrome," explain its origins, and discuss the evidence for or against it. It was a concept originally aimed at traditional female homemakers who devoted their lives to raising their children only to find them grown up and "leaving the nest" by the time these women had reached middle adulthood. This supposedly left them with a profound sense of loss, emptiness, and depression.

In general, the research is mixed regarding empty-nest syndrome today. While some women ***and men*** experience some problems when the children leave home, there is no evidence that it is as devastating for most people as the concept suggests. Many women and men find that with the children gone, they have more time for themselves and each other and their happiness and life satisfaction surge upward.

Chapter 15

Chapter Review

1. occupational (494)
2a. competencies (494)
 b. comprehension (494)
 c. expectancies (494)
3. fall into, what is available at the time (494)
4. economic (to earn a living) (495)
5. 20,000 (494)
6. there are numerous possible correct answers to this, but the three presented in the text are:
 a. the paycheck (495)
 b. fringe benefits (495)
 c. security in old age (495)
7. any five of the following nine:
 a. the opportunity to engage in challenging, stimulating and satisfying activities (495)
 b. the opportunity to broaden social contacts (495)
 c. to fill their days with meaningful activity (495)
 d. the work ethic (495)
 e. self-identity (495)
 f. self-fulfillment (495)
 g. self-worth (495)
 h. social values of work (496)
 i. social roles (496)
8a. fantasy (496)
 b. tentative choice (496)
 c. realistic choice (496)
 d. maintenance (496)
 e. career change (497)
 f. retirement (497)
9. résumé, cover letter (497)
10. summary, one (497-498)
11a. a heading (498)
 b. a statement of your job objective (498)
 c. a summary of your educational background (498)
 d. a summary of your work experience (498)
 e. a list of references (498)
12a. explanation of the purpose of the letter (501)
 b. explanation of how you learned about the opening (501)
 c. comparison of your qualifications and the job requirements (501)
 d. statements of desired salary and geographic limitations (501)
 e. request for an interview or other response to the letter (501)
 f. statement that references will be sent upon request (501)
 g. thanks for the prospective employer's consideration (501)
13. social, test (502)
14. positively, negatively (502)

15.   any five of the following nine tasks:
  a.   making the transition from school to the workplace (505)
  b.   learning how to carry out the job tasks (505)
  c.   accepting your subordinate status within the organization or profession (505)
  d.   learning how to get along with your coworkers and supervisor (505)
  e.   showing that you can maintain the job, make improvements, and show progress (505)
  f.   finding a sponsor or mentor to "show you the ropes" (506)
  g.   defining the boundaries between your job and other areas of your life (506)
  h.   evaluating your occupational choice in the light of supervisor appraisal and measurable outcomes of your work (506)
  i.   learning to cope with daily hassles on the job, frustrations, and successes and failure (506)
16.   stressed, underpaid, underappreciated (508)
17.   satisfaction, health, well-being (509)
18.   esteem, efficacy, emotional (509)
19.   turnover, absenteeism, productivity (513)
20.   use any five of the following nine suggestions:
  a.   improved recruitment and placement (513)
  b.   training and instruction (513)
  c.   use of constructive criticism (513)
  d.   unbiased appraisal of worker performance (513)
  e.   goal setting (514)
  f.   financial compensation (514)
  g.   work redesign (514)
  h.   work schedules (516)
  i.   integration of new workplace technology (516)
21.   worker, performance (514)
22.   control, commitment (515)
23a.   physical environment (517)
  b.   individual stressors (517)
  c.   group stressors (517)
  d.   organizational stressors (517)
24.   exhausted, motivation, detachment, depersonalization (518)
25.   conflict, overload, ambiguity (518)
26.   any five of the following eight:
  a.   loss of energy and feelings of exhaustion, both physical and psychological (519)
  b.   irritability and shortness of temper (519)
  c.   stress-related problems, such as depression, headaches, backaches, or apathy (519)
  d.   difficulty concentrating or feeling distanced from one's work (519)
  e.   loss of motivation (519)
  f.   lack of satisfaction or feelings of achievement at work (519)
  g.   loss of concern about work in someone who was previously committed (519)
  h.   feeling that one has nothing left to give (519)
27.   any five of the following ten suggestions:
  a.   establish your priorities (519)
  b.   set reasonable goals (519)
  c.   take things one day at a time (519)
  d.   set limits (519)
  e.   share your feelings (519)
  f.   build supportive relationships (519)
  g.   do things you enjoy (519)
  h.   take time for yourself (519)
  i.   don't skip vacations (519)
  j.   be attuned to your health (520)
28.   children (522)
29.   15 (522)
30.   workplace, home (523)
31.   three quarters (523)

32.   three (524)
33a.   more realistic career planning (524)
   b.   providing employers with accurate information about women in the workforce (524)
   c.   heightening awareness of the importance of women's careers in dual-career marriages (524)
   d.   maintaining employment continuity and stability (524)
   e.   increasing job flexibility and providing child-care facilities (524)
   f.   recruiting qualified women into training programs and jobs (524)
34.   use any five of the following eight:
   a.   verbal abuse or harassment (525)
   b.   subtle pressure for sexual activity (525)
   c.   remarks about a person's body, clothing, or sexual activities (525)
   d.   leering at, or ogling, someone's body (525)
   e.   unwelcome touching, patting, or pinching (525)
   f.   brushing up against someone's body (525)
   j.   demands to engage in sexual activity that are accompanied by threats concerning someone's job or student status (525)
   h.   physical assault (525)
35.   more, more (525)
36.   aggressiveness, power (525)
37a.   the believe it would be futile (526)
   b.   fear of reprisals (526)
38.   two (526)
39.   use any five of the following nine suggestions:
   a.   convey a professional attitude (526)
   b.   discourage harassing behavior and promote appropriate behavior (526)
   c.   avoid being alone with a harasser (526)
   d.   keep a record (527)
   e.   talk with the harasser (527)
   f.   write a letter to the harasser (527)
   g.   seek support (527)
   h.   file a complaint (527)
   i.   seek legal remedies (527)
40.   balance sheet, psychological tests (528)
41a.   intellectual and educational appropriateness (529)
   b.   intrinsic factors (529)
   c.   extrinsic factors (529)
42.   WAIS, Stanford-Binet (530)
43a.   4 (531)   d. 6 (531)
   b.   1 (531)   e. 2 (531)
   c.   5 (531)   f. 3 (531)

Sample Test

1. D, 495	6. B, 501	11. D, 516	16. A, 530	21. T, 495
2. B, 495	7. C, 502-503	12. A, 518	17. C, 530	22. F, 498
3. C, 495	8. B, 508	13. D, 523	18. C, 507	23. T, 513
4. C, 496	9. A, 509	14. D, 524	19. A, 531	24. T, 523
5. A, 497-498	10. A, 514	15. D, 529	20. C, 531	25. T, 525

26. Your text presents nine different strategies for enhancing job satisfaction (pages 533-536). In your answer you need to identify each of the nine and present a brief (one- to two-sentence) explanation for each strategy. For example:

> Use of constructive criticism: Criticism is sometimes necessary for people to correct mistakes and improve the quality of their work. But it is important that criticism be given constructively, focused on improving someone's performance, rather than destructively, focused on hurting the person or tearing them down. Constructive criticism can make workers feel that you are helping them, whereas destructive criticism destroys morale and can create conflict.

435